D1549094

INTERIBERICA, S.A. DE EDICIONES

MAN AND NATURE
Every Living Thing

Doubleday and Company Inc.,
Garden City, New York, 1976

© 1975 Interiberica, S. A. - Madrid
© 1973, © 1975 Aldus Books Limited, London
SBN: 385 11339 0
Library of Congress Catalog Card No: 75 13117

Also published in parts as
Every Living Thing and Natural Man

MAN AND NATURE

Part 1
Every Living Thing

by Malcolm Ross-Macdonald

ISBN: 84-382-0013-3. Dep. Legal: M. 26.298-1975
Printed and bound in Spain by Novograph
S.A., and **Roner S.A.**, Crta de Irun, Km.12,450,
Madrid–34.

Series Coordinator	Geoffrey Rogers
Art Director	Frank Fry
Design Consultant	Guenther Radtke
Editorial Consultant	Malcolm Ross-Macdonald
Assistant Editors	Allyson Fawcett
	Bridget Gibbs
Copy Editor	Damian Grint
Research	Naomi Narod
	Carol Potter
	Enid Moore
Art Assistants	Amaryllis May
	Michael Turner

Contents: Part 1

Editorial Advisers

MICHAEL BOORER, B.SC. Author, Lecturer, and Broadcaster.

MATTHEW BRENNAN, ED.D. Director, Brentree Environmental
Center, Professor of Conservation Education, Pennsylvania
State University.

PHYLLIS BUSCH, ED.D. Author, Science Teacher, and Consultant
in Environmental Education.

MICHAEL HASSELL, B.A., M.A.(OXON), D.PHIL. Lecturer in
Ecology, Imperial College, London.

ANTHONY HUXLEY, M.A. Author and Editorial Consultant.

STUART MCNEILL, B.SC., PH.D. Lecturer in Ecology, Imperial
College, London.

JAMES OLIVER, PH.D. Director of the New York Aquarium,
former Director of the American Museum of Natural History,
former Director of the New York Zoological Park, formerly
Professor of Zoology, University of Florida.

Foreword by David Attenborough

A small, blue globe, patched with brown and green, wreathed with white streaks of cloud—that was the picture of our planet brought back by the first astronauts. Never before had man got far enough away from earth to be able to view it entire, spinning in the emptiness of space. It is a vision that haunts the imagination.

Of course, men long ago had worked out by sheer power of logic that the earth on which they lived was not flat, but round. Since then they have become aware with increasing force that the living creatures of the earth do not inhabit separate individual worlds, but are interconnected by a web of relationships so intricate that the fate of one creature may affect the fate of all. But that view from space summarized both those truths with an almost shocking vividness. We realized, too, as never before, how vital it is to understand as much as possible about life on earth. Whether we like it or not, we are committed to playing a dominant part.

In the pages that follow, Malcolm Ross-Macdonald surveys the breath-taking variety of life that began in those blue areas of the globe, spread to the green and brown continents and even to the white caps at opposite ends, the Arctic and Antarctic. The closer we look, the more fascinating it becomes. How extra-ordinary it is that life should have developed along so many different lines; how amazing that each organism should be so suited to its particular circumstances. And yet, by examining the details, we begin to comprehend the universal logics of life that determine how one form develops into another and how each becomes molded to match the tiniest characteristics of its environment.

Robert Allen focuses his attention on one particular, unspectacular creature that split away from its primate relatives and began to develop skills and powers that eventually led it to dominate the world. The story of the evolution of man cannot fail to fascinate us. Many of the details are missing, but the overall plot is clear. Since it was deduced almost entirely from fossil bones, it is astonishing that it should be as complete as it is. The way in which this unique creature eventually managed to invade every environment and develop many different ways of organising its societies also provided a dramatic tale. The evidence for this comes from living human beings, not bones, but with the disappearance of many primitive societies, the evidence, too, is disappearing fast. A single living pattern, the one developed by Western European man, seems destined to overwhelm all others. But the story of man's past could be crucially important to us. It was adaptability that, in the past, enabled him to become a global success. To lose sight of how versatile we were might blind us to our future potential on the vulnerable planet that is still our only home.

David Attenborough.

Realm of Life

Life is the greatest of the universe's many mysteries. It clearly obsessed and fascinated our earliest forefathers, who, for thousands of years, drew and painted little else but living forms. And now, despite centuries of detailed and painstaking study that has brought us close to unraveling the forces at the very heart of life, the marvel of it has in no way diminished. Quite the reverse. Knowledge and understanding have added new dimensions to that ancient sense of mystery.

The teeming riches of a plain well stocked with game, the frenzy of a broken anthill, the myriad dark and clamoring specks of a wheeling flock of waterfowl at break or close of day, the lonely grandeur of a soaring eagle, the hoots and shrieks and mysterious rustlings of the natural night . . . these and other sights and sounds must have been an endless source of wonder to our remote ancestors. To modern man they are surely more than wonderful. Even a lifetime spent in their study cannot dim—indeed it can only heighten—our amazement at all the staggering diversity of form and activity.

Yet we must not allow our advancing knowledge to obscure a sense of the *wholeness* of life and of the absolute interdependence of all its forms. The achievements of civilization, its success (in selfish human terms) at taming Nature and harnessing her forces, led us to set ourselves apart from the rest of life. Now we are paying the debt for our arrogance—paying in terms of depleted resources, polluted amenities, and vanishing wilderness. And we are hastily rediscovering all that we had forgotten about the oneness of life.

No longer do we see ourselves as Lords of Creation—a favorite term a century ago. Instead we look around with new eyes and with a rekindled humility. And this new interest reaches far beyond the ranks of professional students of Nature. All around the world people are taking an intense interest in Nature. From such interest it is but a short step to involvement

Herds of gnu and zebra at Ngorongoro Crater, Tanzania. The teeming richness of Africa's plains symbolizes a wealth that is rapidly vanishing from the surface of the earth.

600 miles of atmosphere

4000 miles

Of the approximately 4600 miles of earth and atmosphere contained between the arrows above, only the thinnest shell, some 12 miles deep, is home to living things— even then, only the land surface and the top 500 feet of ocean is at all densely populated.

and responsibility—qualities that spell hope of survival for the living diversity we are now learning to cherish as never before. One of the first fruits of that learning is the realization of how very thin is the sphere of life, the *biosphere*, on the earth's surface.

When the British expedition of 1953 conquered Everest, they saw a small flock of alpine choughs (a small bird like a crow) at around 26,900 feet— the highest altitude at which any animal, or even plant has been recorded. Almost 6½ years later Dr. Jacques Piccard and Lieutenant Don Walsh grounded their bathyscaphe *Trieste* 35,802 feet down in the Challenger Deep of the Marianas Trench in the western Pacific—only 398 feet short of the deepest known spot in the ocean. There, gripped by a pressure of eight tons per square inch, they stabbed their searchlights into a dark and a depth no man had ever glimpsed. Almost the first thing they saw in the pale-rust-colored ooze was a solelike fish. Even at those stupendous pressures there is life.

These are the extremes of altitude and depth at which nonmicroscopic life (other than human explorers) has been reliably reported. To human beings, for whom a trip up even a small sky-scraper or a visit down a few hundred feet of limestone cavern can be dizzying or unnerving, these upper and lower limits may seem awesome indeed. Yet in terms of the earth's vertical geography they span the merest shell—equivalent to no more than a good coat of paint on a foot-ball. Like a thin growth of lichen on a giant dome of rock, life infests the thinnest shell of a planet whose bulk is sterile.

Even these two extremes, some 12 miles apart, are misleading. Over 99 per cent of life on earth actually lives on its land surface or in the top 400 feet of the sea. Of the animals and plants that live out of the water there is not one whose life cycle and habits keep it permanently out of contact with the ground, or with trees and plants rooted in the ground. And the sea creatures that live below 400 feet are like the mice that feed on

The highest flying bird known is the alpine chough, which has been seen at 26,900 feet above sea level

500 feet above sea level

The true biosphere.

500 feet below sea level

One of the deepest known creatures is the solelike fish seen from the bathyscaphe *Trieste* at 35,802 feet below sea level

11

crumbs from the rich man's table, their food falling in a steady rain of manna from the true biosphere above. This biosphere is even thinner, in proportion, than the coat of paint; it would be more like a molecule-thick film on the football.

It isn't really surprising to find that life is so totally dependent on the earth's surface. Like all processes, life has two basic requirements; energy, and something to work with—some raw material. The energy, as we shall see when we study the process in detail in later pages, comes in the first place from the sun. The raw materials are carbon dioxide, water, and minerals. The carbon dioxide comes from the air, the minerals from the soil, and water is available in the earth, the oceans, and the air. Even then, the minerals are of no use if they are in a solid form. They must first be broken down into their individual molecules. And the medium for the breakdown process, the medium in which individual molecules move into and out of living cells, is almost always water. Where do we find the greatest concentrations of light, air, water, and minerals? In the same place, to be sure, as we find the over-

Well adapted to their harsh Arctic environment, polar bears are the fiercest killers to roam the northern ice.

whelming concentrations of life: on the land surface and near the surface of the ocean.

What we have said so far applies more directly to plants than to animals. They need the sun in the most basic sense, for without its energy they could not make new material—150,000 million tons a year by the land plants alone. Animals need the sun for a different purpose, for warmth and for light to see by, and they need its apparent daily rotation to keep their internal clock synchronized. But they do not need it—in fact, cannot use it—directly to make new material. They get that and their energy by eating either other animals or plants or the waste products of both.

Because of this, animals can break the bonds that normally restrict plants to the light-rich surface. Some, for instance, can fly over the Himalayas, and others can scavenge the deep ocean trenches. But they are, nonetheless, totally dependent on the more humdrum, earthbound activities going on at the surface.

The earth's surface itself is by no means uniform. Here it is a high northern mountain, bleak, windswept, and snowbound; there it is a desert, below sea level, bleak, sunbaked, and parched. Here where no rain falls, only snow, the sun makes six months of daylight and then vanishes for a six-month night. There, the temperature never drops below the sixties and the rain appears to fall not in drops but in ropes as thick as the creepers in the forests all around. Here, richly wooded grassland in well-watered, gently rolling country. There, hundreds of square miles of sand shimmering by day in life-quenching heat, shivering at night as that heat disperses through cloudless skies. These are but a few extremes of a planetary surface whose diversity has challenged generations of its students. Yet in each environment life of some kind has its foothold.

However harsh the environment, and whatever its extremes, one or more forms of life will have evolved to cope with its rigors.

Even in Antarctica, within a few degrees of the South Pole, there is a brief flurry of life at the height of summer. The unsetting sun melts a thin film on the crust of the snow. The cold air above may be well below freezing; and the snows below may preserve the harsh cold of winter. But in the

Right: precarious lodgings on cliff ledges keep guillemot and kittiwake fledglings safe from many hungry predators.

thin zone of melted crust there is a temporary alpine microclimate. And here, from spores that have lain dormant all winter long, springs a flourishing rash of red algae, turning the landscape pink. However, like the creatures of the ocean depths, these algae are dependent on nutrients from outside. Water and carbon dioxide are available locally; the rest comes in a fine dust, consisting chiefly of guano, blown down from warmer latitudes.

The alga that brings a blush to the Antarctic midsummer doesn't grow anywhere else. The spiny thorns and cacti that thrive in deserts cease to thrive—and may even die—in wetter environments. In short, the great diversity of conditions on this planet's surface—of climate, of light, of altitude—has molded living things into special communities of plants and animals, each adapted to one or other set of conditions. Later volumes in this encyclopedia will look in detail and in turn at such communities, so here we shall only touch on them in the most summary form. From this point of view it's a pity that there isn't a broad-based, roughly stepped mountain, somewhere just south of the Tropic of Cancer with its foot near the ocean shore and its peak around 25,000 feet. It would form a kind of world national park with examples at different levels of practically every kind of community we can see in the world at large.

Because Nature denies us this giant outdoor tableau of life, we shall have to invent it. Also, if we're not too specific about where we site it, we can concentrate on the most general points. For instance when we talk of tropical forests, we needn't worry about the differences between those found in different parts of the world; we can avoid such details in this general survey.

And tropical forests are where we begin, for they stretch away from the southern foot of our mountain toward the equator. All year around they have a high temperature and a high, evenly spread rainfall, and they are very humid. None of the other land zones is so favored. The plants can grow and produce fruit and flowers all year and this is beneficial for the animals, many of which can specialize their diet to one kind of fruit or to nectar from a single variety of flower. The even, year-around warmth favors the animals that can't make their own body heat—insects, spiders, mites, lizards, snakes, and so on. Elsewhere they become torpid when the temperature drops. Here they remain active, their bodily functions operat-

Vegetation varies with altitude and latitude. This imaginary mountain situated just south of the Tropic of Cancer, with its peak at around 25,000 feet, shows the distribution of plant communities from tropical forest at the foot to alpine scrub near the summit. Similar changes in plant-life zones occur as one travels from the equator to the poles.

Desert

Savanna

Snow and Ice

Alpine Scrub

Coniferous Forest

Grassland

Deciduous Forest

Tropical Rain Forest

ing at a high rate and they can therefore reach giant size: 10-inch centipedes, 6-inch snails, 10-foot lizards, 37-foot snakes—all live in the tropical forest, beneficiaries of its mild conditions.

The humidity is particularly good for animals with soft, porous skins, such as flatworms, leeches, and the strange little caecilians, worm-like cousins of frogs and newts. The humid forests enable them to live on land without the risk of drying out.

The whole pace of life seems speeded up here.

Breeding can go on all year, with each generation hard on the heels of its parents. Competition is fierce and, with so many more chances for genetic change, evolution may be fastest here. One sign of this is the huge variety of species—much greater than we shall find in other zones.

In the twilight gloom, color, light, and sound are important means of communication. Here we find the gaudiest butterflies, the gayest bird plumage, the brightest fireflies. And when the sun goes down and the forest wakes, its raucous cacophony

Left: seedlings spring up from the floor of a tropical forest. Intense competition means that thousands of seedlings must fail for each one that grows.

Below: the dense canopy of an Amazon rain forest allows little light to penetrate to the lower depths, yet in the warm, humid gloom life is more varied and more hectic than in any of the many other environments on earth.

will defeat all attempts at sleep by those who have not experienced such a noise before.

Even in small areas we find many stages of forest growth. Where a recent fire scarred a hillside we shall soon find a lush growth of broadleaved seedlings and grasses. Later they will give way to young saplings and shrubs. When the first saplings mature, we shall find the most typical kind of tropical forest, with enough light filtering down to support the ferns, shrubs, and animals of the forest floor. Halfway up the vegetation layer is another world filled with different plants and animals. And at the top, in the canopy, out in the fierce sunlight, we find another world again. In time the canopy will thicken, and less and less light will filter down, until only a few shrubs, tolerant of the deepest shade, will survive. This is the only kind of tropical forest where creatures like ourselves can wander freely among mighty tree boles that spread like the buttresses of castle walls. This situation does not last long. It needs only one giant to topple, letting

Above: a red uakari sleeping on a branch in the middle story of an Amazon forest. Uakaris are the only short-tailed monkeys in the New World. They feed on fruit and insects and rarely touch ground. When the red uakari is excited its face glows even stronger than the color seen here.

Cloud forest is a cooler and even wetter version of the tropical forest. The moist air encourages mosses, ferns, lichens, and orchids, which can grow so thickly that they festoon the trees.

17

in more light, and life soon strikes up again in the middle and lower layers.

As we climb the mountain, around 2500 feet, we notice that the forest changes character. It grows more humid and, with the altitude, colder, especially at night. Here we see relatively more of the warm-blooded animals, which are now more favored. Rainfall is heavy and the forest is often shrouded in wet mists that condense on every surface. The higher we go, the more marked this becomes. At about 6000 feet the forest is actually called "cloud" forest. Here everything is so permanently wet that tree trunks and branches are festooned with ferns, mosses, fungi, and orchids. So succulent are the plants of these higher reaches that many of the animals that eat them need never drink water at all. Many of the leaves and branches trap enough water to support whole

aquatic communities: for example, it is commonplace to find the tadpoles of tree frogs swimming in these little pools high above the ground.

Farther inland, higher than the coastal plain and away from the dependable rains, we find a belt of grassland. The rainfall is too low to support the rich, teeming forests—in fact, drought is always a threat here. There are many trees but they grow in isolated splendor or in scattered stands near water and along river banks. Between them is the grass that gives this region its name. In the warmest, southernmost parts of our mountain, it is tropical grassland or savanna.

The grassland's most characteristic animal is the browser or grazer—bison, kangaroo, antelope, horse, and so on. All have long legs and a swift gait to carry them to safety beyond the reach of the fierce and fearsome carnivores that

Plains bison, or buffalo, grazing the North American prairie. Once about 60 million roamed the plain. Now, after being hunted almost to the point of extinction, they survive only in national parks, sanctuaries, and zoos, where they are protected.

hunt them. Long legs are not their only adaptation to life out in the open. Many of them live in large herds to give mutual protection. Through long years of evolution the basic plan of the five-digit limb (seen for instance, in our own five fingers and toes) has become modified in the interest of lightness and speed, giving the two toes of the deer and ostrich and the one toe of the horse. Their eyesight, too, is generally much keener than that of forest dwellers. Zebra, for instance, can focus on grass at the end of their nose, yet they are also able to keep a distant object equally sharp. The side-facing eyes of the grazers give them clear all-round vision.

Smell plays an important part in communication on the grasslands, for the wind blows steadily and in a recognizable direction when there are no trees to break or confuse the wind currents. The predators drive from upwind, stalk and ambush from the lee. Most of the larger animals communicate through smell. There are smells for recognition, smells for aggression, smells for sex, smells for every purpose.

Because of their warmth and the high energy input from the sun these tropical grasslands can support a richly varied and abundant life. Even animals that share the same terrain and graze the same patch can do so without competing; for one may graze the coarser, taller grasses while the other takes the shorter, finer grasses in between.

The temperate grasslands, which are higher, cooler, and more to the north of our mountain, have the same general characteristics, and we can find similar relationships among their animals. But they are less prolific, with fewer species and less overlap. Also, there are relative-

Spotted hyenas, largest and strongest of Africa's scavengers, devour the remains of a lion's kill. When they have finished, it is the turn of the vultures, and then a host of smaller scavengers and bacteria take over, until nothing remains of the carcass.

Organ-pipe cactus and fuzzy cholla cactus in the Arizona desert have the succulent stems and spiny leaves typical of many drought-resistant desert plants.

ly fewer reptiles, insects, and other animals that rely on outside warmth to stay active.

The moist air that makes the cloud forest and the tropical forest loses its final vestiges of water in the form of snow higher up the mountain. It's a very dry wind that passes beyond the peak, and a very dry land, a desert in fact, that stands in its lee. As we move around the mountain, across the grasslands, we see its lush pastures giving way to patchy scrub and bare soil. The transition is so gradual that there is no place that we can put a marker saying "desert begins here." We shall take an orthodox definition and say that the desert starts where the rainfall is less than 10 inches a year and the temperature warm enough to evaporate water. Even at this limit an astonishing variety of life can thrive. There are plants that stay almost dormant until a flush of rain (perhaps the whole year's quota or more in one stupendous downpour) quickens them into a frenzy of flowering and seed-building. Then, too, last year's seeds, and earlier ones, germinate and grow, hastily building up enough reserve material to withstand the next long drought. This makes it clear that most sand deserts are not sterile but potentially fertile areas that lack the rain necessary for normal plant growth.

If we look more closely at the plants we shall

Most deserts are not barren or infertile but merely lack water. Even the Sahara Desert, whose massive dunes tower in the background of this picture, can spring into life at oases, where water abounds. Here plants flourish and animals gather.

see that many of them are adapted to resist plant-eaters and reduce water evaporation. Some have thorns and spines, often too small to be seen but robust enough to lodge in the soft flesh of a grazer's mouth and irritate the creature. Others have tough skins that are primarily adaptations for water conservation in the plant. Other adaptations of shape allow them to collect even such traces of moisture as dew and channel it toward their roots.

At dawn and dusk, before and after the fierce noonday heat, the desert springs to life. Most of the reptiles and insects are favored by their tough dry outer coverings and lack of pores. But there are also mice, jerboas, ground squirrels, jack-rabbits, and their predators—foxes and birds of prey. As the sun climbs, these creatures seek shelter. Only a few highly specialized animals, such as the antelope ground squirrel of the Mohave Desert or the oryxes and wild asses of Arabia and Asia and the desert gazelles of Africa, can tolerate the parched heat of midday.

Returning to our mountain slope, we find, above the cloud forest, a temperate zone supporting a rich variety of broadleaved forest trees. On the warmer southward face it is similar to the evergreen forests of Asia and Australia with bamboo and hard, waxy-leaved trees. Animals such as the pandas and macaques, the muntjacs and sika deer of the Asian forests, would be at home here. On the cooler slopes the evergreens give way to the sort of deciduous forest that once covered much of the Northern Hemisphere, before man. Here, there are frosts to damage the leaves. In winter the groundwater often freezes or lies inaccessible as snow. Responding to these harsh conditions, the trees shed their leaves and lie dormant until warmer, wetter days.

Hundreds of different organisms get to work on the annual fall of leaves to produce a rich humus; they include fungi, bacteria, and other plants, through springtails, lice, mites, and ants, to snails, millipedes, and beetles. These, in turn, support a host of lizards, snakes, frogs, moles,

mice, hogs, hedgehogs, and birds. Farther above ground, from the undergrowth to the branches of the trees, is an even richer community—deer that graze on bark, young shoots, and grassy clearings, squirrels, dozens of insect-eating songbirds, and again mice and beetles. The predators of this group are animals such as wolves, cougars, foxes, and badgers, through raccoons, skunks, and possums, to magpies, crows, and woodpeckers.

Except for the tropical rain forest no environment offers so many opportunities for living things to find a niche especially suited to them. (If climate and geography permitted, all kinds of land would tend to become forest land, temperate or tropical. Only cold, drought, low light input, high wind, or man can prevent it.)

The rich leafy humus, the moderate temperatures, and the generally thin canopy of a deciduous forest encourage a flourishing and varied undergrowth.

Below: the old world badger lives in woodland in Europe and Asia. It is a shy animal, much less aggressive than its relative the weasel. It feeds at night on insects, small rodents, and vegetation.

Higher still up the mountain, where it becomes even colder, we have a belt of coniferous, chiefly evergreen forest whose thin needle-shaped leaves are adapted to resist frost and drought and to make the most of the available light all the year around. It supports a similar diversity of living forms to the deciduous forest, though on a lesser scale.

Above the forest comes a mixed zone of hairy shrubs and dwarf trees. The hairs and the dwarf stature help to protect them from the frost and wind. Animal life at this level is noticeably more sparse. Higher still, above the tree line, is a zone of hardy alpine shrubs and grasses. The air here is thin, offering less protection from solar radiation and less blanketing warmth at night.

Without trees to hinder them the winds are strong, cold, and biting. The steep slope hastens the downward movement of the soil, which is already thin and poor. What is more, the mountain top is isolated by long stretches of quite different country from the next mountain top. As far as the plant and animal communities up here are concerned they might as well be on islands afloat among or above the clouds.

Almost all the plants here are perennial, growing toward maturity in stages that span the years. They tend to have a very concentrated cell fluid to act as antifreeze. Many of them are like tufted cushions, conserving heat the way a bird does when it fluffs out its feathers. Some can actually use their starch to make enough heat to

The red squirrel is among the most agile and graceful of all small mammals. Once the only squirrel in Britain, it was almost annihilated during this century by the introduction of the American gray squirrel. Its comeback, which dates from the middle of the century, is providing ecologists with a fascinating case study in the long-term equilibrium between competing animal species.

Left: mature coniferous forest forms a thicker canopy, and dense undergrowth is found only where that canopy is broken, letting in the light.

melt the snow that accumulates next to their roots.

The larger animals tend to be well insulated, surefooted climbers. Often they winter lower down, in the forests, returning to the heights with the thaw—the only time they can find unfrozen water up there.

The birds have adapted to rest on steep escarpments and in precarious clefts. Neither they nor the insects fly much; strong winds could buffet them so easily. But plenty of them can soar, eagles, lammergeiers, condors—all are at home here, all can use the rising currents to lift them up and keep them buoyant at very little cost in effort. Other birds are adept at crawling along sheer rock faces. gripping every tiny foothold with strong claws that are both sharp and long.

The richness of life in these extreme conditions is further demonstration that living things will use the resources of any zone, however harsh and inhospitable, and use them to the full. Nothing is wasted for long. For some plant or animal will adapt or invade from somewhere else and use any untapped resources. Even above this most forbidding zone there is yet another, harsher still, where life persists. Above the tree line, above the soil line, up there on bare rock, dormant for most of the year, coming alive only when the snows briefly melt and a pauper's dole of minerals can dissolve from the damp face of the rock, are the lichens, hardiest of all plant life.

Our trip up the mountainside, a stiff two- or three-day walk up about 21,000 feet, has been equivalent to a much longer walk—say about 4000 miles northward from the 20 degrees longitude where our imaginary mountain stands to about 80 degrees North. On the way we have passed through practically all the world's main kinds of land habitat and seen briefly the typical plant and animal communities they support. In later pages we shall see in greater detail how such communities arise and where they gain the energy and materials that keep them going. Before doing so however, by way of preparation, let us survey the two kingdoms of living things— animals and plants—seeing how they are organized, how they behave, and how their individual members fit into the great scheme of things. We begin, as befits the egocentric, self-obsessed creatures that we are, with man.

Left: the alpine ibex lives in small herds, high among glaciers. Males, such as this one, often stand on isolated peaks keeping watch while the females and young are hidden in the rocks.

Above: alpine choughs are among the highest-living birds in the world. Birds' very efficient lungs enable them to thrive at altitudes impossible to mammals—the only other animals that are warm-blooded and that therefore have a great demand for oxygen.

Below: the bright colors of alpine flowers help attract pollinating insects during the short flowering and ripening season.

Living Kingdoms

Every species is unique in some way, but man is unique in so many respects that it is hard to know where to start. We begin by relating him to other animals. He is obviously a primate, a close relative of apes and monkeys. In fact he and they had a common ancestor about 35 million years back. He has a sparser fur than they have but he compensates for this by wearing clothes. He has an upright posture and gait for which he is badly adapted anatomically; for instance, his nasal sinuses drain the wrong way, he has a weak hip joint, and his backbone has some of the weaknesses of an archway stood on its side. All of these give him constant trouble. His eyesight is acute, his hearing moderate, and his sense of smell lamentably defective.

Man lacks natural armament such as fangs or talons, and has a somewhat puny frame compared to other ground-dwelling primates. Human young are helpless for many months after birth and have a childhood that endures at least a decade. Full growth and sexual maturity is delayed even longer.

If this sounds like a prospectus for a doomed creature, that is because it leaves out the one outstanding advance that *Homo sapiens* shows: intelligence. Everything that has made him lord and potential destroyer of creation can be traced to this one attribute. His intelligence can beget language, writing, mathematics, and technology. It fosters the desire to understand and feeds the urge to control. It also makes it possible to learn from experiences gained and handed down through the centuries. It is, in fact, a breakthrough in evolution.

Until man appeared, evolution rested on the interplay of random change and opportunity—the random changes between parents and offspring,

There is only one living species that annexes territory and fundamentally changes its character on the scale shown in these pictures—man. Since the dawn of farming, man has applied this process to the very limits of his technology. As long as that technology remained primitive, the natural world around could contain his onslaught. Since industrialization, however, the process has become increasingly unbalanced.

White-handed gibbons

Baboons

Red-faced uakari

Long-tailed macaque

Despite their puny stature, comparatively small numbers of offspring, and other seeming drawbacks primates have used their high intelligence and their ability to form strong social groups to such advantage that they are now widely spread around the world and thrive in many different kinds of habitat, as shown in these pictures. Baboons live in scrub and open grassland in much of Africa and Arabia. They are poor climbers and prefer to stay near the ground. White-handed gibbons are found high in the forests of southern Asia.

and any opportunities that those changes gave their possessors to thrive and breed. No consciousness, and certainly no conscious effort, was involved. Many an early, short-necked giraffe must have stretched like a kitestring for succulent upper-branch leaves, but the effort had not the slightest effect on its offspring. The long neck had to wait for random changes in the makeup of giraffes—changes that giraffes could do nothing to hasten or prevent. But the appearance of intelligent self-consciousness has made the evolutionary process aware of itself. Its future course can never again be entirely haphazard; our deliberate actions must now, to no small degree, direct it. If you seek to know precisely what makes man unique, it is this: he

alone of all creatures controls the destiny of life on this planet—including his own—and he alone is equipped to make the necessary choices. Such sobering knowledge must color our study of all the other living things whose home we share.

The primates—which include lemurs, monkeys, apes, and man—are among the more ancient mammals in terms of bodily specialization. One need only look at the foreleg of the horse or hog, for instance, to see how they are much more developed for specific purposes than are the fairly unspecialized five-digit primate arm and hand.

Primates evolved as tree-living creatures. Their diet included insects, fruit, and nuts. The need to grasp branches, which grow at all angles,

Baboons

Uakaris are confined to small areas of the Amazon forests, where the numerous rivers act as barriers to their spread. By contrast the long-tailed macaque, or crab-eating monkey, is a powerful swimmer and a good diver. It can swim quite long distances and has become established on many Pacific islands. Its near relative, the Japanese macaque, thrives in snow for part of the year—a rare feat among primates other than man. It lives on forested mountain slopes in communities of up to 200 individuals.

and to pluck and skin fruit or pick insects out of the crevices, explains why the limbs of primates are as they are. They have so many tasks to perform. With rare exceptions primates need all five digits, and especially they need the thumb, which can oppose the others for gripping, grasping, holding, and manipulating. The great flexibility of the primate wrist and the ability of the forearm to rotate are other responses to the same requirements. In fact, the human hand and arm—the most highly developed of all—can make at least 54 movements of their 18 joints (counting bending and unbending as two movements).

In the treetop environment, sight becomes more important than smell, not only for seeing food and enemies but also in the swift coordination of eye and body during rapid movement through a maze of branches. The resulting enlargement of the visual centers in the brain is one of many cerebral developments that led ultimately to man. Each favored the development of the cranium and the shortening of the jaw.

Although some primates (for instance, baboons and man) have moved down from the trees, and others (such as chimps) spend only part of their time off the ground, the typical primate is still a tree dweller. And even those that have deserted the branches for the ground can still trace many of their physical traits and social behavior to their former environment.

Life in the treetops does not favor large families. Primates tend to have just one offspring at any one time and there is a corresponding reduction in the number of nipples, usually to a single pair. The resulting concentration of parental care is impossible where litters number 8 or more individuals. Pairs that produce 80 or so offspring can afford to lose 10 times as many individuals on the way to adulthood as can pairs that produce only 8 or so. In short, primates had to develop more elaborate arrangements for individual survival. The task was made doubly difficult by their relatively puny stature; they have no armored hide like a rhino, and no lethal claws and fangs like lions, although the canine teeth of chimps and baboons go part-way along that road.

Below: a young male chacma baboon uses a termite heap as a lookout post while guarding the troop from predators.

Below: two chacma baboons and a baby at a waterhole. Somewhere nearby a sentry will be keeping a keen watch.

Two dominant male gelada baboons from Ethiopia's Simien Mountains fight over the control of a harem of females. Such fights can profoundly change the order within the troop, although the general structure will remain unaltered.

Their most important response to this need was the development of a new form of social cohesion; primates reveal some of the most highly organized social groups in the whole realm of nature. Their organization is based not upon the sort of rigid and mechanical behavior we find in ant colonies, but upon a more intelligent and adaptable hierarchical system. Primates have no set mating season and thus enjoy a practically uninterrupted sex life. This creates a constant bond between male and female—a powerful cementing force among animals whose intelligence and adaptability must tend to favor individualism and personal aggrandizement.

These socializing characteristics are most marked among primates that have left the protection of the trees to live on the forest floor or even outside the forest altogether. Take, for instance, the baboons that live in the hills and rocky plains of Africa and Arabia. These gregarious and well-organized primates live in groups of 30 to 300 members, led by the older males. Whether primates are monogamous or prefer harems of females, the males guard their mates zealously, sometimes punishing infidelity with death; and rarely does one male court another's female. Yet aggression is well controlled by a number of ritualized behavior patterns. In general each baboon knows his or her place and defers to those above in order of dominance. A dominant individual, in return, is placated when a threatened subordinate (of either sex) presents its hindquarters as if for mating. The dominant individual may even make a few ritualized movements of copulation, as if to reassure the other that his aggression is subdued. Grooming is also a device for promoting cohesion and peaceably establishing dominance—especially among the young,

31

which must test their relationships without lethal struggles that would seriously weaken the troop and even threaten the species.

A troop on the move, with its chiefs and subordinate "officers," its sentries and outriders, its vanguard and rearguard, is one of the most fascinating sights in Nature. It can stand off leopards and even whole packs of wild dogs. The more one studies a troop in action, the more one marvels that the organization is achieved without any benefit of spoken and learned language.

Mammals have hair and suckle their young. These two features are more closely connected than you might think. Way back in evolution, when animals were first facing the problem of living away from water for extended periods, Nature came up with several solutions. The first to succeed on a large scale was that of the reptiles, which developed a hard, impervious skin that prevented water loss from the body. This was a successful answer to the problem of drying out but it left little possibility for the animal to develop temperature control systems, too. This is where we see the ingenuity of the mammal-type solution. Each mammal hair has a muscle to raise and lower it, and the skin between the hairs is richly provided with oil and sweat glands.

A white rhino cow nurses a calf. Young mammals in general are dependent on their parents for much longer than the young of most other animals. For this reason the offspring of mammals tend to be fewer in number and better cared for.

The fastest land animal is the cheetah (top speed 63 miles per hour), here seen chasing a Thomson's gazelle (50 miles per hour). The gazelle stands an even chance of survival by darting and swerving until the cheetah tires.

Between them these structures help to prevent the animal from drying out and are also important in the ability to control its temperature within very fine limits. This is why we call mammals "warm-blooded." Some of the secretion glands in the skin developed into milk-secreting glands with their outlets concentrated at the nipples. Without the hair and gland solution to the problem the suckle-feeding system could not have developed. On these two features the whole mammalian way of life depends.

Because the mother must make the food for her young within her own body, she cannot support big litters, the typical mammal litter being less than 10. You might think that mammalian survival is thus more precarious than for animals that produce thousands or even millions of off-spring at a time. But, there are compensations. Parental care among mammals is prolonged and intense, so that each individual is much better fitted to survive. Mammals also have a much more advanced basic design—something they owe to being warm-blooded.

A generally constant body temperature allows all the internal chemical reactions to go at a constant rate. This means that every body organ can function more precisely. Kidneys and livers can purify the blood to a finer degree. In turn this makes it advantageous for the circulation to divide into two circuits: one takes spent blood from the body organs to be replenished in the lungs; the other takes the replenished blood to the body. Only birds and mammals have this refinement. In fact, whatever system we look at in the mammalian body we find to be more sophisti-

Above: bats are the only mammals to have successfully taken to the air.

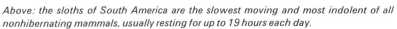

Above: the sloths of South America are the slowest moving and most indolent of all nonhibernating mammals, usually resting for up to 19 hours each day.

Below: although they breathe air, like all other mammals, white seals are among those that have successfully returned to a life in the sea.

cated, more efficient, and more finely controlled than in any earlier life form. This paves the way for the most significant mammalian feature of all, intelligence.

Intelligence is a property of the nervous system, especially its center, the brain. A brain that is irrigated by blood of constantly varying composition and is housed in a body of constantly varying temperature is never going to be or do anything very sophisticated. But a brain that is protected from such variations is open to enormous capabilities. And the mammal that possesses it has a formidable power. For along with the improved brain goes a generally improved sensory network—keener sight, more sensitive smell, better hearing—and a more efficient body, too. Longer legs for swifter movement, hip and shoulder joints of greater strength and flexibility, more highly developed and specialized teeth, and more efficient circulation are just a few of dozens of improvements that we find among the mammals and, to a different degree, the birds.

Mammalian development was spurred on by intense competition. The mammal flesh-eater—the fox, say, or the tiger—with its keen senses, powerful jaws, and intelligence, is one of the most formidable hunting-killing creatures in the entire history of life. In response to this quite unprecedented challenge, plant- and insect-eaters developed special defenses: extra long legs with

Dolphins are even more aquatic than seals. Among the most intelligent and likeable of all mammals, they have a large "vocabulary" of sounds whose meanings are now being intensely studied. It has been reported that they can even mimic human voices.

fewer toes for the horses and deer; greater climbing dexterity for the tree dwellers (some of which, such as flying squirrels and bats, even went so far as to develop gliding and flying ability); thicker armor for the rhinos, anteaters, and porcupines; better digging claws for the burrowers; and protective coloring for many of them. Even the smaller flesh-eaters had to defend themselves against their larger fellows. The repellent odor of the skunk is just one such defense.

Competition for food has also played a major role in shaping the mammal orders. The complicated guts of the grass- and leaf-eaters allow them to process large quantities of low-grade food. The streamlined bodies of the swimmers enable them to chase and catch fish, just as the light bodies and filmy wings of the bats, the only true flying mammals, help them to catch insects in flight or to eat fruit on normally inaccessible branches. The long snouts, tongues, and claws of some insect grubbers, and the fearsome talons, fangs, and colossal neck muscles of the big carnivores are more obvious examples of how competition for food has shaped the mammalian body.

As one new form developed from another, the mammals pushed out into new habitats. From the tropical ferny scrub in which they probably made their first appearance they spread into the swamps and marshes, the rivers and seas, the forests and mountains and even into the air. Now they are found in every continent and climate. Each of these new environments, in turn, has further modified and refined the mammals that ventured into it, producing, for example, the water-repellent hide of the seal, and the almost hairless skin of man, the self-renewing teeth of rodents and the bone-crunching molars of the dog, the 330-degree field-of-view of the horse and the ultrakeen stereoscopic vision of some monkeys, to name just three contrasts.

Yet, despite their diversity of form and life style, mammals have a surprising number of features in common, especially their basic body plan and life cycle. The way they reproduce, for instance, is very similar across the whole range; only monotremes such as the duckbilled platypus (which lays eggs) and marsupials such as kangaroos (which nurture their fetuses in a pouch instead of a womb) differ in this respect. Interestingly enough, both kinds of animal are near or at

A fur seal bull surrounded by a harem of females—all of them won in fierce combat with rival bulls.

Two male lions fighting. Although living in prides has advantages in hunting and communal rearing of young, lions are competitive and aggressive and such flare-ups are common.

the bottom of the mammal intelligence scale. Biologists link this with the relative inefficiency of eggs and pouches compared with the wombs in which all other mammals rear their fetuses.

A fetus in an egg is living off a fixed food supply, can be subject to great temperature fluctuations, and is surrounded (until the shell breaks) by a mounting accumulation of its own toxic wastes. A fetus in a pouch has no direct bloodstream-to-bloodstream connection with its mother—to supply food and remove wastes—but must rely on the slower processes of digesting the food it absorbs from tiny nipples in the pouch, and excreting the waste products. By contrast, a fetus in a womb is at constant temperature and has minute-to-minute adjustment of the foods and wastes in its bloodstream—ideal conditions in which to develop the delicate and complex struc-

tures of its brain and other organs.

After it is born, the parental attention given to a mammal is markedly different from most other animals. Its parents will continue their intensive care for a long time after birth. They will protect it from the worst consequences of its own lively curiosity, which itself is an outstanding mammalian feature. A young mammal will explore and probe the world around it, learning what it can control and what it must avoid or abandon.

Part of that surrounding world will consist of its fellows. In relating with them in what we call "play" (which is by no means a trivial or frivolous activity) the young mammal learns to fit the hierarchy of its social group. Such social groups are extremely common among mammals, from elephants to mice and from seals to bats. They depend on a general observance of a code of behavior in which dominant and subordinate individuals accept duties and obligations to one another. The code is rigid but the individuals may change their rank with changing circumstances. This makes mammal societies much more flexible and adaptable than, for instance, insect colonies. The dominant animal may establish itself by actual fighting, but most mammals have worked out a system where the *threat* to fight is enough, and the animal that threatens most convincingly wins.

In cold climates mammals tend to breed once a year, the young being born at the most favorable season, spring to early summer. Often these mammals are solitary or they may live in loosely organized feeding groups until their usually dormant sex organs become active again. Then the male tends to establish a territory, fighting off other males and jealously guarding his mate or even a whole harem of females.

In warmer and more constant climates mammals tend to breed all year, the female going on heat at a certain time after her last offspring was born. Between heats she is sexually indifferent and ignores or repels male overtures. Mammals organized in societies with dominant and subordinate strata tend to belong to this group, which includes dogs, elephants, lions, many rodents, and, as we have seen, the primates.

Some advanced mammals have an ability unique among animals: they can communicate by facial gesture as well as by the more usual means

Left: a male mule deer closely following a doe on heat during the breeding season. This is the only time during the year that the sexes take any particular interest in one another.

—vocal sounds, drumming or ground beating, touch, and smell. Man is unusual in that his sense of smell is limited. The marvelous universe of scents and odors, in which his dog takes such an obvious delight, is forever barred to him. And to go for a walk with a dog in woodland after a spring rainshower is to know blindness in a world of magical colors.

Mammals produce odors from complex glands in different parts of their bodies. Lemurs have them on their wrists and shoulders, some antelopes and deer have them under their eyes, muntjacs have them on their feet, hamsters on the flank, and in many other mammals they are near the tail. Like the milk-giving mammary glands most of these scent glands evolved from the oil glands that keep the fur in condition and so are an essential mammalian feature. In fact, mammals usually smell each other when they meet, and thus exchange information about their present state and condition.

Mammals that live in cool or very cold climates face severe problems in the depth of winter, especially the smaller ones, which lose body heat much more rapidly than the larger ones. Unlike birds, they cannot swiftly migrate to a warmer climate; instead, many hibernate. Some, such as the bears, experience a drop in body temperature but retain all their faculties, waking several times between snowfall and thaw. Others, such as dormice and some kinds of squirrels, reduce their temperature greatly and their heart-rate falls to around five beats a minute; they go into a true torpor from which they do not naturally waken until spring. The edible dormouse, which is found in temperate climates, regularly hibernates at least six months, from October through April, and one ground squirrel has been cooled to a body temperature less than one degree above freezing with no untoward effect.

Even mammals that are active all year around spend a large part of every day asleep. Most people think of mammals as either daytime (*diurnal*) or nighttime (*nocturnal*) animals. In fact by far the greatest number are *crepuscular*— active morning and evening, sleeping or resting at the height of day and dead of night. Visitors to national parks said to be rich in wildlife are often disappointed until they realize this fact.

The bigger a mammal is, the longer it tends to

A lesser horseshoe bat deep in hibernation and a black bear in its somewhat shallower winter sleep—the mist is actually the bear's breath. Mammals tend to hibernate during the winter months whereas birds usually migrate to warmer parts.

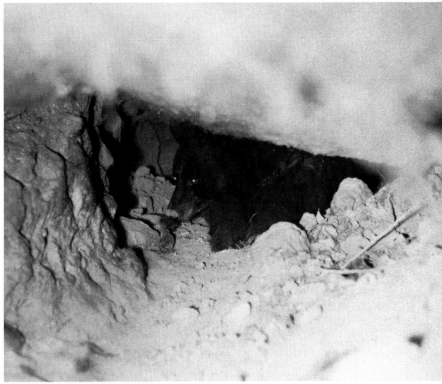

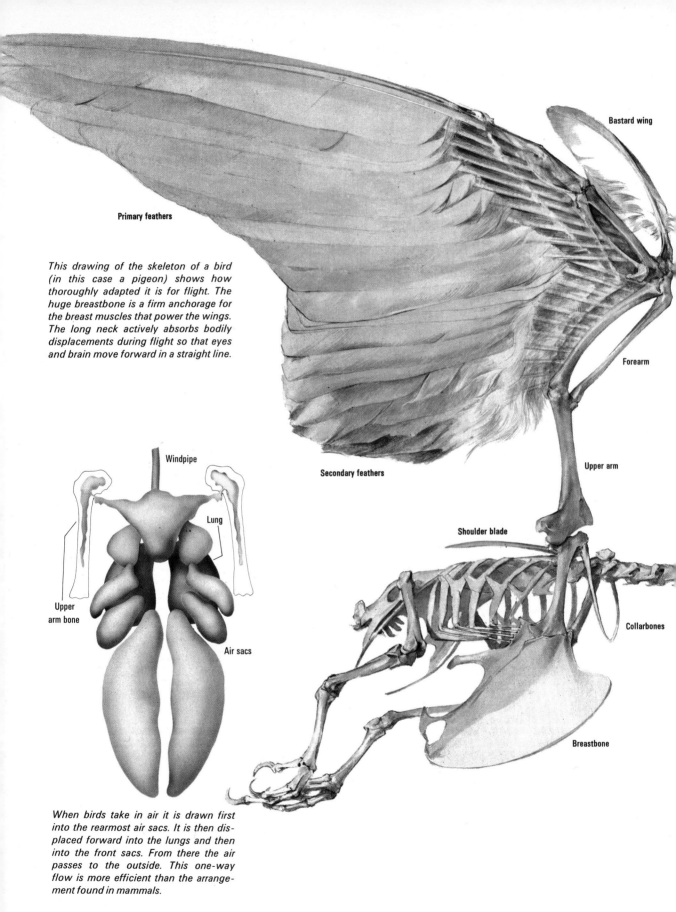

Bastard wing

Primary feathers

This drawing of the skeleton of a bird (in this case a pigeon) shows how thoroughly adapted it is for flight. The huge breastbone is a firm anchorage for the breast muscles that power the wings. The long neck actively absorbs bodily displacements during flight so that eyes and brain move forward in a straight line.

Forearm

Secondary feathers

Upper arm

Windpipe

Lung

Shoulder blade

Upper arm bone

Collarbones

Air sacs

Breastbone

When birds take in air it is drawn first into the rearmost air sacs. It is then displaced forward into the lungs and then into the front sacs. From there the air passes to the outside. This one-way flow is more efficient than the arrangement found in mammals.

40

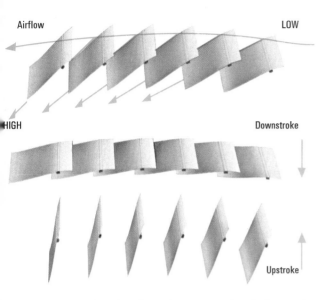

Arrangement of feathers in a wing ensures that during soaring air is moved from above to below the wing (1). On the downstroke of the wings the feathers automatically overlap (2) and on the upstroke they open (3)—like the slats of a venetian blind—to offer minimum air resistance and save energy.

live. Maximum life spans range from just over one year for the pygmy shrew, through 22 years for the tiger, 33 years for the bison, 54 years for the hippo, to 69 years for the Asiatic elephant. To be sure, these are maximums; the average life expectancy of the elephant is only around 15 years. A major exception to this trend is the order of primates, with maximums up to 52 years (a chimp). And the greatest exception is man, whose average life expectancy in the developed world is about three times as long as his size and weight would lead one to expect.

We can recognize birds most reliably by their outer covering of feathers. These and wings are found on all birds, even those that cannot fly. Yet behind this basic similarity lies an astonishing diversity. The smallest bird of all, the bee hummingbird (at $\frac{1}{8}$ ounce) could just about cover one eye of the largest, the ostrich (at 340 pounds). The ostrich cannot fly, whereas the common swift stays airborne for at least nine months each year. The king eiderduck can search for mussels 150 feet under water, and the alpine chough, as we saw at the beginning of this book, has been seen over 26,000 feet up in the Himalayas. In fact, so diverse and successful are birds that, central Antarctica apart, there can be very few square miles of the earth's surface on which the shadow of a bird does not regularly fall.

The key to their success lies in the solution, about 100 million years ago, to a problem that human aero-engineers are just learning to tackle: the problem of drag. In an efficient wing, bird or

The widely spanning wings of the gannet are perfectly adapted to take advantage of the slightest updraft around the cliffs and coastal waters it inhabits.

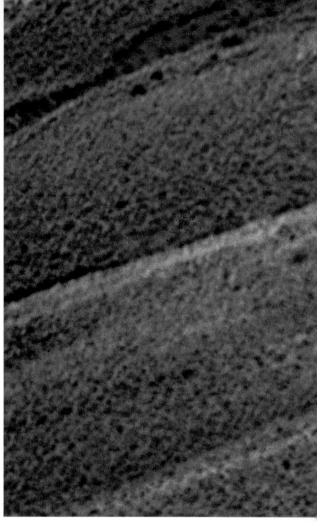

Penguins huddle on an ice floe in the Antarctic. Their webbed toes and flipperlike wings are evidence of how completely adapted they are to an aquatic way of life.

airplane, the air must pass more quickly over the upper than the lower surface; the higher pressure in the slower-moving air helps lift the wing. The forces that resist the forward movement of the bird or plane are called drag. One way of reducing them, we are now learning, is to remove air from the low-pressure upper surface and pump it into the higher pressure region below. When you look at the spread of feathers in an outstretched bird wing you can see just how this is achieved. The bird's anatomy is even more fascinating, for the feathers automatically rotate like the slats of a venetian blind so that the wings offer little air resistance in their upward sweep.

The shape of a bird's wing is closely related to its life style. The wing is a modified forelimb and has the same elements as our own—an upper arm, a forearm, and a number of digits. A bird that needs to accelerate quickly, such as a grouse or a corncrake, has short broad wings. Such birds spend long periods perched or earthbound and little or no time in gliding flight. Birds that spend most of their time soaring tend to have long, thin wings. These allow them the fullest advantage of the dynamics of air currents over land and sea and, like the thin wings of supersonic aircraft and gliders, have minimum drag. Albatrosses and tropic birds are good examples of these. In between we can find every kind of variation. Swifts and falcons, for instance, have short forearms and long hands, which sweep back, V-wing style, to give stability in high-speed diving. Owls have special feathers at the wingtip and trailing edge to make their flight absolutely silent. This not only enables an owl to take small rodents by surprise but also allows it to glide and fly in silence, listening for tell-tale rustles and scratchings in the undergrowth—tiny noises that could

Above: the Andean condor is the heaviest bird of prey and among the longest-lived of all birds. Its vast wings enable it to soar effortlessly at heights up to 20,000 feet.

Below: hummingbirds are remarkable not only for their small size but also for the wide range of environments they inhabit—including forests, deserts, and mountain snows.

easily be drowned by wind sighing through wings close to the bird's ears. In this way an owl can swoop upon an unsuspecting mouse in woodland in near-total darkness. There are even wings that are perfectly adapted for "flying" underwater, such as those of the Peruvian diving petrel and the pelican.

The feathers that make up the wing and that cover the rest of the body are a miracle of natural design. Look at a plucked bird trussed for cooking and you will clearly see tracts on the skin from which the feathers grew. In most birds these tracts cover less than two thirds of the body area (excluding the legs, whose scales recall the birds' reptilian ancestors), the rest being naked or sprouting only hairlike feathers or down. Birds have only one oil-secreting gland, found at the tail, and called the *uropygial* gland (from Greek words for "tail" and "rump"); but not all

An electronic flash captures an owl moments before it swoops on an unsuspecting mouse. The owl is superbly adapted for this kind of raid: soft down hushes the swish of its wings, and powerful night vision and acute hearing help it to home in on its quarry.

birds have even this. When a bird preens itself, it is not only spreading oil from this gland over its feathers and generally grooming itself, but also instinctively realigning its feathers for peak aerodynamic efficiency.

Plumage colors are of two kinds. Some result from actual pigments in the feathers, these tending to be white, yellow, black, brown, red, or buff. Others are produced by thin transparent plates and prismlike formations in the plumage that bend, reflect, and alter the light in such a way as to create colors, especially greens, blues, and purples. Often both types are superimposed. The green-blue-purple sheen seen in some black-colored birds is one example. Another is the iridescent green of a parrot feather, produced by a yellow pigment overlying an iridescent blue layer. If you compress the feather you can destroy the blue, turning that part of the feather yellow.

Most of a bird's body weight is taken up by the muscles used in flying. The wings are anchored with especial firmness in what amounts to a double set of collarbones. Each rib is strengthened by a bony process that projects backward to overlap the one behind and the whole rib cage is further protected by a long shoulder blade. The breastbone has a deep keel to anchor the flight muscles. Practically every muscle in this region is devoted to flying, even the muscles that, in mammals, are used for breathing.

Birds have very different lungs from those we see in mammals. Instead of a larynx at the top of their throat they have a syrinx at the bottom of the windpipe, where they make their calls and songs. In flight the ribcage expands and contracts with the rhythm of flying. Perched or earthbound they can use the throat muscles to assist their breathing. But in both cases the air is pumped into one set of sacs, through the lung to a different set of sacs, and then out again. Because the air goes only one way through the lungs, they are much more efficient at extracting oxygen and passing it to the blood than are the mammalian lungs. Many birds can stay chirpy and active at altitudes where men need oxygen masks.

Birds have remarkable eyesight. For instance, they have two "yellow spots"—regions of sharp vision—instead of the single yellow spot in the human eye. One gives sharp vision on each side, the other gives sharp binocular vision forward, as in our own eyes. Moreover birds have about 10 times as many light-sensitive cells in these spots as we have, which perhaps means that they can distinguish the shapes in this |||||||||| as clearly as we can in this █ █ █

Their reproductive systems, too, are very different from those of mammals. Except for ducks and some flightless birds the males have no penis. When they copulate they drop their sperm into the *cloaca*—a cavity near the tail—and turn it inside out to meet the female's cloaca, which she also turns inside out. Immature females have two ovaries and ducts but only the left one becomes functional; the right one withers to a mere rudiment. The sperms travel up the oviduct and fertilize ova already descending and well supplied with yolk. The fertilized ova become covered with egg-white, then with a double membrane (soft shell) and finally with a shell, which is often colored or patterned.

With many birds the males and females are so different that they look like separate species; peacocks and birds of paradise are well-known examples. Often this kind of difference goes hand in hand with polygamy or at least with the kind of monogamy that lasts only briefly. Here the males must fight for their mates or harems. In birds with harems, such as the farmyard fowl, this differentiation is often extreme. The male chooses the roosting site, protects and fusses over the hens, foraging for food and giving them first choice when he finds it. But he shows little interest in nest-building, brooding, incubating, or rearing the chicks. At the other extreme are birds such as hemipode quails and painted snipes, where the females fight for the males, mate with them, lay eggs, and then seek another mate, leaving the first to do all the brooding and rearing.

Most birds are monogamous, choosing a mate and pairing off until the fledglings have flown, and sometimes forming two or even three such pairs in a season. Usually it is the males who fight, not so much for the females as for particular territories. Males that win territories then mate with available females. Males that gain no territory do not come into mating condition and so do not sing the song that advertises "male and territory available." Some birds, it is thought, pair for life; among them are parrots, swans, geese, pigeons, and many birds of prey. Certainly they form stable bonds over many years.

Fights between males often do not reach actual physical violence and bloodshed, for that would imperil the survival of the whole species. More often they merely threaten to fight and the resulting behavior is among the most entertain-

The brown pelican fishes in salt water from southern United States to southern South America. It cruises at about 20 feet above the water until it is certain of its prey and then dives clumsily, relying on speed to make a kill.

ing in the whole animal kingdom. Partridge cocks will pursue and flee from each other with apparent malice or terror; but watch closely and you'll see how careful they are to preserve a sort of traveling no-man's-land between them. Among ruffs no two cocks are alike when, in spring, they grow the huge circles of colored neck feathers that give them their name. They stand on special "hills" (display grounds), erect their ruffs, and shiver at each other most menacingly, but hardly ever do they fight. Woodpeckers with chisel-sharp beaks rarely peck one another, and birds of prey do more play acting than harm in their elaborate aerial encounters.

Displays, too, are a prominent feature of courtship among birds. The huge red throat of the cock great frigate bird rouses the hen to great sexual excitement. The little Adélie penguin continues to display long after it has paired off. In courtship it stretches its head and bill slowly up, clapping its flippers, throwing out its chest, and making a noise like a drum. When they have paired and nested, either bird visiting the nest will bring a sort of goodwill offering to the other, which may be a bit of fish or just a stone. Then they will bow deeply to each other or stand face to face, bills up, crests erect, and rock from side to side shouting raucously—a sound that carries up to half a mile.

Coloration has many other uses among birds. Dotterels, nightjars, and other ground-nesting birds are so well camouflaged that they can be almost impossible to find. To most carnivores the black korhaan is nauseous and its plumage conspicuous; but the highly edible Rüpell's korhaan is well camouflaged. The high-contrast plumage of kingfishers, drongos, and some honeyeaters may have a similar function.

The Australian frogmouth can gape, displaying a flowerlike mouth and throat, to attract the insects it feeds on. The eastern kingbird and royal flycatcher have flowerlike crests that may serve the same purpose. Another American bird, the pygmy owl, has a false face on the back of its head to confuse birds that may seek to mob it during daytime. And there are many birds that can flash sudden and confusing patterns of bars, stripes, and eyelike spots in the face of a predator.

Courtship displays lead, naturally, to mating, nesting, egg-laying, and incubation. Birds have a higher body temperature than mammals because they need to deliver energy to their muscles at a

The complex courtship display of Africa's greater flamingo climaxes in the wing salute shown here. Such displays play an important part in arousing the sexes and leading them into mating postures. Flamingos breed in vast colonies of up to a million pairs.

The male great frigate bird has an orange pouch that turns brilliant red and becomes inflated during courtship.

Flamingo chicks cannot survive without the help of their parents. Here, in the midst of a breeding colony and safe from most predators, a greater flamingo feeds its young chick small crustaceans and worms filtered out of the mud.

Below: two male golden pheasants fighting. Although they can wound each other, their fights are rarely to the death. The flapping wings, fluffed-up neck feathers, sudden leaps, and flashing spurs look aggressive but they are partly a charade.

Above: the ruff takes its name from the beautiful neck feathers the male displays at mating time. The males congregate, each on its own "hill," and strive to outshine one another as females choose among them for a mate.

Above: the beginnings of a weaver-bird nest. Sometimes many individuals work together to make a communal home. Below: the completed nest. These remarkable structures, some of which house hundreds of birds, are found in many parts of Africa.

much higher rate. The average temperature is around 110 to 112°F. Unhatched chicks need the same sort of temperatures, and this is easiest to arrange in a nest. So nests are almost universal among birds, ranging from the simplest heaping-up of mud to complex structures like the bower-bird's bower, the mallee fowl's self-heating heap, or the vast hanging communes of the sociable weavers. The long-tailed tailor bird is an extraordinary nest builder. It makes a typical bowl-shaped nest of sticks, stems, and down, but slings it in a cradle made by sewing large leaves together. For thread it uses vegetable fiber or fibers stolen from houses. It stabs holes in the leaves and pulls the thread through before securing it with a stopknot. Some birds make no nest of their own at all. The tiny elf owl uses old woodpecker holes. Nutcrackers drive out squirrels and expropriate their drey. Cowbirds, honey guides, and most species of cuckoo simply lay their eggs in other birds' nests.

The most extraordinary incubation story of all must surely be that of the emperor penguin of Antarctica. This is the only bird that never normally sets foot on dry land. In April and May, when the Antarctic winter closes in, the emperors make for the bleak wastes of winter ice. There, in the last rays of the dying summer, the females lay their eggs and return to the food-rich waters around the ice. During the winter-long night, in temperatures that may reach below −80°F and in winds that may gust up to 100 miles per hour, the males huddle in "pods," taking turns to share the warm center while each incubates his egg on the tops of his feet and beneath a warm, feathered fold of skin. To expose the egg could mean instant death to the chick inside.

During his two-month vigil, a typical male loses one third of his 75 to 90 pounds weight, yet when the chick hatches in July or August, the father can still disgorge a little nourishment from his crop. Just before the eggs hatch the glossy, fattened females come back. From then on the males and females take it in turn to feed and tend the chicks. Then, by January, when the summer comes and the ice breaks, conditions are most favorable for a young emperor to fend for itself.

Chick-rearing habits are as varied as those of nest-building and egg-incubation. Among domestic fowls, ducks, gulls, ostriches, and others the chicks are born covered with down, open-eyed, and able to leave the nest at once. They have reserves of fat that carry them through until they

49

can find their own food—which is why day-old domestic chicks can safely be express freighted. But most perching birds, birds of prey, pigeons, and woodpeckers have chicks that hatch naked and blind and that need a great deal of parental care before they can fend for themselves. Pigeons feed their young on "pigeon's milk" that they regurgitate from the crop at the base of the food pipe. Others spend a large part of every day foraging for grubs, worms, seeds, or other food for their ever-ravenous brood. The bright colored throats of the gaping nestlings are a powerful display signal triggering the foraging and feeding activity of the parent.

The way birds respond to seasonal change is also markedly different from the pattern we have seen among mammals. Only the poor-will of America is known to hibernate. The rest either stay put and make the best of it, like the ptarmigan, or they migrate. Almost half the world's bird

species have two homes. Of Greenland's 64 regular species, 36 vanish southward in winter. And even in tropical Mexico, with 950 species, some 200 are winter visitors only, or just passing through. In the temperate lands between, migratory birds are in a clear majority.

It is possible that birds have migrated since their earliest days on earth, although some naturalists point out that the Ice Ages must have added a powerful impetus to the habit. Today billions of birds pour down the world's flyways each fall. Most of them migrate from their northerly summer homeland to the warmer climates in the south. Some, such as the black-capped chickadee or the rosy finch, merely fly from the mountain top, where they summer, to the valley below, where they winter. At the other extreme is the Arctic tern, which breeds in the Arctic summer, then in fall spans the globe to enjoy the Antarctic summer. Great shearwaters make a slightly shorter journey at the same time but they breed in the Antarctic.

Wherever possible, migrants fly overland. For instance, North American birds favor routes through Mexico, or Florida, to Yucatán, instead of more direct routes over the Gulf or the Caribbean. Naturally they are most vulnerable to predators, especially man, at the times when they gather; and there is no doubt that if the United States government had not established a network of refuges along the flyways, many migratory birds, especially wildfowl, would long ago have joined the extinct passenger pigeon, whose migrating flocks once darkened the noonday sun. Similar action is surely needed in Europe, where Maltese, Sicilians, and other islanders on the flyways wreak annual carnage among exhausted fall migrants.

How birds navigate is still something of a mystery. Birds have been trapped, transported, and released far beyond their natural range yet have found their way back within days, even across the Atlantic. Sun and stars have something to do with it for many birds stop halfway and roost or forage if the sky is overcast. And birds released in planetaria have flown the predictable course southward according to the layout of the constellations being projected.

Undoubtedly many thousands of birds die each year as a direct result of migration, through exhaustion, straying, or predation. Yet the habit is so widespread that it must offer advantages that far outweigh this toll in lives. Among them are a year-around best-of-both-worlds environment and an enormous adaptability. Much of the success of birds can be traced to this feature.

The strange incubation of the emperor penguin's egg begins in total darkness and bitter cold around early July. For six weeks the males cradle the eggs between their feet and their bellies. When the winds blow they huddle in groups, taking turns to stand at the warm center. The eggs hatch just after daylight returns to Antarctica. Then the females come back to care for the young.

Above: a young black-shouldered kite puts on a threat display to ward off a carpet python. Pythons have no venom and kill their prey by wrapping themselves around it and crushing or strangling it to death before finally eating it.

Below: an Australian copperhead snake devouring a frog—whose contorted limbs show the effect of the snake toxin. During the process the snake covers the frog with a lubricating saliva, some of which can be seen in the picture.

Above: this western rattlesnake shows clearly the forked tongue, which flickers in and out capturing small particles and transferring them to smell organs in the roof of the mouth. The heat-sensing pits, behind the nostrils, help it find warm-blooded prey.

Below: the open jaws of a red diamondback rattlesnake show clearly its poison fangs. In the background is the snake's rattle.

Reptiles were the first animals with backbones to overcome the problems of living away from water for long periods without drying out. They developed a hard scaly skin that, unlike the skin of fish and amphibians, has few or no glands. As a result, their skin is not tacky or slimy but dry. The only way the reptile can renew it is to grow a new one underneath and then cast the old one entirely. This modification, among others, made them one-time Lords of the Earth. For over 100 million years their supremacy was unchallenged. But conditions changed, the environment became less favorable, and the birds and mammals, with better basic design, began to take over. Now only four kinds of reptiles survive: snakes, lizards, turtles, and crocodiles. One lizardlike reptile, the tuatara of New Zealand, is in fact the sole survivor of an order whose other members died out 100 million years ago.

The reptile blood circulation is much less efficient than that of mammals and birds. In most reptile hearts spent blood from the body partially mixes with freshly oxygenated blood from the lungs. As a result they can get only enough oxygen to their tissues to do the minimum essential work of movement, digestion, tissue repair, and so on. Birds and mammals can afford to use foodstuffs simply to keep up their body temperature. But not reptiles—for body warmth they rely almost entirely on sunshine and the warmth of the air around them. This, in turn, restricts their normal range to temperate and tropical lands; most reptiles cannot live for more than a few minutes in snow, even at melting point. Nevertheless some of the forms that *have* survived are remarkably like their ancestors of 200 million years back, so in the general scheme of life they can hardly be called unsuccessful (and certainly not by a species that has not yet lasted through one hundredth of that span!).

Snakes are probably derived from other burrowing reptiles that progressively lost the need for limbs. They range in size from about 37 feet, the maximum authenticated length for the anaconda, down to the four-inch West Indies thread snake, which could crawl comfortably through the hole left in a pencil from which the lead has been extracted. Many of the snakes between these extremes are venomous. Those with poison fangs at the back of their jaws tend to be mildly so; front-fanged ones include the more deadly. The poisons work by clotting the blood, or destroying the blood vessels, or paralyzing the nerve system of their victim.

All snakes are carnivorous. Having no limbs makes eating difficult, so snakes often swallow their victim whole. The largest African rock pythons can swallow animals up to 150 pounds. To help the process, the snake's jaw is not hinged like ours but has a wonderful system of levers that allows for great flexibility of movement.

Although almost deaf, snakes are extremely sensitive to vibration. The reason we rarely see them is that our lightest footfall can send them scurrying long before we come into direct view. They also have a keen sense of smell, using an organ in the roof of the mouth together with the tongue, which flicks in and out to pick up air-borne particles and carry them to the smell organ for sampling. Pit vipers (bushmaster, copperhead, and rattlesnakes, among them) have a heat-sensing pit between eye and nose on each side of their face. Equally remarkable is the rattle of the rattlesnake. Made of dried skin from previous casts, it must have saved many from being trampled by buffalo herds on the move.

Considering they have no legs snakes can move extraordinarily fast. In fact they have four ways of moving. The commonest is *serpentine:* wiggling over soft soil or through water, and pushing back on it at each bend of the body. If the soil is very loose snakes can *sidewind,* i.e. roll sideways with a looping motion. For moving along crevices snakes will *concertina* themselves forward pressing their bodies firmly against the wall. Heavy-bodied snakes can also move their belly skin *caterpillar* fashion, using their scales to get a

good purchase. The fastest a snake can move is about four miles per hour (although greater speeds are claimed), a pace that even young children can easily outrun.

Male snakes are generally smaller than females and have relatively longer tails. They live apart except at breeding time. Boas, pythons, and a few other snakes have the remains of back legs near their cloacas, which is where the male's penises are found (each male snake and lizard has two penises). They use these vestigial legs to scratch the back and sides of the female and excite her into offering her cloaca. When she does so the male uses one of his penises to inject his sperm. Many other snakes go into a kind of intertwining dance to line up their cloacas; it may last several hours with every appearance of

Above: there is a strong tendency among some groups of island-dwelling reptiles to evolve smaller and smaller species. Day geckos of the Seychelles, such as the one above, for instance, are at least 30 per cent smaller than their cousins on the far larger neighboring island of Madagascar.

The Komodo "dragon," a monitor, is the largest living lizard, sometimes exceeding 10 feet in length. Despite its enormous size it was totally unknown to Western science until 1912. It inhabits the Indonesian islands of Komodo and Flores.

55

intense excitement. The embryos grow inside soft-shelled eggs. Sometimes they hatch inside the mother and take their first nutrient as secretions from the walls of her egg duct, a forerunner of the mammal system. Some hatch as they are laid; others are left to hatch later. There is generally very little parental care and most die before maturity, their death being balanced by large numbers—10 to 100—in each clutch.

Lizards are the most numerous reptiles of all, in terms both of species and of absolute numbers. Considered as a piece of structural engineering their skeleton is clumsier than that of the mammals, especially in the way their limbs join onto the trunk. Despite this they can, when warm, move at dazzling speeds over short distances. There are some in which limbs have atrophied to mere stumps, or have even vanished completely so that they are often confused with snakes. None of the snakelike lizards is venomous: in fact, there are only two venomous lizards in the world, the Gila monster and the closely related beaded lizard of the south-western states of America and western Mexico.

Lizards range in size from the Komodo "dragon" (really a monitor), which has been recorded at just over 10 feet and lives on certain Indonesian islands, down to the tiny gecko measuring just 1.4 inches and found only on Virgin Gorda, one of the British Virgin Isles.

Some lizards burrow in the soil but most live on the ground or in the trees. Many of them, especially geckos, are active only at night. Geckos have soft scales, which is probably an adaptation to their very active life style, but which also makes them vulnerable. They have suction pads on their fingers and toes, which enable them to run upside down on overhangs and straight up sheer vertical surfaces. One lizard, the marine iguana, feeds under water although it is a land-based, air-breathing animal. A naturalist living in the Galápagos Islands, home of the marine iguana, has domesticated several of them and found that they will eat a wide variety of vegetables, but in the wild they browse only on seaweeds, which they will dive several fathoms deep to find.

The flying lizards of Southeast Asia have a thin veil of skin that can be stretched out, supported by the ribs, to resemble wings on each side of the body. They don't actually fly, but can glide or parachute from high in one tree to low in another over clear (and potentially dangerous) ground. Most lizards eat insects, eggs, or small mammals;

Above: marine iguanas are found only in the Galápagos Islands, living in large colonies. They forage several fathoms deep (below) for the seaweeds that form their diet.

Below: a chameleon in the act of shooting out its concertina-folded tongue to trap the incautious insect that has landed nearby. Binocular vision gives it accurate aim.

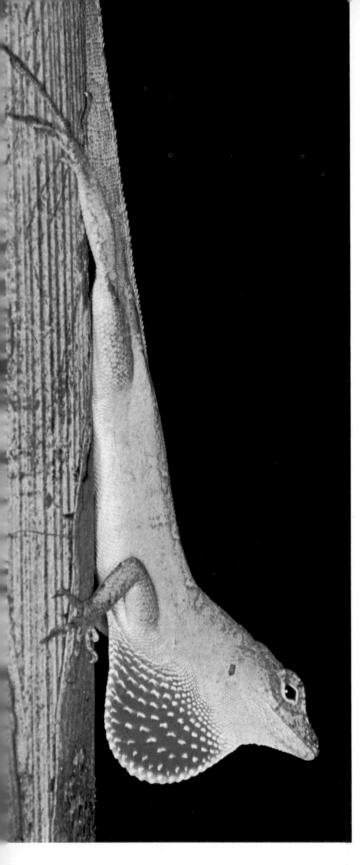

the Komodo dragon eats pigs and even other Komodo dragons. Perhaps the smartest hunters of all are the chameleons, which have an uncanny ability to settle on a stone or branch and take on a color to match their surroundings. They do this by automatically varying the size of black, yellow, red, and white pigment cells in the skin. Then they lie patiently until the insect prey comes within reach. And what a reach! A chameleon's tongue at full stretch is almost as long as its body, so that a little fellow only a foot long can easily pick up a fly eight inches away, on the sticky part of its tongue.

Some lizards have developed a faculty for sexual display almost as colorful as we have seen among birds. The flying lizards have brilliant yellow or orange sides and dewlaps. The anoles of Florida and the Carolinas can flush from dark brown to green, and excited males display a distended throat sac. It has always puzzled biologists to note that females seem totally indifferent to male displays. Indeed the males themselves show scant preference in their choice of mate; if two males fight and one submits, the other will often copulate with him just as if the submissive one were female. The behavior of a partner, rather than his or her actual sex, seems to trigger the mating urge in male lizards. Fighting among them for possession of females is usually fierce and sometimes ends in death. The victor seizes the female in his jaws and legs, forcing her to be still while he inserts his penis into her cloaca. Copulation lasts only a few seconds but there may be many repeats over a few hours.

Like the snakes, most lizards lay eggs (from 10 to 60 in a clutch) and leave them to hatch; but a few hatch either just before or at the moment the eggs are laid.

Turtles, as a group, are the strangest reptiles of all. They have a hard panlike shell from which only their legs, heads, and tails protrude and into which these vulnerable extremities can be drawn. Most are sea-, river-, or pond-dwellers although a few, sometimes called tortoises, are strictly land creatures. Many of the water-dwellers are able to breathe some oxygen from the water through the soft skin of their cloaca so that they need come to the surface much less than one would expect considering their great bulk. (The Pacific leatherback, for instance, weighs up to 1500 pounds.) When they sleep, their oxygen requirements are even further reduced and cloacal breathing is enough to let them slumber comfortably on the

A male anole lizard shows the brilliantly colored dewlap that it uses in its territorial displays against other males and in courtship.

Above: the frilled lizard of Australia opens out its eight-inch frill to display aggression when its territory is threatened. It walks upright and leaves tracks strangely resembling those of extinct dinosaurs.

A collared lizard eating a western fence lizard of around its own size—about a foot long, excluding the length of the tail. Lizards' jaws and throats are less accommodating than those of snakes, so this collared lizard will have to bite the victim into several pieces before finally eating it.

shallower parts of the ocean floor. They use the same ability when hibernating in mud or sand.

Practically all large areas of water in the tropics and temperate zones are home to turtles, some of which live by scavenging dead or dying plants and animals. Land turtles live on vegetation, small animals, and carrion.

The poet Ogden Nash wrote:

> The turtle lives 'twixt plated decks
> Which practically conceal its sex.
> I think it clever of the turtle
> In such a fix, to be so furtle.

To a biologist this is doubly witty, not only for its obvious humor but also for its accuracy and observation. In fact, throughout the animal kingdom there can be few creatures that have so hard a time mating as the turtles. Aquatic ones copulate in water, which helps take some of their weight; but the male has to work hard to keep his partner still. He will bite her, pull out the scales on her head and sometimes blind her before she is still enough for mating. With land turtles it is even more hazardous. Despite his longer claws and tail and his more concave belly, the male still has nothing to grip, and he now has gravity as well as a mate to fight. He has to ride around partly on her until she becomes still enough to let him rear up almost vertically and, in one precarious movement, get his penis in. Anyone who has watched the long-drawn-out frustrations of this drama has to marvel that 250 turtle species survive and that the group as a whole is at least 200 million years old.

All turtles lay eggs and leave them to hatch. All, even the most oceanic, come to the land, to the shore or river bank, and lay up to 100 eggs, which they often cover with mud or sand. Survival among the youngsters is, naturally, very low. Those that do survive, however, can reach an age of a century or more. The oldest authentic turtle was the Marion's turtle brought from its Seychelles home to Mauritius in 1766. It went blind in 1808 and was accidentally killed in 1918, aged at least 152.

Crocodiles (including alligators and caimans)

A green turtle laying eggs in a scooped-out hollow in the sand. Normally she lays about 100 eggs. One, uncovered for photography, is shown hatching right. Usually they hatch under the sand and excavate their way out before scrabbling down the beach to the sea, where their flipperlike limbs are highly efficient.

Pacific Ridley turtles mass-nesting on Nancite beach in Costa Rica. Unlike the green turtle, whose nest above the high-tide line is so obvious, these creatures lay between tide lines, where all trace of their nests is obliterated by the advancing water.

Above: crocodiles often bask in shallow water or beside lakes and rivers, sometimes in fairly large groups. Above right: alligators courting in Florida's Everglades. Males often undertake long journeys in search of females. Pairs always copulate in water. Below right: the eyes of the crocodile can poke above the water line when the rest of the animal is submerged. When the crocodile dives below the surface its eyes are covered by a protective membrane. The vertical pupil can open widely to give good night vision.

are as a group, the bulkiest reptiles of all. There is some evidence that they may be more efficient at controlling their temperature than other reptiles, although they are by no means warm-blooded. Certainly their hearts are *almost* four-chambered. A wall divides the large pumping chamber (the ventricle) and gives near-perfect separation of used blood coming from the body and fresh blood coming from the lungs. All of them live in or near the tropics and all are aquatic. Alligators and caimans (which have short, oval snouts) reach a maximum length of 20 feet. True crocodiles (with long thin snouts) grow up to 27 feet long (the estuarine crocodile). All of them have powerful bone-breaking jaws with up to 60 teeth set firmly in sockets. The musculature that gives them this closing strength, however, is of little use for opening, so much so that a man can hold their jaws shut with one hand.

They have eyes, ears, and nostrils on the top of their heads so that they can float or cruise along almost totally submerged and well concealed. They swim with powerful tail movements and with some assistance from their flattened feet. Many also use their tails to sweep small animals that come down to drink into deeper water, where they are easier to kill. Around the world they kill about 2000 humans each year, many of them in this way. Their main diet, though, is fish; gavials rarely eat anything other than fish, which they catch with a sideways sweep of their long thin snout.

Crocodiles have well-developed voices and their loud bellowing, especially at mating time, carries far from the river bank. Their mating habits are similar to lizards' except that the males do not fight quite so viciously, although their frenzied lashing of the water and fierce puffing-up of their

Right: the "congo eel," a North American salamander, lives in running water. It has rudimentary limbs and lungs, but it breathes chiefly through gills, which persist in the adult form.

A spotted salamander eating an earthworm. This species of salamander lives in the forests of eastern North America although when it lays its eggs it seeks out slow-moving water or ponds.

bodies can seem frighteningly savage. At such times the males emit an overpowering and nauseating odor of musk (which, in minute doses, is in fact an ingredient of the costliest perfumes!). A triumphant male copulates very roughly with his mate and always in water. The female lays from 10 to 90 eggs, close to the water. Sometimes she may cover them with rotting vegetation, whose fermentation helps to incubate the young. Sometimes, too, she stays nearby and drives off predators, especially raccoons, skunks, and certain lizards, for whom the eggs are a favorite diet. As with other reptiles, the rate of survival of the young is very low. They are nowhere near as long-lived as the turtles, the greatest authenticated age being 56 years.

The word "amphibian" means "double life." It refers to the two distinct life forms of most animals in this group: a juvenile form that is more fishlike than not, and a mature air-breathing form, often based on land. Thus they come between the fish and reptiles in life style and they were, in fact, the first animals with backbones to overcome the problem of living above the surface of the water. Even so, their solution was incomplete; few of them can live very far from water, and most of them return to it for mating and egg-laying. All breathe to some ex-

tent through their skins although many possess functional lungs.

There are three basic kinds of amphibian: salamanders, frogs and toads, and the limbless caecilians. The group containing salamanders also includes newts and mudpuppies. Except for a few species in Central and South America they are found only in North America and Eurasia, where they live mainly in cool, damp places. They all have four limbs and a lizardlike body except for the sirens, which have no hind legs, and "congo eels," which have only vestiges of limbs. In size they range from the 1½-inch pygmy salamanders of Tennessee, North Carolina, and Virginia to the five-foot Japanese giant salamander. All are flesh-eaters.

A few, such as the sirens, mudpuppies, and "congo eels," never go through a double life; they become sexually mature in their juvenile form and remain in water all the time. Newts have a strange double life. Their juvenile form, the "eft," is not at first sexually mature. It lives on land for a year or two before returning to the water, where it lives as an airbreathing swimmer-diver and finally gains sexual maturity. Most salamanders have a curious mating ritual. The male performs a complex dance to stimulate his partner. Some annoint her with secretions from the throat or tail. When she is aroused she joins him

Spotted newts of the eastern United States mating. Their position ensures that their hind parts will be correctly aligned for the transfer of sperm. The fertilized eggs are then hidden among water plants, which give them some protection until they hatch.

in a tail walk, her nose to his tail. Soon he lets out one or more small parcels of sperm from his cloaca, which she scoops up into hers as she passes over it or them. A few partners actually clasp together and transfer the sperm directly. The female keeps it (sometimes for months) until egg-laying time and then lets a small amount of sperm meet each egg. Some American newts make nests of damp moss and stay around until the eggs hatch. Most salamanders, however, abandon the eggs to their fate, which is usually premature death, but the number of eggs is compensatingly high.

Frogs and toads are the most successful land-dwelling amphibians, especially the toads, whose dry, thick skin allows them to live for long periods away from water. Frogs and toads are found in all continents except Antarctica, some even as far north as the Arctic Circle, where they hibernate in the 40°F water at the bottom of surface-frozen lakes. They have many other fascinating adaptations to life away from water, most of them concerned with the survival of their young, the tadpoles. Typically they mate in water, the male broadcasting his sperm over the jelly-like spawn. The young then hatch as tadpoles, and gradually lose their gills and tail and develop lungs and legs until they are miniature adults, several months short of full maturity. The number of eggs varies from about a dozen (Camp's frog) to over 25,000 (Woodhouse's toad, which lays more than any other land vertebrate).

Some, however, such as the obstetric toad, carry the spawn around with them until it hatches during one or other visit to the water. In others, such as the Surinam toad, the eggs drop into niches in the female's back, where the young hatch and develop, emerging only when they have transformed from tadpoles to toads. Some breed in small pools in hollow trees or even in flowers. And there are a few that make a kind of foam under leaves overhanging a river. There the tadpoles swim and are nourished until an exceptionally high water level releases them. In one group of frogs, confined to high-altitude lakes in South America, the tadpoles actually grow much larger than the adults that spawn them. They don't grow, so much as *shrink* into maturity.

Frogs and toads are the only amphibians with "voices," and their croaking is often the most characteristic sound of the area they inhabit. These noises are made by the males, usually as

Above: the yellow-bellied toad is a small, dark-colored creature that lives in pools and streams. It exposes its surprisingly yellow belly when an enemy approaches or threatens.

Common frogs mating. The female's belly is distended with spawn: spawn from other frogs is seen in the background.

Above: tadpoles of the common frog still clinging to the jellylike spawn from which they have just hatched.

The chorus frog makes the call for which it is named by expelling air from its vocal pouch. This frog is very common in America where it is found in swampy forests.

they puff up their throats with air and then expel it in one loud croak or piping sound. The spring peeper, an eastern tree frog, is familiar to most Americans for its extended springtime chorus from the pools where it congregates to mate.

Color variation among frogs and toads is almost as extreme as among reptiles. Some can change color in moments, almost as well as a chameleon. Some have bright colors—reds, yellows, and white—that contrast strongly with nearby patches and streaks of black. These warn likely predators that the frog or toad is nauseous or even venomous. Sometimes these bright patches are exposed only in the sudden jump that a frog makes to escape a pursuer. The bright flash vanishes as soon as the frog lands, which confuses the predator.

No frog or toad is lethal to handle, although several in South Africa can severely irritate the skin. But when the poison is swallowed or gets into a cut, the story is quite different. The one-inch-long Kokoi tree frog of South America produces a poison so deadly that less than half a millionth of an ounce will kill a man. The Choco Indians collect this venom by shrinking frogs over a fire to expel it from the skin. The juice from one of these frogs tips about 50 arrows, each

of which can instantly paralyze a deer.

The caecilians are nobody's idea of a typical amphibian. Except for a mouth and sometimes a pair of eyes they look remarkably like earthworms; but their smooth-skinned, segmented, legless bodies conceal a skeleton, a spinal cord, and a skull. They must be among the least studied and least known of all land vertebrates, for they are difficult to locate even by hunters. Most live in soil burrows; a few stay in water all their lives. Adults range in size from $3\frac{1}{2}$ inches to $4\frac{1}{2}$ feet. All are found in tropical and warm temperate forests.

Fish are the most primitive animals with backbones. In fact their ancestors are also the an-

Below: the fearsome teeth of the shark are, in fact, modified skin scales. Even its scales, with their core of pulp and layers of dentine and enamel, are extraordinarily toothlike. Right: the flattened shape of this fish combines with its wide gape and long powerful tail to make it one of the most ferocious of the sea's predators— more than a match, for instance, for the dolphin.

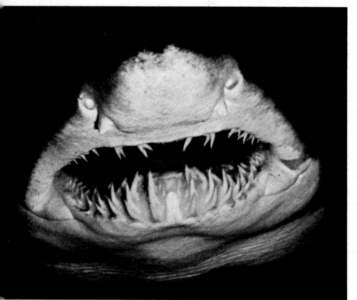

cestors of all the animals so far studied in these pages. They live in water and swim with the aid of sinuous wagging movements of their tails and fanning movements of their fins. Most live in salt water, some in fresh water, and a few inhabit both at various stages of their lives.

The typical fish, the kind that most people picture if you simply say the word "fish" to them, is represented by the mackerel or herring, to name two saltwater kinds, and by the trout, to name a freshwater kind. It has a double-wedge stream-lined body almost circular in section near the middle and tapering toward its snout and tail. It has two fins in line on its back, two paired fins, one pair on the side, and one pair underneath and well forward, a central fin farther back un-

derneath, and tail fins. With various extremely subtle and coordinated movements of these, it can dart, hover, rise or sink vertically, back up, and do sudden turns of more than 180 degrees.

It breathes through gills, delicate structures full of blood vessels, behind and to the side of its mouth. The fish gulps water and passes it out over these gills, which are usually loosely covered by a hinged bony flap. Oxygen dissolved in the water passes into the blood, while carbon dioxide travels the opposite way. As with reptiles and amphibians this system is much less efficient than our lungs, so fish cannot acquire enough oxygen to use food merely to keep warm. They are all cold-blooded.

Our typical fish has a two-layer skin. The outer,

thin layer is a coat of dead, protective cells. The inner layer has nerves, blood vessels, and sense organs, and is similar to our skin. This is the layer that makes the scales. These remarkable structures, which both streamline and protect, have basically an outer layer of enamel, an inner one of dentine, and a core of pulp, exactly like our teeth; and the scales of fish are in fact the forerunners of teeth. Even in the fish itself these scales may be modified into rasplike teeth on the rim of the jaw and the roof of the mouth. With these it grips, shakes, and tears its food into lumps that it then gulps.

Our typical fish shows very few sex differences. At mating time the male may have an extra spot or two of color, the female may be a little fatter with her thousands or millions of eggs; but at other times they will be hard to tell apart. Their mating, too, is fairly casual. They usually swim beside each other and shed their eggs and sperm into the water, leaving the rest to chance.

There are countless departures from this basic form and habit. They range from the 60-foot whale shark, which—unlike most of its kind—is a harmless vegetarian living off plankton, to the tiny 0.2- to 0.3-inch-long dwarf pygmy goby of Luzon.

Members of one group, the most primitive of all, have no jaws. Instead they have a sucker-type mouth and live by parasitizing other fish or rooting around in bottom mud. Other fish that live on the bottom tend to be flat and well camouflaged. The anglers and the rays are well-known examples; they have bodies compressed horizontally. Others, such as plaice and soles, have tall, thin bodies and spend most of their lives lying on one side, the lower eye migrating around to the upper side.

Any change from the double-wedge streamlined shape of the mackerel type involves a sacrifice of speed; so there must be some compensating advantage for fish of other shapes. For rays and flatfish it is concealment on the bottom. For tall, thin angelfish and many coral fish it is the ability to squeeze among fronds of seaweed with the

minimum of hindrance and turbulence while predators pass by. For porcupine fish it is the thickset rows of spines that cover their squat unstreamlined bodies, whereas trunkfish have an armor whose toughness repels most predators. Eels have rounded bodies well adapted to life in mud and weeds and hiding in nooks and crannies along riverbank and lakeshore. The strangest of all is the seahorse, the only fish whose head is at right angles to its neck. It swims upright with the help of its pectoral (neck) fins. Its spiral tail can coil and grasp weed and rocks. Its skin is toughly armored and may develop long filaments that closely match the weeds it lives among.

A few fish have the ability to produce electricity. In some South American and African fish the currents are weak and form a continuous field around the fish. When another fish—prey or predator—swims into the field, it sets up changes that the creator of the field can detect. Such a field has the same function as a perimeter trip-wire alarm in a guarded area. But in electric

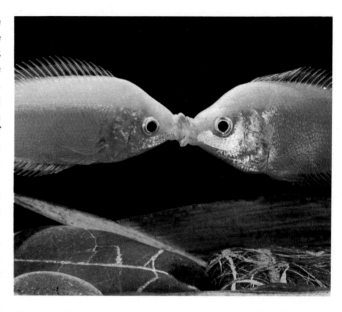

Above: in fresh water shallows these fish use their large lips to browse algae from the rocks. They practice the same movement on one another, possibly as a form of social communication—hence their name "kissing gouramis."

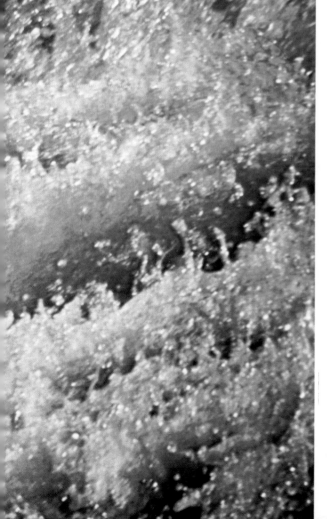

Above: pufferfish, widely found in warm waters, discourage would-be predators by inflating themselves with water so as to erect the spines that cover their skin. The striking effect that this produces is clearly seen in the picture.

Left: a salmon leaps rapids on its long journey from sea to spawning ground. The highest such leap has been measured at over 11 feet, requiring a velocity of around 20 miles an hour.

71

eels, rays, and catfish the current is powerful enough to stun nearby small creatures, leaving its generator free to pick and choose among the unresisting morsels.

There is also much variation in the way fish reproduce and rear their young. The number of eggs a female lays each time varies from one or two for the topminnow to over 50 million for the ocean sunfish. Those that lay large numbers of eggs take no further interest in their young and play no part in their rearing. But some more modest producers go to fair lengths to protect their offspring—salmon, for instance. After an epic journey that may span up to 2000 miles from ocean to mountain stream, the female salmon swishes a shallow pocket in the stream bed by fanning her tail violently, creating a calm hollow in the turbulent water into which she and her mate drop their eggs and sperm. Then she scoops up the gravel immediately upstream to fill the hollow and cover the eggs. A female bullhead will get into overhung cavities and crevices where she nods violently to attract the males. When a male enters the crevice she turns upside down and lays her sticky eggs in one lump on the overhanging stone, leaving him to fertilize them.

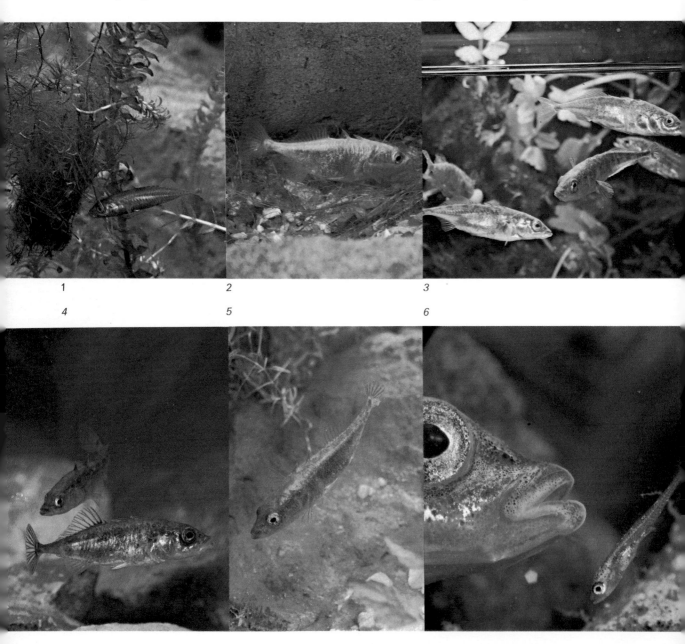

1   2   3

4   5   6

Lumpsuckers lay eggs in a similar way under the shells of crabs; and bitterlings use the mantle cavity of freshwater mussels as a nest for the development of their young.

The stickleback is the best-known example of nest-building fish. Early in spring the male begins to make copious quantities of a sort of glue with which he sticks vegetation together to form a nest. Then he develops bright patches of color to attract a succession of females, each of which lays 50 to 100 eggs inside. He drives away each in turn, fertilizes the eggs, and guards them during their two- to three-week incubation. Some

male paradise fish make a nest of bubbles anchored to vegetation. The female turns upside down and lays buoyant eggs below the nest, while the male fertilizes them; both retrieve eggs that float up but miss the bubble raft.

Some fish show even greater parental care. Male seahorses and pipefish have pouches into which the female lays her fertilized eggs, for him to brood and hatch. Dogfish and some other sharks mate by putting their cloacas together, thus coming closest to the sort of copulation that typifies land vertebrates, in which the male deposits his sperm inside the female. The young

The reproductive behavior of the stickleback shown at left:

1 The male ten-spined stickleback builds a nest among weeds.

2 Its three-spined cousin makes a nest in the river bed.

3 In both species the male's belly turns red when in breeding condition.

4 A female heavy with eggs triggers the male's courtship dance.

5 While the eggs develop he guards the nest and fans it with fresh water.

6 Even after the young are hatched he protects them from predators.

Above: anglerfish, creatures of the ocean depths, lure their prey toward themselves with luminous bait, which is attached to rods on their heads. They can swallow relatively large fish, which are prevented from escaping by the anglerfish's backward-pointing teeth.

Right: lampreys are parasites of fish, and attach themselves to their prey by means of tubular mouths. Their saliva contains chemicals that stop the blood coagulating. As water is prevented from reaching the gills through the mouth it is pumped over them by way of gill openings on the side of the lamprey's body.

are then incubated inside the mother and in some cases are actually nourished from the walls of her egg duct.

The prize oddity among fish is possibly the Amazon molly. Sperm (usually from a male molly but almost any sperm will do) enters the female and triggers egg growth, but without fertilization! The young, all females, hatch inside her before swimming to the outside world. There, some of them undergo a sex change. In turn, their sperm will repeat the process, but there will never be any mixing of genetic material. An equally strange situation arises with one kind of angler. The male, early in life, becomes a parasite of the much larger female, gripping her with his mouth. Gradually they become, quite literally, one flesh with a single bloodstream. Almost all his organs, except his reproductive ones, wither away and he becomes totally dependent upon her. These are sluggish, solitary fish, living on the deep seabed; obviously in some past age this drastic expedient offered a better chance of securing a mate than more traditional methods.

This brief account has barely scratched the surface of the amazing variety in the world of fish. For instance, the lungfish, which normally relies on gills, can breathe through a primitive kind of lung, and, although it needs moisture to survive, can generally tolerate drier conditions than can many amphibians. At the other extreme are the little-known fish of the ocean depths. Surely as our exploration of the abyss grows more regular and systematic we shall uncover many surprises, not only among fish but perhaps even among other groups long thought to be extinct. We have already had a foretaste in the 1938 rediscovery of the coelacanth off the southern coast of Africa— a fish that the textbooks, until then, had said was extinct 70 million years ago. (Curiously enough, the professor who identified a later specimen of the coelacanth was told by local fishermen that this fish was so common among them that they used its rough skin to scuff up the inner tube of a punctured bicycle tire before sticking on a repair patch! How many more animals are known to man yet still remain *un*known to science?)

The name arthropod comes from Greek words for "joint" and "leg." All the animals in this vast group, except velvet worms, the most primitive type, have jointed legs and hard outside skins or exoskeletons. In other words, whereas all the animals we have so far looked at are built of

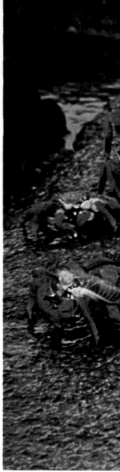

Above: this head of a flea, highly magnified, shows the amazing construction of these small wingless insects.

Below: house-dust mites, magnified 120 times, "grazing" on scales of human skin. Even the cleanest household harbors thousands of these useful scavengers.

Above: the brilliantly colored land crabs of the Galápagos Islands left the sea at some stage of their evolution. Now they live exclusively on the shore. Many Pacific islands have their own land-crab species because each was colonized separately.

Below: a male garden spider approaches its much larger mate. Its ritualized gestures help to "switch off" her aggression and so allow him to mate with her.

fleshy bodies surrounding skeletons of bone or cartilage and covered by skin of varying hardness, the arthropods are built on precisely opposite principles. Their skeleton is on the outside, in the form of a hard tubular or boxlike structure; the fleshy parts are fixed and protected inside it. This puts obvious limitations on such animals, the most important being growth restriction. The basic body plan limits the development of a rich sensory-nerve network and therefore of a brain and of intelligence. It also limits the possibility of temperature control and so of the ability to be warm-blooded.

You might think, therefore, that arthropods are a small and unimportant group on the fringe of life. In fact, they are the most numerous and successful of all animals. Insects alone, with more than 900,000 known species, outnumber all other animal species by about four to one, and arthropods as a whole have conquered every known habitat, from the Antarctic mainland and the ocean trench to the most parched of deserts. Apart from insects, the two other main kinds of arthropod are the crustaceans (lobsters, crabs, and barnacles, among others) and the arachnids (spiders and their relatives).

Arthropods are not only the most numerous animals, they are also our closest territorial neighbors, we share our homes with between 5000 and 50,000 of them on average, and if our home is old, the number is many times greater. They range from the tiny mites that thrive on dead skin flakes (and which are found in the cleanest mattresses in the most spick and span of homes), through house-dust mites, cheese mites (again, found in the freshest cheese), silverfish, carpet bugs, clothes moths, woodlice, woodworms, and timber beetles, not to mention such obvious guests as houseflies and spiders—all of which we feed and shelter.

What is the secret of their success? What features of their bodily form and life style make them so numerous and universal? High on the list come a basic simplicity of form and a hard protective covering. The ancestors of all arthropods looked something like a large woodlouse. They had a wormlike train of segments each with legs, a hard shell, and a simple array of sensory elements (eyes and feelers) and mouthparts at the front. Modifications to this simple plan have produced the million-plus forms of arthropods today.

The centipedes and millipedes kept the multiple segments but developed roundish bodies, often with hairlike spines. Millipedes are sluggish, harmless plant-eaters that move with concertina-like ripples of their legs. Centipedes are carnivorous and have evolved poisonous pincerlike fangs to kill their prey; they move fast with a left-right-left-right leg action.

In other arthropods we see more unusual use of the ancestral 3-layered skin: an outer, often waxy, layer, a middle hard layer, and an inner soft layer. The hard layer, chief component of the external skeleton, is interrupted at joints, leaving the soft flexible layer to bridge the gap. Such an arrangement would be mechanically unsound in large land-based animals, which is possibly why all the large, heavy arthropods are water-dwelling; the buoyancy provided by the water compensates for the mechanical weakness of their joints. (Also, as we shall see, breathing through gills is more efficient than relying on the air that gets diffused or forced through special air tubes in land arthropods; this greater efficiency also permits greater bulk.) But for small land creatures the arrangement of the skeleton has two great advantages: it is watertight, so the animal can live away from water without desiccating itself; and it is capable of almost infinite variation, ranging from the fragile spindly legs of the daddy-longlegs or the giant Japanese spider crab (the largest arthropod, with a claw span of at least 12 feet) to the bold markings of the Goliath beetle (the heaviest insect).

In almost all arthropods the ancestral form of body segments has been reorganized into two or three basic regions. The head has the brain, the jaws, the silkmaking mechanisms (except in spiders), the eyes, ears, and feelers; the thorax has the stomach and the legs and any wing muscles; the abdomen has the lower parts of the gut, the sex and excretory organs, the heart, the lung, and any sting and (in spiders) silkmaking mechanisms. To be sure, there are many departures from this pattern.

Arthropods vary in the way they feed, prey, or defend themselves. Many insects have strong jaws and they may have a poison sting in their tail. Arachnids tend to have pincers and may have poison fangs. Ants (insects with poison bites) and scorpions (arachnids with poison tails) are exceptions. Crustaceans tend to break up their food with appendages around the mouth, which they also use for defense.

Although many land arthropods have simple lungs (called "book lungs" for their resemblance

Above: the 4-inch-long Goliath beetle, at 2 ounces, is the world's heaviest insect.

Right: this large black hunting wasp has paralyzed a baboon spider with her sting. Now she is dragging it away to a suitable nest. There she will lay her eggs on or near its still-living body. When the larvae hatch, they will feed on the spider until they mature; although paralyzed it will not die until it is nearly all consumed.

Below: this large hermit crab has taken over an empty whelk shell as a home. The anemones on its back are always associated with this kind of crab. They benefit from fragments of food the crab discards. The crab is protected by their powerful stings and camouflage effect. When it grows and moves to a larger shell it will take these anemones to its new home.

to the pages of a book), they cannot get all the oxygen they need through these elementary structures. Often, instead, a fine network of air tubes penetrates into every part of the body. Air diffuses slowly through it, assisted by the natural pumping effect of the walking and flying muscles. Those that live under water breathe through gills, although some microscopic ones manage by simple diffusion through the skin.

A major innovation, found in arthropods only

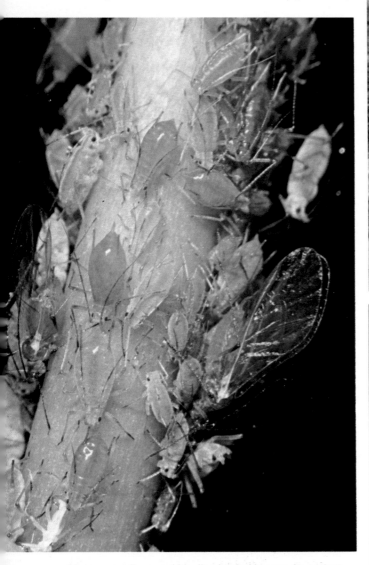

Above: greenfly, or aphids, live by sucking sap from plants—which makes them one of the worst botanical pests. They not only distort and stunt the plants, but also transmit diseases.

Right: a monarch butterfly emerging from the cocoon that it spun around itself when it was a caterpillar. When its wings have hardened it will fly away and mate. The resulting eggs will give rise to a further caterpillar generation.

Scorpions engage in a mating dance during which the male deposits a blob of semen on the ground; he then maneuvers the female onto it so that it enters her body. Young scorpions are either produced alive or hatch immediately after birth.

among insects, is the development of one or two pairs of wings. All except the most primitive insects have them, but in some advanced kinds that have returned to earthbound living (fleas, lice, and worker ants, for example) the traces are only vestigial. Small size gives insects advantages denied to birds. Weight for weight the smaller animal is stronger, has more aerodynamic lift, and can flex its muscles more rapidly. As a result many insects can do things that birds cannot do or that only certain highly specialized birds can achieve: fly backward, for instance, or hover, or take off at eye-baffling velocity, from zero to full speed in milliseconds.

Reproduction among arthropods is as varied as their bodily form. At one extreme is virgin birth, which is normal among water fleas, some scale insects, and aphids. At the end of the summer female aphids, for example, lay large numbers of eggs that hatch into females in the following spring. These females reproduce without the

assistance of males, producing live young females. In late summer males also begin to be produced. These males and females mate to produce a smaller number of hard-covered eggs that are well adapted to withstand drought or cold, until the next favorable season triggers their hatching. Male ants, bees, and wasps are also the result of virgin birth. Among horseshoe crabs (which are not true crabs but allies of spiders) the female lays eggs in shallow, sandy hollows while the male strews semen over them. A scorpion male lays blobs of semen during ritual courtship dances, then he maneuvers the female over the blobs, which she scoops up into her body. One male spider spins a short thread and lays droplets of semen on it. These he scoops up into leglike palps on his head before he approaches a female, pacifies her by visual or stroking rituals (some of which are very complex), and then pushes the semen into her egg duct.

Rituals play a vital role among insects, too.

Many species are so alike in looks and life style that only minute variations in courtship characteristics prevent them from mating with one another. The trigger may be a sound, as with the chirping male cricket, or a scent, as with many moths and butterflies, or a buzzing of wings, as with the mosquito, or a flashing light, as with fireflies, or a visual sighting, as with grayling butterflies. At the end of the ritual the male usually deposits semen into the opening of his mate's egg duct, using a kind of penis. Mostly this happens on the ground or in vegetation, but midges, mayflies, and dragonflies mate on the wing. The strangest example of insect reproduction is that of the bed bug. The female has a special pouch in the side of her abdomen. Sperms put there by the male tunnel through the pouch wall and migrate through her body tissues until they reach her ovaries and fertilize the eggs.

The number of eggs laid varies from more than 80,000 a day, which one kind of queen termite maintains for long periods, down to the few eggs, each in its own elaborate nest (complete with a food larder packed with succulent grubs), laid by the potter wasp. Most arthropods lay hundreds or thousands of eggs and undertake no brooding. Their behavior is dominated by instinctive activity and rituals, which learning or training can do little to modify. Even among social colonies the young are instinctively fitted to their role rather than trained to it. Nevertheless, there have been remarkable cases of seemingly intelligent behavior. A red ant colony in the gardens of a French laboratory learned to form a fire brigade that could extinguish lighted matches and cigarette butts dropped near their nest by laboratory workers. Nearby colonies, on *their* first exposure to fire, behaved like a panic-stricken mob, many of them burning to death.

The newly hatched arthropod often bears scant resemblance to its adult relatives. Because they can grow only by shedding their tough outside shell, many arthropods have taken advantage of the process to adopt different life styles, each suitable to a stage in its growth. The most extreme form is the transformation from caterpillar through chrysalis to butterfly or moth; in some species most of the caterpillar actually dies in the chrysalis, leaving small disks of embryo tissue that grow into the winged adult. On the other

Termite heaps dot the plains of East Africa. Their construction is resilient enough to withstand wind and storm, and even a determined man with a steel spade may find entry difficult. A complex colony of insects is housed within each nest.

South American swallowtails and sulfur butterflies, measuring five or six inches in wingspan, congregate on mudflats where they drink from minute pools of water.

Above: worker termites, their nest disturbed for photography, remove exposed eggs to a place of safety. Survival of these social insects depends on such cooperative efforts to protect each other.

An octopus displaying its eight tentacles, each with a characteristic double row of suckers. With these it can hold its prey of fish and shellfish in a strangulating grip while at the same time devouring it with the help of sharp, powerful jaws.

hand there are creatures, such as spiders, crabs, dragonflies, and silverfish, in which the young are recognizable miniature adults that in successive stages grow more obviously mature—for example, any wing pads will grow into wings, sex organs will appear, and so on.

Because arthropods are so small, so successful, and so adaptable, and because they scavenge among so many of the wastes of civilization, they do more harm to man than any other animal. Just one insect, the common housefly, has been indicted as a carrier of no fewer than 30 diseases and parasites, including dysentery, cholera, typhoid, leprosy, bubonic plague, smallpox, polio, diphtheria, scarlet fever, and cerebrospinal meningitis. Locusts do over 300 million dollars' worth of damage every year. Bees and wasps kill more people each year than the 40,000 killed by snakes and the 2000 eaten by crocodiles. And then there are termites, mosquitoes, tsetse flies, scabs, ticks, lice, woodworms, cockroaches . . . and an even longer list of pests that infest our domestic animals, crops, and foodstores. Even so, we could not manage without them, for arthropods do a remarkable job of scavenging and cleansing the world—testimony to the amazing economy of Nature, which dictates that nothing, from the tiniest discarded flake of human skin to the mightiest trunk of fallen redwood, shall long remain unused.

Ranked beneath the arthropods on the evolutionary scale are tens of thousands of simpler animals, from the wily octopus to the microscopic creatures that make pondwater so interesting to anyone with even a low-power microscope.

Octopuses are among the most fascinating of this group. They belong to the mollusks, which include a great many shelled creatures, from garden snails to giant clams. Octopuses have lost their shells during the course of evolution. As if to compensate they have developed eight versatile arms, eyes of a complexity to match that of many vertebrates, and a nervous system so advanced that they can learn tasks and relationships more easily than many insects. And their close relatives the 10-armed squids, which are more difficult to keep in captivity and so have not

been studied so closely, are probably even more advanced—indeed, are probably the most intelligent of all animals without backbones.

It is difficult to account for this development. One theory is that they evolved from mollusks that crawled along the seabed and that then developed gas bladders to give enough buoyancy to reach up into the middle waters. There, as the dominant form, they were free to develop further, first by losing their shell, later by increasing intelligence and maneuverability as more advanced arthropods invaded their realm.

Mollusks show a characteristic that runs

throughout most of the animal kingdom: they are bilaterally symmetrical—that is, if you cut them down the mid-plane from head to foot, the right half is more or less a mirror image of the left. Even those complex parts that show no trace of bilateral symmetry (for instance, the human chest with its heart and nearby blood vessels) have had such a symmetry at an early stage of their development. There is, however, one large and important group that has no obvious mid-line—at least in their adult forms. These are the echinoderms—the starfishes, sea urchins, and their kind. Their radiating kind of symmetry is, in

fact, more suited to their sedentary kind of life than a left-right symmetry would be.

The typical starfish has five arms that radiate from a central body. (The largest starfish is one yard in diameter, the smallest only $\frac{7}{10}$ inch; both come from the North Pacific.) On the underside of each arm are unique little organs, found nowhere else in the animal kingdom, known as "tube feet." To extend the foot the animal pumps in water. Touch an extended tube foot and it at once turns into a suction pad of remarkable tenacity as the muscles in it tighten; the tube feet in one square inch can jointly lift a nine-pound weight. With this suction, which they can maintain for hours on end, they can pry open a clam or oyster enough to digest it—with the help of a most unusual kind of stomach. The starfish's stomach is like a fine sheet of semi-transparent plastic. An opening in an oyster shell as thin as the paper of this page is wide enough to let the starfish insert its stomach and wrap it around the succulent flesh inside. Then from this fine sheet comes a stream of digestive juices that kill the mollusk and digest it. The starfish can then relax its merciless grip and use those same tube feet in a coordinated way to move off after fresh prey at a rate of up to six inches a minute.

Also among these lower animals are the sponges, worms, flukes, rotifers, jellyfish, and thousands of single-celled microscopic creatures. Many of them, but for their lack of green color, one could easily mistake for plants—sea anemones and corals, for example. Although their forms may be complex, the systems of which they are composed (blood, nerve, and digestive systems, for instance) are all simple compared with those we have looked at in higher animals. Thus none of them has eyes as we understand the term, although most of them have light-sensitive cells that enable them to respond to light in simple ways. Many of them have a saclike gut in which they digest their food and which they can turn inside out to get rid of the remains.

All lower animals produce large numbers of offspring, which may go through one or more larval stages before settling into their adult form. In the sea these larvae are an important constituent of the plankton—the floating population of tiny plants and animals on which many sea creatures, including the whales and whale sharks, feed.

Only now are naturalists beginning to grasp the predator-prey relationships among these simpler animals. Already we know enough to feel daunted by their complexity, for it is not just a question of sorting out what eats what but of noting how the pattern changes with the seasons and with the different stages of life cycle.

To give an example very much in the news in recent years, many people have heard of the crown-of-thorns starfish, which has destroyed hundreds of miles of coral reefs by eating the little coral polyps that inhabit and create them. It is not nearly so well known that the larvae of the starfish are themselves eaten by the free-swimming larvae of many corals—a fact that will obviously affect any plans we may make to save

Above: a starfish moves and clings by contracting a series of small suckerlike appendages called "tube feet"; acting together such feet are powerful and tireless enough to exhaust the muscles that hold together the two parts of shellfish such as clams, mussels, and oysters.

Despite its plantlike appearance and name the sea anemone is an animal. It feeds by poisoning any unwary intruder by means of tiny stinging cells on its tentacles and then, as here, eating it.

Above: Heron Island, a nature sanctuary in Australia's Great Barrier Reef. Parts of this vast coral structure, one of the great natural wonders of the world, have been irreparably damaged by the crown-of-thorns starfish shown at right, which is a predator of coral polyps. In recent years an epidemic of them has threatened coral reefs and their residents over wide areas of the Pacific Ocean.

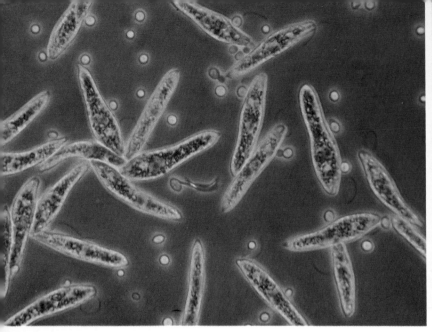

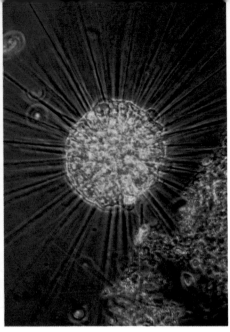

Above: Euglena *is a single-celled creature that straddles the borderline between plants and animals. They are plantlike in having the green pigment chlorophyll, which they use to make food, yet they have the animals' ability to move about freely, in this case by waggling their flagella in the water.*

Above: Actinosphaerium, *a single-celled inhabitant of acidic waters, has hairlike processes that trap food and carry it inward to the cell.*

Around most of the world's rocky shores the zone between the tides is the kingdom of the algae—the brown and green seaweeds. They anchor themselves to the rocks to prevent being carried away by the tide, but draw all their raw materials from the seas around.

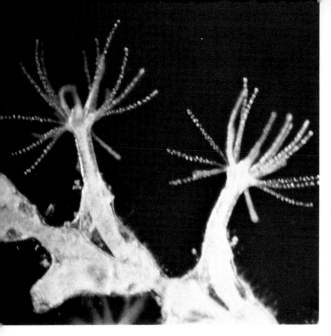

These hydroids are part of a colony—an association of semi-independent animals. They feed by waving their "arms," or tentacles, to trap floating food and pass it into the mouth.

Above: marine plankton, a collection of small-to-microscopic plants and animals in the upper layers of the sea, are the basis of all ocean food chains.

the greater part of Australia's Great Barrier Reef from this voracious creature.

However bizarre their life forms and however complex their food-getting relationships, they all share with higher animals an inability to manufacture food from simple substances. They all need to take in complex foodstuffs in ready-made form (which, after all, is the basic definition of an animal). Some of the lower animals have taken the process so far that they are incapable of independent life and must live exclusively as parasites. To do so they have had to develop extremely complex life cycles, which explains why even those that have cost us dearly—in terms of either our own health or that of our livestock—down the ages, are only now being brought under control.

The tapeworm is a well-known example. In one form the adult lives in the human gut and sheds eggs that find their way through sewerage or drainage to open water. Here each hatches into a free-swimming larva that is eaten by a shrimp-like creature. Instead of being digested, it burrows into its host's flesh and develops a wormlike body. Then a fish eats the host; again the larva escapes digestion and develops still further in the fish's flesh. If a man catches the fish and cures it or undercooks it before he eats it, he gets a new tapeworm to feed—and to shed more eggs. Other kinds of tapeworm live in man and pigs, or man and sheep's brains. One can only marvel at the evolutionary pressures that have forced these creatures into such convoluted life cycles.

At the very bottom of the complexity scale come the simplest creatures of all—the single-celled animals or protozoans. All live in wet or damp environments. These animals are a favorite starting point of biology textbooks because they reveal all the basic properties of living things in the most elementary form. They take in nutrient molecules, break some of them down to yield energy, and build some of them up to make new material. To gain that energy almost all of them take in oxygen, combine it with the broken-down products of large molecules and return it in carbon dioxide. They reproduce sexually in the simplest way, by directly combining their genetic material. But many can also reproduce asexually, by splitting into two or forming spores.

Some protozoans have a kind of hollow skeleton made of silica compounds; among those that live in salt water are some that can separate out the salt to make a freshwater "pool" inside them.

Right: young golden orioles are totally dependent on their parents, whose feeding activity is triggered by the powerful stimulus of those gaping, brightly colored beaks. Below: zoologist Desmond Morris has called the pouch that harbors a baby kangaroo a "womb with a view."

Above: the mouthbrooders are among the few fish that take any interest in their young. When danger threatens, they will take them into their mouths for protection. Right: human infants are dependent on their parents for longer than the offspring of any other species.

Prolonged parental care is a notable feature of primate life. This baby Japanese macaque clings firmly to its mother as she leaps to the safety of a rock amid a torrent of water. The young macaque remains with its mother for two to three years.

Fresh water being lighter, this gives buoyancy that keeps them near the surface.

Protozoans reveal every mode of animal life—from hunting-killing and browsing to parasitism. The best-known parasite among them is the malarial parasite, which lives by devouring human red blood cells and is transmitted from person to person by bloodsucking mosquitoes. Another causes amoebic dysentery. Some are *commensals*—harmless parasites. Run your tongue around the line where your teeth sink into your gums and you are stirring up thousands of them. They mop up bacteria and small remnants of food in your mouth.

Some protozoans move with the aid of tiny mobile hairlike structures called *cilia*, which act as banks of oars. Others, such as amoebae, move by bulging out in the direction they want to go and then drawing the rest of their one-celled body toward the bulge. Some can wriggle tail-like processes called *flagella* to propel themselves along.

In short, we can find among the protozoans almost all the activities that are common elsewhere in the animal kingdom, but fewer complexities—no nerve systems, no special reproductive organs, no separate digestive tracts, and so on.

This brief survey of single-celled animals completes our review of the animal world. Looking at this world as a whole we can see certain marked trends that span the entire range from the simplest to the most advanced. For instance, there is an increasing tendency toward a more complex nerve system, a better-organized brain, and intelligence. Hand in hand goes an increasing refinement of all the systems that control the internal environment—maintaining temperature, and purifying and reoxygenating the blood and controlling its chemical levels. Although almost all behavior is instinctive there is a noticeable increase in the ability to make responses based on learning, experience, and, at the highest levels, reasoning. This has its effects on social

behavior, as we can see by comparing the totally programmed life of the simplest creatures with the rigid ordering of insect colonies and the looser and more adaptable social structure of groups of primates.

Another major trend is found in the ways that animals produce and care for their offspring. At the simplest level there is total reliance on numbers. They reproduce to the limits of available food as fast as possible, with no parental care and no training of the young. In adverse conditions billions die, millions survive in some resistant, dormant form. Moving up the scale there is less reliance on sheer numbers and an increasing degree of parental involvement in the survival of the young. At the peak of this scale is the human child, which is biologically dependent for 6 to 10 years and socially dependent for up to twice that span, or between a third and a quarter of its average lifetime.

There is one other feature common to the entire animal kingdom. Start with any animal, list the things it eats, then list the things that those things eat . . . and so on until you run out of edibles; however complex the chains may be, the last name at the end of each branch will be that of a plant or a plant product. No matter what animal you start with, no matter what stage of that animal's life you take, it ultimately feeds on or by courtesy of the plants.

Plants have shaped the world we know today. The original earth, before life began, was utterly different—so much so that all plants and animals alive today would die in moments if they were transported back to it in time; only a few highly specialized bacteria and viruses might survive. The planet then was perhaps surrounded by an envelope of carbon dioxide mixed with the gases methane and ammonia—both poisonous to us. It had no free oxygen at all—and so no protective layers of ozone (a form of oxygen) to shield out lethal ultraviolet and shorter-wave radiation from the sun. The seas, too, were a thin soup of water, simple alcohols, and ammonia lapping barren, lifeless rock.

The steady rain of high-energy radiation, plus energy from lightning storms and volcanoes, fused the simplest molecules of that thin soup

In some of her moods earth can still recall her primordial days. Imagine that these are clouds in an atmosphere of methane and ammonia, and you have some idea of how earth-before-life may have looked over four thousand million years ago.

91

into more complex ones. These, by straight-forward physical and chemical processes, using the same sources of energy, became amino acids, the building blocks from which proteins are made. Over countless aeons the thin soup was enriched by these acids, turning slowly into a broth that could sustain life.

In time the amino acids fused into proteins, and different proteins came together to form cell-like structures. In time, too, a different set of acids (nucleic acids, formed by the same processes as amino acids) became organized as part of these primitive protein cells. This was a powerful step forward, because nucleic acids, properly organiz-ed, act as patterns on which new proteins can be quickly and regularly assembled.

Somewhere in that sequence we can put a marker labeled "life begins"; precisely where depends on how you care to define life. For our present purposes it is more important to realize that this life was living off capital—exhausting that rich broth of chemicals that had built up slowly over millions of years. Perhaps it *did* exhaust that broth. Perhaps there was a slow and worldwide ecocatastrophe as the rundown went on, until a mere remnant army of cells was reduced to living on the small trickle of new compounds, built up each day by the radiation still pouring in. If any geological record of that time survives, we have not yet learned to read it.

But perhaps, before that exhaustion could happen, a new and giant leap forward occurred among those primeval one-celled creatures. Perhaps one or more of them developed a struc-ture, a pigment, that could capture the sun's energy directly and use it to make complex molecules from simple ones.

The first cell to achieve that was, by definition, the first plant. What a breakthrough it was, and what a mammoth advantage it gave! No longer did such a cell have to wait for the haphazard and slow creation of new food. It could make it, regularly, reliably, every time the sun shone, every hour of daylight.

The snag was oxygen, the inevitable by-product of the building-up process, and a gas just as lethal

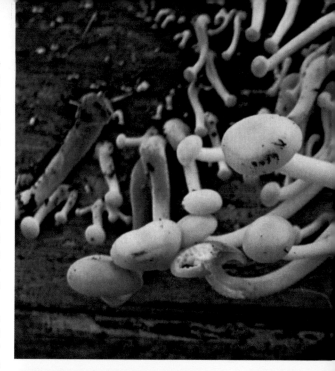

Above: puffballs thrive on compostlike material. In summer they grow a globe-shaped fruiting body, which in the fall will burst and puff out a cloud of spores into the air.

Lichens are formed by a partnership between two plants, an alga and a fungus. The alga has chlorophyll to make new material, the fungus determines the appearance and provides a moist environment. Lichens are an important winter food for caribou, lemmings, and some insects in cold northern regions.

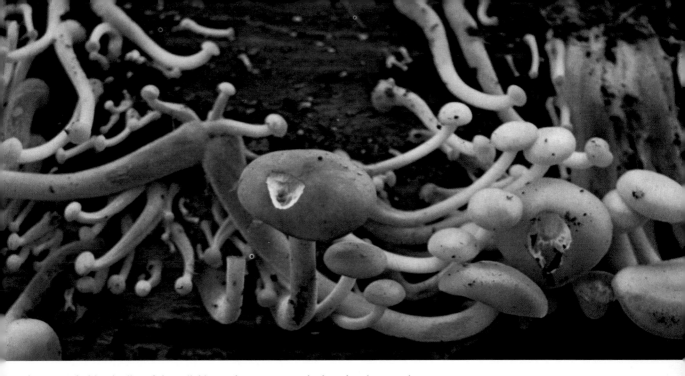

Immature fruiting bodies of the collybia mushroom, exposed when the photographer peeled away the bark of the fallen log on which it had been feeding.

to ammonia- and methane-using cells as those gases are to us. Still, a long, long time passed before the new oxygen built up to lethal levels—time enough for life to adapt, for new, oxygen-tolerant forms to evolve, as the original methane-dependent forms gradually disappeared. And it was even longer before oxygen became the second most common gas in the atmosphere—nearly 21 per cent, after nitrogen at 78 per cent. But it happened, so successful is the plant formula for survival.

Simultaneously with this development there must have been other new kinds of organism. Some were scavengers, cleaning up dead plant matter, breaking it down into simple compounds that would, in turn, make new nutrients for another generation of plants. Others fed off plants directly, creating the sort of competition for survival that has always been the most powerful spur to evolution. So even at the earliest stages of life as we know it (oxygen-tolerant life) there were the foundations of two distinct life styles: the plant style, in which the individual sits tight, absorbs energy, and uses it to build up complex foods from simple molecules;

Right: most fungi live by breaking down dead plant or animal matter. Here a bracket fungus has consumed the dead part of a tree and has grown a large fruiting body, which, when ripe, will shed into the air millions of dustlike spores.

and the animal style, in which generally the individual moves around and forages for ready-made foods.

To be sure, with increasing complexity goes increasing interdependence. To start with, all the give might have been among the plant types, all the take among the animal types. But that is certainly not so today. The plant world as we know it is as dependent on animals as vice versa. And not just in obvious ways such as needing bees to carry pollen. Many delicate grasses would not thrive unless there were animals to graze out the coarse ones. Many grasslands would not survive unless there were animals to nibble off the tender shoots of invading tree seedlings. The plant kingdom that we know today is conditioned and shaped by animals.

The very simplest plants have no *chlorophyll* (the green pigment that catches the sun's energy) and we call them plants only because they are in all other respects plantlike in their way of life—they have no definite body plan and do not move about freely like most animals. (In fact, some people put them in a separate kingdom called

Below: the lordly tree fern, like all the more primitive plants, has neither flowers nor seeds. It will produce, asexually, spores that grow into a structure containing male and female tissue; sexual reproduction will then result in another tree fern.

Above: the development of flowers and seeds was an enormous advance in the world of plants. The tree-living male and female generation had been confined to moist areas, where the sperms could swim to the female plant. Flowering plants, however, with their many dispersal mechanisms, were free to colonize other habitats—especially plants such as the dandelion whose seeds (here magnified 12 times) can drift long distances on the wind and colonize areas far from the parent plant.

protista.) They include bacteria and slime molds. Bacterial cells can manage without a nucleus: the central governor, rich in nucleic acid material, found universally in higher-order life.

Slime molds, by contrast, have nuclei but no cell walls, so that their living material spreads in a slimy mixture over decaying matter in the damp woodlands where they live. Fungi are closely related, and most of them, too, live on decaying plant or animal matter.

Curiously enough the simplest organisms that contain chlorophyll show a mixture of plant and animal features diverse enough to baffle the most enthusiastic classifier. They are single-celled creatures that move with the aid of cilia or

The stigma of a flowering plant (this one, magnified 12 times, is of a campanula) is where the pollen lands and sends down a long "arm" to reach and fertilize the egg in the egg chamber, or ovary. The pollen grains and eggs are evolutionary remnants of what were once free-living male and female plants.

flagella and are capable of absorbing complex food products every bit as efficiently as their animal relatives without chlorophyll. Organisms such as those we have so far mentioned make it impossible to draw rigid distinctions between plants and animals.

The simplest unequivocal plants are the algae—seaweeds and some pond weeds. They have chlorophyll or other similar pigments colored blue, brown, or orange. The lichens are an interesting combination of fungi and algae living together for mutual benefit. Slightly more complex still are the mosses, ferns, and horsetails. Once, when the giant reptiles were Lords of the Earth, these were the dominant plants. Great forests of tropical ferns formed the backcloth to the aeons through which the big reptiles moved; and the decomposing vegetation, compressed under hundreds or thousands of feet of later rock deposits, eventually formed coal.

Most of the plants so far mentioned can reproduce in two ways: asexually, by forming spores; or sexually, either by direct fusion of single cells or by forming "male" (mobile) and "female" (static) cells that fuse to produce a new individual. Where they reproduce sexually they undergo a curious process called "alternation of generations." We have already seen examples of this in the animal kingdom where, for instance, coral polyps anchored to their reefs give rise asexually to small, free-living, jellyfishlike forms that breed sexually. This alternation of sexual and asexual generations is universal among the plants already listed. In a very different way it is also universal among the plants we are about to look at—the trees, shrubs, flowers, and grasses. Among *them*, however, the sexual generation has no separate existence but is reduced to a small part of the flower.

The ferns are the most advanced of the plants we have so far looked at. Yet they have not overcome their problems of living and sexually reproducing far from water. Almost all of them live in moist, shady, or humid areas. To survive outside such areas, most plants need roots that can reach wide and deep in search of water, and stems and leaves that can prevent evaporation

when water grows scarce. Yet they must not prevent evaporation altogether, for the simple reason that if water were not lost from the leaves it would stop entering at the roots.

One of the major differences between animal and plant tissues is related to the basic difference between their ways of life, the one generally roving and active, the other normally sedentary. An embryo animal grows to a form in which it can live in the outside world, with or without parental help. All its tissues are the same age, although they are constantly renewed and repaired. You cannot have a teenage ear enraptured by spring birdsong up at one end, and a 70-year-old big toe dying of gout down at the other end of the same body (not yet, anyway). But that kind of discrepancy is quite normal in the plant kingdom. The 3500-year-old bristlecone pine still has plenty of embryo tissue, creating new stem wood and new leaves. Even a flower that survives just one summer has tissues of different ages, some laid down in early spring, some laid down only days before the frosts seize and wither it.

Because the parts of a plant appear and mature at different times and rates, a plant has no predetermined shape as an animal has, although its general form *is* determined. For example, all beech leaves have a particular pattern of serrations and that pattern is the surest guide to identifying a beech and distinguishing it from a hornbeam, which is very similar but has a different pattern to its serrations. Even so, you can search a long time before you find two identical leaves. Similarly the branches of a larch tend to grow downward, those of an Indian cedar to grow out more or less horizontally, and those of the poplar to grow as vertically as their heavy burden of leaves will permit. But within these broad patterns there are so many possible variations that the chances against any two trees of the same species being identical are too large to calculate.

In this respect plants have greater freedom than animals. They grow continuously from seedling to maturity — allowing for seasonal spurts among those that survive more than a year. The seat of their growth is embryo tissue called *meristem*. It is found in buds and the growing tips of stems and branches. It also occurs, named *cambium*, as a thin layer in the main stem or trunk and any side stems or branches. From this layer come more specialized cells: fibers for support, tubelike cells that transport fluids and foodstuffs, canals for resin, cork for bark, and others. In long-lived plants, such as trees, there are annual spurts of new growth, leaving the old tissue to turn into supporting fiber. The resulting growth rings are a sure guide to the age of a tree.

How dead is dead in the plant world? The bulk of each of these cedars in the Sierra Nevada is dead and already beginning to decay. Yet parts, as shown by the leaves, are still young and alive. This coexistence of dead, old, and young material is quite common in the plant world, much less so among animals.

Many orchard fruits will not develop unless the flowers are fertilized with pollen from another tree—and sometimes even from a different variety. Growers ensure this cross-fertilization by deliberately over-populating their orchards with bees; competition then forces the bees to range far afield for nectar and they transfer the pollen at the same time.

The way these tissues are laid down is far from haphazard. Where the main job is to withstand compression, as in the trunk of a tree, the fibers tend to line up vertically, but where there are torsional forces, too, as where a branch grows out from a trunk, the fibers intertwine and knit to resist shearing stresses. Anyone who has ever split logs will know the difference. A log from the trunk will usually cleave in two at a single stroke; but one from a junction can take half a dozen skillfully placed steel wedges and several dozen blows with a sledgehammer to split.

And this tendency to lay down fibers in response to stress usually affects the outer form of the plant—not just in the elementary sense that they are thicker at the base than at the outermost ends but also in details of cross section.

Furnished, then, with these basic tissues—roots to take in water and nutrients; leaves to catch the sun's energy and allow excess water to evaporate; strong, well-knit fibers to support the transport system that links the two; and continuing meristem tissue to lay down new material —the plant is equipped to survive well away from water, away from the conditions in which the great ferns thrived.

Another change was necessary before this new type of plant could exploit its capacity to survive in other habitats. The fern-type alternation of generations was too hazardous for drier conditions. So among trees, shrubs, grasses, and flowers we find a new modification. The free-living generation of tiny male and female plants becomes absorbed into the other generation. We see it in the male and female cones of cone-bearing plants and in the male and female parts of flowers (*anthers* and *ovules*) in the others. The anthers produce pollen grains (the actual rem-

In reaching for nectar, bees brush past the pollen-bearing parts of a flower, thus carrying pollen from flower to flower and ensuring cross-fertilization.

nants of the free-living generation) that are carried—by wind or water, birds or insects—to the female element. There the pollen grows a tube reaching into the egg (the other remnant of the free-living generation) and fertilizes it.

The flowers that contain these structures must make it rewarding to any insects or birds that visit them and carry the pollen from one to another. They produce a rich nutrient, nectar, usually deep down inside, so that the insects have to crawl past the anther and the *pistil* (where pollen settles and grows its fertilizing tube). It is from such nectar that bees make honey.

The seed ripens to maturity. It may be naked, as in the cone-bearing plants, or it may be hidden in the fruit, as in the others. The result may be fine as dust or bulky as a coconut. It may be poisonous, discouraging animals from eating it. Or it may be a hard, indigestible pip in a succulent and nourishing fruit. It may have wings or down, to enable the wind to carry it far from its parent. It may be glutinous, or sticky, or barbed, to fasten it to the coat of passing animals. It may grow in pods that develop an immense tension as they dry, eventually tearing apart with explosive violence that shoots the seed far from the shade of the parent.

An extreme example of this is the jack pine, whose cone is so tight that only the heat of a forest fire can spring it open. The cones lie on the forest floor, tightly shut and inaccessible to birds, squirrels, and other creatures. Then comes a

The Kirtland's warbler is one of America's rarest birds. It probably winters in the Bahamas, but in summer it lives only in large tracts of jack pine forest in northeast Michigan. The young trees, regenerated after a forest fire (right), provide a thick ground covering and low branches, which conceal the bird's nest. Four small forests are now dedicated to the preservation of the warbler.

forest fire, destroying all. And when it has passed, the air is thick with flying seeds and the noise of explosively opening cones. The seeds would have had a hard struggle to survive in the dark of the forest, but now they find light and plenty of nutrient from ash and decaying trees. This particular story has a twist to it, worth pursuing for the general point it illustrates. There is a bird, the Kirtland's warbler, that nests on the ground among the growing trees of jack pine forests. The low branches of the saplings and the thick ground cover provide protection for the nests. Once this bird was common in North America, wherever jack pines grew and natural forest fires were frequent. But as forests were cleared and fires were brought under control, the Kirtland's warbler was threatened with extinction. Indeed it would now be extinct if Audubon Societies in eastern Michigan had not got together with state conservationists and the United States Forest Service to dedicate four small forests, totaling 18 square miles, to its survival. They produce carefully controlled burns each year to support about 1000 birds.

Here we see how closely the lives of animals and plants can interweave, to the point of total dependence. In this case the advantage is all one way, for it is hard to see that the warbler benefits the jack pine greatly. But the squirrel that buries hundreds of nuts in dozens of hoards and then fails to locate several of them, or the thousands of animals that feast on fruit and berries and then either spit out the stone or defecate the pips, perhaps miles from the parent plant—these are playing an essential role in that plant's life cycle.

This deep-seated interdependence of flowering plants and animals, which stretches right back to the origins of those plants, in the days when the overlordship of the great reptiles was dwindling, goes far to explain the great diversity of form and life style of both. The bare definition of an animal as something that lives either immediately or ultimately off a plant carries implications that the benefits are all one way. This, as we have seen, is far from true.

Now that we have briefly surveyed the two great kingdoms of animals and plants, we can start to dig beneath the surface a little. We can throw some light on the great themes that unite all forms of life.

Survival Systems

"To every thing there is a season, and a time to every purpose under the heaven: a time to be born, and a time to die."

The Bible is not alone in pointing out the inevitability of death. The sacred Hindu book, the Bhagavad-gita, says less eloquently: "For that which is born, death is certain." In fact, one could say that all the world's great religions are founded on the mystery of death.

To the student of Nature the mystery is no less acute. Most living things die prematurely. Again and again in our survey we have seen that one sexual act between two individuals can lead to hundreds, thousands, or even hundreds of thousands of eggs or seeds. In the very nature of things, if that couple is not to inundate the world with its progeny, most must quickly perish. In fact, Nature's most characteristic product, apart from eggs and seeds, is a creature heading for premature death. Of all the plants and creatures, young and old, alive at this or any other precise second in time, the majority are actually dying— not in the general sense that "in the midst of life we are in death," but in the precise sense that they have only moments left to live. And ranked behind them are billions of juveniles, and behind them still further trillions of eggs or seeds, all heading for that same early death. To put it another way: the mature adult is the rarest and least typical member of over 99 per cent of the earth's species. (These figures—"billions" and "trillions"—are not literal. It is unlikely that anyone has ever calculated—or, having done so, would dare claim any great accuracy in the result—how many juveniles or eggs and seeds burden the earth at any given moment. But it is a figure far greater than one that has any direct meaning to our puny minds.)

It is only when we state the truth in such stark terms that the full force of the mystery is borne home. On the one hand, we have the universality and frequency of death; on the other, the most astonishing tenacity and determination to sur-

Adult mayflies have no feeding or digestive organs and so live only a day or two. Their sole purpose is to mate and lay eggs— thousands of them, most of which will be eaten. Its short life is the living embodiment of ideas quoted in the text on this page.

vive. The evolutionist can provide a partial (and negative) explanation by pointing out that creatures that lack the quality of tenacity would be quickly extinguished by the rest. This accounts for the universality of the quality and even explains why it is inevitable, but it leaves untouched the central question of how that tenacity arose in the first place and how it is expressed in the hereditary matter that each generation passes to its successor.

We simply have to accept it. Just as in chemistry we accept that all nitrate minerals dissolve in water, so in studying living things we must accept that all of them have a built-in urge toward survival. Certainly survival is the key problem to face all living things.

Survival has two major aspects. There is the obvious sense of *individual* survival. Plants and animals need ways to obtain food, water, and oxygen; they need defenses against large and small attackers; and they need systems for sensing and responding to their surroundings. There is also the slightly less obvious sense of survival as a *species*; for this they need ways of reproducing and ways of providing for the resulting offspring. Each of these aspects will repay more detailed study.

The immediate difference between the living matter inside a cell wall and the nonliving matter outside is that the living matter is made of complex organized molecules, whereas the nonliving matter consists largely of simpler molecules. The cell's basic problem is to get nonliving material inside the cell and to assemble it into useful things. Each stage costs energy.

We use energy in daily life at a very crude level: we light a gas flame or we start a car, for instance. In both cases we are applying a vast stimulus (a match or spark) to a huge reservoir of fuel, either pouring out through holes in a burner or compressed inside a cylinder. The energy we liberate by so doing is molecular—the energy that binds atoms together in a molecule. In the gas flame, for instance, the molecule is *methane* (natural gas), a combination of carbon and hydrogen atoms. Put methane and oxygen together at ordinary temperatures and nothing much happens. But excite the methane molecules with a spark so that their atoms vibrate and the ties that bind them loosen, and then with a violent suddenness they rip apart and attach themselves to the oxygen, making carbon dioxide and water. As they combine with the oxygen, they let loose

energy, *more* energy than it took to pry them apart. And there's the point: *more than it took to pry them apart.* So if you keep mixing methane and oxygen at ordinary temperatures and pouring it into that high-energy zone, you will go on ripping apart carbon and hydrogen atoms and combining them with oxygen to give an ever-mounting surplus of energy, for cooking with, or welding, or whatever you are using the gas for.

That is a very crude way of getting at the energy in the methane, however. It cannot be done with just a few thousand molecules at a time because that would not keep the temperature high enough; it has to be done with billions of molecules at a time. However, it cannot work like that for a living cell. The cell needs to tap energy—that *same* energy—in a much subtler way, a few hundred or thousand molecules at a time and without any high temperatures to start the whole process.

There are countless thousands of different molecules rich in energy and used as its source by living things. But there is one that is used by every living cell in every plant and animal in the world, except some bacteria. No matter what the plant or animal starts out using—whether it is a yeast cell busy fermenting sugar into alcohol, or yourself digesting a steak—the energy from that source gets converted step by step into one universal compound. Its name is adenosine triphosphate, familiarly known as ATP. The diagram explains how energy is stored in, and released from, ATP. The reaction shown there is happening several billion times a second in your body, even when you are deep in slumber.

The process is, however, much more efficient than our way with natural gas and matches, or gasoline vapor and spark plugs. The living cell contains minute powerhouses where individual molecules are taken apart and the energy is put immediately to work—and no priming shot of high temperature is needed to start it going. It is the difference between dismantling a machine with, on the one hand, a sledgehammer and, on the other, a full set of engineer's tools.

When we looked at plants and animals as complete organisms, we saw that every food chain sooner or later led back to a plant. The same is true—*has* to be true—down at this molecular level. The steak you swallow and use for forming (among other things) ATP came from a cow. The cow got its energy and building materials from grass. But where did the grass turn for *its*

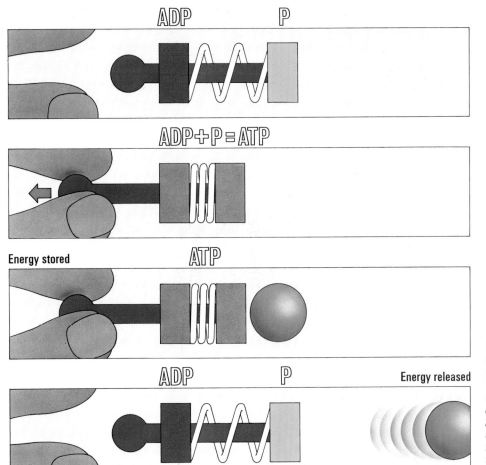

ADP   P

ADP + P = ATP

Energy stored   ATP

ADP   P   Energy released

This diagram outlines the operation of adenosine triphosphate, or ATP. When a phosphate group is added to ADP (adenosine diphosphate) it recharges it, so to speak, to make energy-rich ATP. When the process is reversed, the stored-up energy is released and put to work.

energy and raw materials? Or to put it generally —where do plants get their energy and raw materials from? We saw parts of the answer when we looked at different plant tissues, let us now put the parts together and see how they work.

Some raw materials come in with the water that is drawn in through the roots. The water, too, is a raw material even though much of it evaporates from the leaves. The other raw material is the gas we—and virtually all other living things breathe out: carbon dioxide. Water and carbon dioxide. If those two products sound familiar, that is because we have already mentioned them when we looked at what methane turns into when it burns with oxygen. Here, in the leaves of the plant, the opposite happens with the water and carbon dioxide. The plant puts them together and instead of giving out energy the process absorbs it. The product, it so happens, is not methane but another carbon-hydrogen compound, one that also has a few oxygen atoms: a very simple sugar called glucose.

The energy required for this process comes, of course, from the sun, and the pigment that absorbs the energy and makes it available is chlorophyll. The little powerhouses that hold the chlorophyll take individual molecules of carbon dioxide and individual molecules of water—six of each at a time—and use the captured energy to force all 12 molecules to unite and make one large glucose molecule. The glucose has all the carbon and hydrogen, but only one-third of the oxygen of the 12 starting molecules. The rest of the oxygen comes out of the leaves as a gas.

It sounds a very humdrum, dull little process: take six molecules of carbon dioxide and six of water, add a little energy, make one molecule of glucose and liberate six molecules of oxygen. But not only is that simple reaction the starting point for *all* the living processes now going on around the world (as if that weren't important enough), it is also the basis of a vast, worldwide balancing act between plants and animals. For the carbon dioxide the plants take in and use for making glucose is the same gas—the same actual molecules—that animals breathe out. On two

105

All the energy consumed by every living thing—whether it be gazelles leaping across a plain (above) or a conductor leading an orchestra through the intricacies of a concerto (above right)—is derived from the break-up of one compound: ATP.

counts, then, this simple reaction can claim to be *the* fundamental reaction of life.

The energy in the glucose molecule is instantly available. In a fraction of a second the living cell can send the molecule along a chain of 12 reactions that break it down to give two lactate molecules and recharge two ATP molecules. In a further twinkling of an eye each lactate molecule can be sent through 11 further reactions whose ultimate yield is 18 more recharged ATP molecules—plus, naturally, all the carbon dioxide and water in that original glucose molecule. To make the carbon dioxide and water the cell had to take in the six oxygen molecules the plant let free. There's the balancing act. And look at the energy it makes available: from breaking up one glucose molecule we get 38 recharged ATP molecules— 38 little coiled springs ready to travel through the cell's energy pathways and power its activities, build new protein, lay down new reserves of oil or fat, repair damage, destroy poisons, parcel up wastes, carry messages . . . the thousand and one jobs each cell does all the time.

Look more closely at that list of activities and you will see they can be sorted into three broad categories. Running messages, dealing with wastes, repairing damage; activities like that are part of the cell's daily economy, and keep it ticking over. But laying down new material is like saving and investing capital. It is part of the cell's long-term survival strategy, and the survival strategy at the level of the whole animal or plant.

There are three basic kinds of new material the plant or animal can build, and it is an important part of the organism's health to maintain a proper balance between them. The glucose molecule is a carbohydrate, a compound of carbon, hydrogen, and oxygen atoms. Its energy is so easily available that it is like ready cash in the cell's economy. But to keep going the plant cell must make a lot more glucose than it needs momentarily; what can it do with the surplus?

First it can make other carbohydrates, more complex than glucose, with bigger molecules. The energy in these is not quite so easy to get at; they have to be broken down into glucose again first. So if glucose is like ready cash, the other carbohydrates are like cash in a checking account—ready enough but demanding a little effort to get at.

Just as you don't gain anything by keeping more cash in a checking account than you need for "normal emergencies," so it is unprofitable for the cell to store more carbohydrate than *it* needs. The surplus can be turned into oils or fats,

which, in our cash analogy, you can think of as long-term deposits—more difficult to get at, but valuable savers. What, you may ask, is the equivalent of the interest that long-term deposits can earn? Well, an important by-product of all these energy transactions in the cell is heat. In animals, fats are good thermal insulators and save a lot of heat—a lot of energy that the cells need not squander their glucose to produce.

But here the analogy gets a bit stretched. Long-term deposits are somewhat passive, but fats play a very active part in the cell. For instance they are a vital part of every cell wall, stopping outside fluids from entering in an uncontrolled way. Also, fats around the nerve fibers in your body stop the electrochemical current that travels along them from leaking and so help to speed up the messages and cut down the energy they consume. Fats—and their near-neighbors, oils—are a vital part of the energy store of many plant seeds and animal eggs. So, although the most important role of fats is to act as an energy store, which makes them akin to money on deposit, they also play a vital structural part in the day-to-day economy of the cell, which makes them akin to fixed capital assets (plant, buildings, machinery, and so on).

But the true counterparts of the fixed assets are the proteins. They *are* the fabric of cells. They are muscles, skin, the nucleus, and the coating over the fat in the cell wall. They form the powerhouses in which energy is made and burned. They are responsible for the transport of messages. They control the activities. In fact proteins determine the structure, function, and character of the whole operation, both at the cellular level and at the whole-plant or whole-animal level.

The glucose in the simplest plant cell is identical with the glucose in your body; and most of the other carbohydrates are common to vast groups of plants and animals. But not so with proteins. Unless you have an identical twin, there is not even another human being, let alone another animal, who can make proteins *identical* to yours. The differences may be minute—far less than those between two "identical" cars off the same production line or two copies of this book—but they would be there, and they are what make everything that lives unique. The fats come somewhere between the uniqueness of proteins and the universality of most carbohydrates.

Just as fixed assets, deposits, and cash are all ultimately convertible into one another, so too are carbohydrates, proteins, and fats. Starve yourself and your body will utilize the fats and proteins already present, rendering them down from complex molecules to that simple molecule of glucose and then breaking them down further to carbon dioxide and water.

Carbohydrates, as we saw, are made up of carbon, hydrogen, and oxygen. Fats are chiefly made of carbon and hydrogen, with very much less oxygen. Proteins are similar to fats except

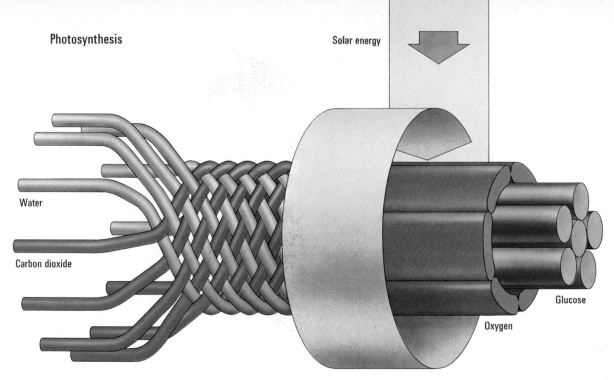

Solar energy

Water

Carbon dioxide

Glucose

Oxygen

This diagram summarizes the main elements in photosynthesis —the process whereby plants make new material from water taken in through the roots, and carbon dioxide absorbed by the leaves. In the leaves, too, are structures containing chlorophyll—a pigment that captures energy from the sun. The plant then uses that energy to bind the raw materials together to make simple sugars such as glucose. An important by-product of the complex photosynthetic reaction is oxygen.

that they also have another essential element, nitrogen, incorporated in their molecules. How does the nitrogen get there? Again by courtesy of the plants. Nitrogen is a fairly inert gas, and does not form compounds with other substances very readily, because it takes a lot of energy to tear the two nitrogen atoms in a nitrogen molecule apart. But lightning can do it. A flash of lightning can rip nitrogen atoms apart and in that state they will readily combine with nearby oxygen to form oxides of nitrogen. These in turn will combine with water in the air—rain or cloud vapor—to make nitrogen-containing acids. When they fall on the soil the acids react with minerals there to form nitrates, especially calcium nitrate, for calcium is a major element in many soils. There are about 1000 lightning flashes every second around the world, so this is quite a rich source of nitrogen.

As we saw in the opening paragraphs of this section, *all* nitrate minerals are soluble, so the water in soil is loaded with them. That is one way nitrogen from the air gets into plants and becomes raw material for proteins. There is another way. There are some bacteria that can break nitrogen atoms gently apart and use the energy thus made available. Although some live freely

in the soil, one important group lives in the roots of leguminous plants such as clover, peas, and beans. They create even more nitrogen compounds than lightning does. There is evidence that many plants outside the legume family can themselves make small quantities of nitrate.

Those are the ways in which *new* nitrates are made and incorporated into the world of living things. There is, of course, a much vaster quantity that is simply recycled. When you realize that one kind of animal alone in the U.S.A., the domestic dog, creates 3500 tons of dung and $9\frac{1}{2}$ million gallons of urine *each day*—all rich in nitrogen compounds—you can imagine the truly mind-boggling quantities of nitrogen returned to the soil daily by *all* the world's animals. Then add to it an even greater quantity in the form of dead and decaying animal and plant matter and you begin to see the reservoir and turnover of nitrogen in its various compounds.

There is another group of bacteria that live by breaking up nitrogen compounds and returning the nitrogen gas to the atmosphere. In the long term their activity is precisely compensated for by the agencies that add new nitrogen to life's stock. In other words, life's nitrogen is like a vast lake with a trickle of fresh supplies running in at

Above: the leaves of broadleaved woodland trees spread out in thin light-absorbing layers that are rarely dense enough to stop the sun's rays from penetrating directly down to the forest floor. Thus even the lower branches are well furnished with leaves and are able to play their part in making new material by photosynthesis.

Right: a diagram illustrating the worldwide gaseous balance between animals and plants. The arrows indicate that the sum of plant and animal respiration, which uses oxygen and produces carbon dioxide, is balanced by photosynthesis, which uses carbon dioxide and gives off oxygen as a by-product.

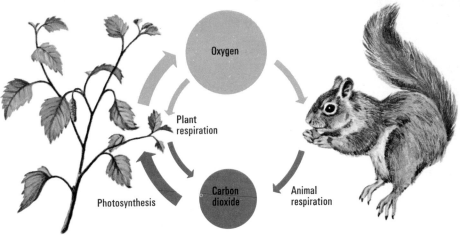

Oxygen

Plant respiration

Photosynthesis

Carbon dioxide

Animal respiration

109

Many human myths picture the origin of earth and its life in a flash of lightning and a thunderclap. In a way these ancient tales enshrine at least an element of truth; such flashes must have played a key role in fusing small and simple molecules together to make larger and more complex ones—a major step in the process that led ultimately to life on earth.

Plants build nitrates into protein

Lightning fixes nitrogen gas as simple compounds

Animals convert plant protein to animal protein and return nitrogen compounds to soil in wastes

Soil bacteria liberate nitrogen compounds from animal and plant remains

Bacteria in clover and other legumes (and also in many other plants) fix nitrogen gas as simple compounds

Animal protein is transferred from prey to predator

Soil bacteria release nitrogen gas from nitrogen compounds

Soil bacteria fix nitrogen gas as simple compounds

Around the world lightning flashes help fix gaseous nitrogen in simple compounds. Bacteria in soil and legumes also fix nitrogen, an important element in all proteins. The diagram shows how nitrogen is cycled around the living world and returned to the soil.

one end and waste running out at the other.

Briefly, then, the plant takes in nitrates, builds them into amino acids and builds these into proteins. Animals eat the plants, break down the plant proteins into amino acids, and build them up in a different way to make animal protein. Other animals eat those animals, break down their protein again to amino acids, and build them up yet again into other proteins . . . and so on. The bits they cannot use, together with breakdown products of the wear and tear and repair of life, get passed out, mostly in feces and urine. These, like the dead matter to which all living things return, are fodder for a host of other animals, plants, and bacteria, some of which liberate the nitrogen, although most merely return it as simple compounds to the soil, where the whole cycle starts again.

The ingenuity of the system shows up especially well in those plants that live in places where the cycle is difficult to start. In stagnant bogs and wet heaths, for instance, the water and soil may be so acid that nothing much decays and newly released material may be hard to come by. It is in these places that we find plants such as the Venus's-flytrap and the sundew, both of which trap insects and digest them. In this way they add to their stock of nitrogenous materials, which their environments would otherwise prevent them from acquiring.

We live in a world where every individual seems bound by an inexorable law to preserve its own integrity and resist invasion. Resistance has two main aspects: how to resist at the microscopic level, and how to do it at the whole-plant or

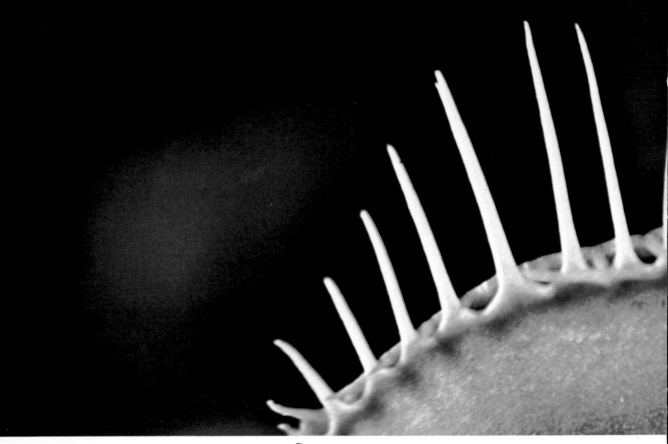

Above: a dying frog trapped in the embrace of a Venus's-Flytrap. This plant evolved in moist areas where nutrients from decaying matter are slow to recycle. The ability to supplement its diet in this way gives the plant a decided advantage in such conditions.

whole-animal level. Because for most of the previous section we were focused on the small-scale, molecular level, let us stay down there to start with and look at resistance to attack on that same scale. For our main example we shall take the human system, because for obvious medical reasons it is by far the best-studied system and the most highly responsive in the whole realm of life. It is also more interesting to us.

The simplest thing that can invade you is an inert foreign body—a small fragment of flying metal, such as shrapnel or buckshot. It is probably sterile, so it will not infect you and it is probably chemically inert, so it will not irritate your flesh. If you can stop other things tracking down the wound, your body will simply tolerate this kind of invader. In biological terms, something inert like this has no existence. The body will build clean scar tissue around it and go on as

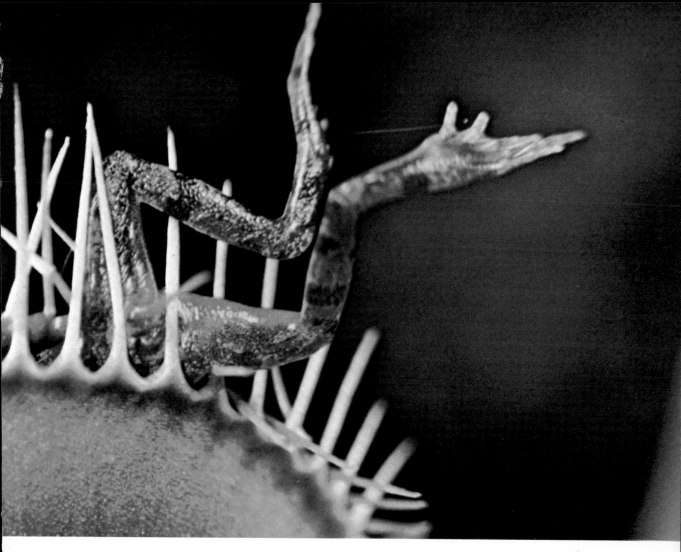

Below: this sequence of pictures shows a Venus's-flytrap closing on a harvestman, or daddy longlegs. When the sensitive hairs on the surface of the leaf are touched the two halves rapidly close together and the teeth interlock, trapping the creature within.

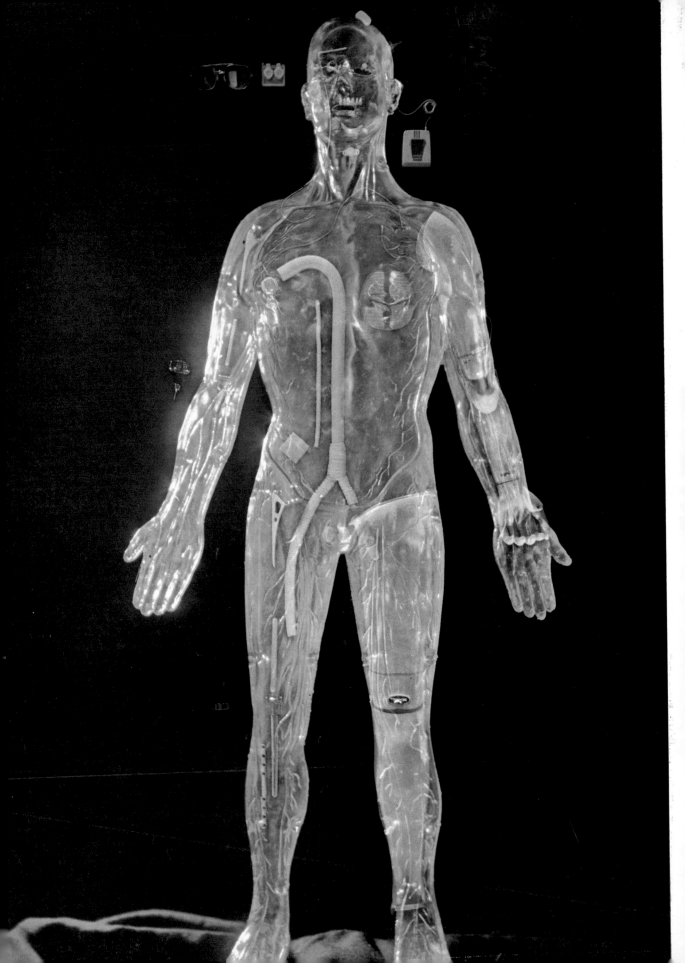

if nothing had happened. But steel and other inert things are artificial. It is hard to imagine a likely situation in nature where small sterile inert objects could be hurled into living flesh and imbed themselves there. So it is not really surprising that the body has no readymade defenses against them. We take advantage of this loophole when we put artificial spare parts in an ailing body—anything from heart valves through plastic eye lenses to hip joints. We use the same loophole to put transmitters inside animals or fine tubes inside plant stems, to study the intimate details of their behavior or physiology in natural conditions that no laboratory could simulate. Still, it is an artificial situation and so has no real lesson for anyone seeking to understand the grades of resistance one living thing can offer another.

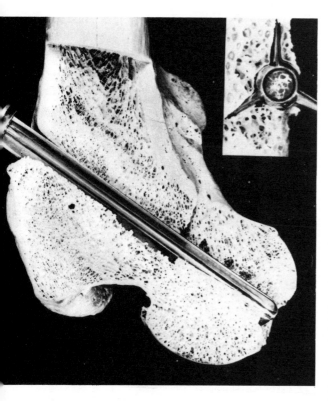

Left: this model shows a number of man-made spare parts, many of which can be surgically implanted inside the human body. The surgeon takes advantage of the fact that such man-made materials do not challenge our white-cell defenses and so are not rejected. One example is a stainless-steel hip joint around which good healthy bone can form. The stainless-steel tube, inserted to strengthen a weak thigh bone at its hip end (shown above), is even more astonishing, for healthy bone has regrown inside its hollow body, as seen in the inset picture.

The next most complex kind of invader is a chemical that is *not* inert—a toxin, or poison. Some are so active, so virulent, that nothing can withstand them: for example, the poison of the koikoi tree frog, of which a fraction of one millionth of an ounce is enough, as we saw, to kill a man. Somewhere, however, there may be one man who by some freak mutation, is immune to that poison; perhaps it may merely make him ill, or perhaps it is no more harmful to him than sliced bread. If the frog or the Indians who use its venom began to multiply in uncontrollable numbers and used the venom to take over the world, the unguessed-at resistance or immunity of this man would have immense value. While others died around him, he would survive. The example is not as fanciful as it sounds. It is precisely what has happened this last decade among rats. For almost a quarter of a century we have been poisoning these rodents with bait containing warfarin, a substance that stops blood from clotting and that can therefore turn even the most minor injury into a fatal one. In the trials that preceded its introduction not one rat showed any immunity to the poison. In the two decades that followed its introduction it was the most dependable rat poison ever. Then increasingly in the 1960s reports began to come in that the bait was being eaten but the rats were not dying. Somewhere in the rat population were a few lucky individuals with the unsuspected and hitherto useless ability to eat warfarin and thrive; they were quickly called Super-rats. They are now a threat to food industries in many areas.

That, then, is how living things evolve the ability to resist poisons. The precise mechanism varies. In one case it may be the ability to make a chemical that will combine with the poison and neutralize it. In another case—as with the warfarin—it may be the ability to tolerate the poison. In extreme cases, especially among bacteria, the threatened life form may completely turn the tables on its would-be poisoner. For instance, there are now some strains of bacteria that cannot live without hexachlorophene, which when it was first introduced was an extremely powerful bacteria killer. They actually use it as *food!*

The most complex kind of invader of all is another living thing. If you were a small, single-celled creature, dependent on a capricious environment for warmth, food, water, and protection from blistering sunshine and freezing dark, your chances of survival would be fairly slim.

You might get by as an individual, but life would be a lot easier if you found a larger living thing with better chances of survival and invaded it for a free ride. If the one you found was warm-blooded, mobile (giving *you* the chance to spread, too), and ate a richly varied diet, you would have found the perfect vehicle for your ride.

Hundreds of different kinds of bacteria have, in fact, used us in this way. Many of them have found a life style that does not directly threaten us. They stay in our mouths, throats, or intestines, doing a useful job of cleaning up and scavenging. Some even do essential work; millions of them are at this moment making vitamin B in your gut. But technically they are not *inside* our body tissue, they are in a cavity *within* our bodies. The real invaders are the ones that get into our bloodstream—through cuts, through breathing, through eating, through sexual contact, or straight through the skin.

Our response is to meet like with like. Just as we can meet chemical invaders with a neutralizing chemical, so we can meet living ones with a living force—a whole army, millions strong, of white blood cells. What they respond to is foreign protein invading the body.

We saw earlier that the proteins a living creature makes are unique to itself, and this is the basis of an effective anti-invasion strategy. Foreign protein is an alarm call for the white cells, that, like prowl cars in the streets, constantly rove through our bloodstream ready for such an emergency. They vigorously attack the new invader and usually kill it. The secret of this

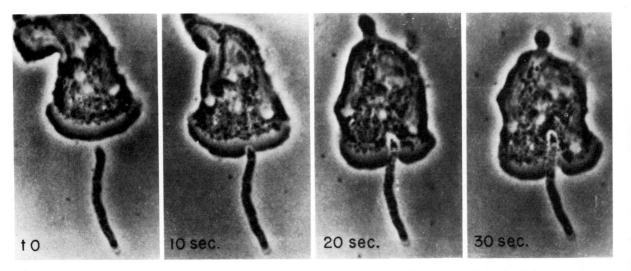

Photomicrographs taken at 10-second intervals show how a white blood cell can engulf an invading bacterium in just over a minute. Elements in the cell at once begin to "learn" the chemical nature of the bacterium. Then even if the white cell dies, as it probably will, it will release chemicals that will inform other white cells of all it has learned. In this way the body gains immunity to invaders.

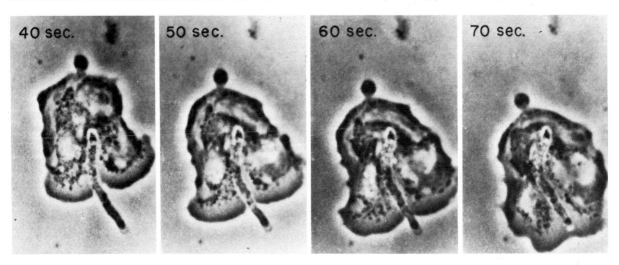

success lies in the fact that practically every organism that can invade your body has already done so. If you cut yourself, you let in thousands of bacteria of many types, but the overwhelming chances are that all those types have invaded you before. Your white cells are already adapted to respond to them and are prepared. The first time any given type invaded you, it was different. The struggle was probably hard fought and dearly won. But the white cells are rarely caught the same way twice. The next time that type of bacteria invades, they will finish it off in a very short time—no fuss, no temperature, no open illness at all. That second-time readiness is what we call *immunity*. We have even learned to take advantage of the process by deliberately infecting ourselves with weak strains of common invaders, or their dead bodies, or their poisons, so that the first exposure gives our white cells both an easy victory and that vital immunity.

Elsewhere in the animal kingdom we find similar defensive systems. Insects, for instance, have a much simpler system of internal defense. Their blood cells engulf invaders as ours do, but they do not in any way become adapted to respond to them, so that insects cannot acquire immunity as we can. In addition to this kind of system, insects are like all other animals and most plants in possessing a wide variety of external defenses.

One almost universal external defense is an outer protective layer: hide, horn, bark, shell, or whatever form it may take. Even your thinnest skin, on your eyelids, is 200 times thicker than a typical bacterium—equivalent to a quarter-mile-thick wall for something man-sized. And if you habitually walked barefoot, you would get a half-inch layer of horn on your soles, equivalent to a wall over 10 miles thick. For most of that thickness the substance is dead, withered, and dry, offering little nourishment to would-be invaders. In fact, so thick and protective can this skin become that a man who had never worn shoes has been known to stand on a red-hot branding-iron and remain unaware of it until he smelled his own soles burning! And when we come to the 9-inch-thick hide of the whale shark, which may turn aside harpoons and stop high-velocity bullets, comparisons become meaningless. Even so they do make clear what a formidable defense even the softest, most delicate of skins can be.

Starfish have an *actively* defensive skin, covered with minute scissorlike projections that snip away larvae and seaweeds that might otherwise settle. At certain seasons the bottom dwellers of tidal waters live in a constant shower of young creatures seeking a growing place, and every surface would soon become infested without such a response.

Other active defense systems used by animals against small invaders are more obviously behavioral than that of the starfish. At the simplest level they amount to an ability to live in close association with other creatures that do a good close-up scavenging and cleaning job. Our own skin and clothing is home to millions of creatures, from bacteria to the house dust mites we looked at in earlier pages, which live off complex foodstuffs we cannot use or have finished with. Most of these fellow creatures can be seen only through a microscope, but elsewhere in the animal kingdom there are examples of such cooperation that do not need a visual aid before we notice them. Damsel fish, for instance, have a slimy skin that protects them as they swim unharmed and safe from predators among the poison tentacles of sea anemones. In addition they scavenge debris on and around their protectors, which has obvious advantages for both partners in the association. Tick birds eat ticks that infest rhinos, and the rhino's acute sense of smell and the bird's keen eyesight make the partnership collectively more vigilant. One type of goby fish scavenges for encrustations and scabs on the skin of tiger rock fish, which, if they do not get these regular groomings, grow very unhealthy.

Simply keeping clean is another excellent defense against all small-scale attackers. We can find examples of grooming, preening, and bathing throughout the animal kingdom. Houseflies, as soon as they settle, start rubbing their legs together to rid them of dust and other adhesions. Birds preen and groom endlessly. Cats lick and smooth their fur, Dogs nibble and scratch for fleas. Horses roll in dust and wet grass. Elephants, hippos, hogs, and many others wallow in clay and mud, which, although it is usually a means of cooling, has the added advantage that when the mud dries, shrinks, and flakes off, it takes a good scraping of dead skin, shed hair, and other matter with it. The primates, as we saw earlier, have taken the business of grooming to an extreme, using it as a kind of "social glue" to hold their group together.

When it comes to resisting large invaders, as opposed to mites and microbes, the best passive defense is often an aggressive posture. Even

Vampire bats

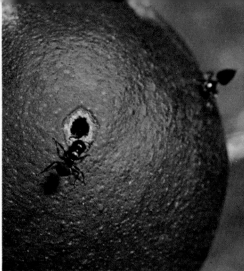

Gall ants

Leech

Most nonmicroscopic living things are protected by a tough outer layer be it hide, bark, skin, or shell. In different ways the animals shown here have overcome these defenses. Vampire bats can bite the flesh of a sleeping animal without waking it; their saliva stops blood clotting. Gall ants provoke plant tissues to develop a gall, which the ants then use for a nest! The leech clings by suction and

plants can play such a role. The spines on a cactus prevent most thirsty animals from using it as a living water resource. The thorns on briars and other members of the rose family send hungry animals elsewhere to graze. Nettles, with their stings, are not the first-choice food of most grazers; and the younger, more tender, and more succulent, a nettle shoot is, the more vicious its sting. Evil-tasting foliage is a variant of this type of defense, but it is directed at the forager's

sense of taste instead of pain.

Poisonous foliage is a subtler defense. It depends on the slow unwinding of evolution rather than on the immediate rebuff of pain. In time, as the animals that eat the poison die, the majority of survivors will seem to have a natural and knowledgeable aversion to the plants. Among them there may be a minority that can occasionally browse on the poison with only a minor upset; they are the nucleus of a population of

Ticks

Ichneumon fly

bites through the skin with serrated teeth in three powerful jaws. The ticks in the picture have penetrated the weakest spot in the turtle's shell—the junction between plates. And the ichneumon fly is laying an egg on the paralyzed but still living body of a wood wasp larva; to do so it must first locate the larva and drill through solid wood. It then paralyzes the wasp grub and deposits the egg.

poison-tolerant animals, like the super-rats and their warfarin.

This type of defense has evolved in many animals, too. Often nauseous-tasting or poisonous individuals are brightly colored or strongly marked, their distinctive appearance acting as a warning to predators. For instance, the poisonous painted jezebel butterfly of New Guinea and Australia displays vivid colors on the underside of its wings, which make the butterfly particularly conspicuous when at rest and easy prey. Painted jezebel caterpillars feed voraciously on mistletoe, the poisonous sap of which is thought to be the source of the butterflies' inedible quality. In the same way, the monarch butterfly of America feeds on the poisonous milkweed plant and birds have learned to leave this distinctively marked, ill-tasting butterfly alone. This combination of warning coloration and offensive nature has reached extreme forms in some

Above left: this buffalo is using the detergent quality of wet mud—and later the abrasive quality of dried mud—to rid its hide of invaders and pests. Above right: the ostriches taking a sunset dustbath are using the dust for a similar purpose.

animals. No one who has ever startled a skunk, for example, and taken a full blast of its evil-smelling fluid, is likely to seek a repeat performance. But just in case you do forget the skunk's powers, you may be reminded on meeting it again by the warning coloration of its fur.

The skunk's behavior takes us to the realm of active defense against large invaders. Here the simplest strategy is flight, on foot or on the wing, to some inaccessible place. Some animals, such as snails and turtles, are lucky enough to carry their inaccessible place around with them; their flight consists simply of withdrawing their softer extremities. Hedgehogs come into this category, too, with their ability to roll up into a tight prickly ball if alarmed or in danger.

For some animals the inaccessible place is an especially prepared nest or hole. The rabbit, which cannot outrun a dog or a fox, develops complex underground warrens over many generations. But the hare, which can usually outpace a fox, has no such bolt hole. Other small animals rely on escape into the trees to foil a pursuer. And when the pursuer can itself climb trees—the chimpanzee, say, or the leopard, both of which find small monkeys tasty—they depend on being smaller and lighter, so that they can shelter on thin branches that would break under the weight of the heavier predator.

There are plenty of other ways a small animal

can escape. One frog, which seemingly vanishes in mid-flight, has a brilliant stripe on its side, revealed only in the early part of its leap when its legs are fully stretched; when it bends its legs again the stripe—and apparently the frog—vanishes suddenly. Similarly, the butterfly with bright markings on the upper wing seems to vanish when it settles and folds its wings together; and brightly colored tropical fish that are vertically flattened seem to vanish when they turn head- or tail-on to a predator.

Other strategies include the ability to shed a limb or a tail, leaving it in the grasp of a baffled predator, who is doubly distracted if the limb or tail goes on moving. The intended victim then either hides or goes carefully while a replacement grows. Playing possum is another effective defense, for movement itself is a powerful trigger of predatory attack. If freezing is inappropriate, running is the next strategy. And when that fails, the animal either submits or turns and fights for its life. These strategies assume a different importance in different groups of animals. Even those that would normally flee may be powerfully equipped to fight—the wild boar, for instance. Although the dog is more maneuverable and has stronger jaws, it is no match for the boar's chisel-sharp tusks and colossal neck muscles; it takes many dogs to finish off a boar.

Among birds, too, there are individuals

Above: a young impala buck lowers its ear for the red-billed oxpecker to remove any ticks that may have crawled inside. Such mutually beneficial associations are quite common among animals. Another example is the tiger fish (below), which soon becomes unhealthy if deprived of regular skin cleanings given to it by the much smaller goby fish here seen near its mouth.

Above: baboons spend many hours grooming one another and removing ticks, lice, and fleas. The habit has the dual function of maintaining cleanliness and promoting social cohesion.

Left: a standoff between a wolf and a skunk. If this is the wolf's first such encounter, he is in for quite a surprise—and next time he will not ignore the skunk's coloration and warning posture.

equipped to fight although their usual reaction is to flee. The ostrich, for instance, is a flightless, grassland dweller. Its long neck and side-facing eyes give far-reaching all-round vision, and its powerful legs can carry it at 45 miles per hour. But if an ostrich turns and fights, those same legs are the most formidable weapons in the whole world of birds. In captivity, one kick by a single angry male bent a half-inch iron bar to a right angle. An unarmed man's only defense is to lie flat on the ground, where the kick has no power. At a less spectacular level there is the powerful wing of the swan, which can break the leg of a dog or fox and can painfully bruise and repel any larger-boned intruders.

Some of the larger animals concentrate on the ability to outdistance a pursuer. Many animals owe their form to the need to satisfy this one demand, as we saw with the double-wedge shape of the typical streamlined fish, the long two- or one-toed feet of grassland animals such as deer and horses, and the short, broad wings of the quick-take-off birds such as grouse and partridge.

Where individual strategies fail, group strategies may succeed. The world of living things has thousands of examples of animals that form groups to stand off almost any attack, although any one of them would be easy prey for a predator. A man may crush an ant without pausing in his stride, yet whole villages of men will flee before an advancing column of driver ants. A musk ox, because of its bulk, is a poor distance runner and no sprinter at all. An individual is fair game for two or three wolves; but when a herd of them forms a defensive ring the only mortal thing they need fear is a man with a bow and arrow or gun. Similarly, a flight of starlings threatened by a falcon will move from a loose, open formation into a tight bunch. In this way they not only present less obvious individual targets, but also force the falcon to risk collision and possible injury if it still dives down and tries to pick off one of the flock. And there are many small song-birds and perching birds that will mob intruders even though the intruder could make

Right: baboons easily frustrate a marauding lioness by climbing a tree. One of them, probably the one highest up in the tree, would have stood sentry and given good warning of the cat's approach toward those on the ground.

The land turtle's tough shell is its main defense against attack; it also helps prevent the animal from drying out.

Left: by shamming death in this highly realistic way the grass snake sometimes induces would-be predators to ignore it. Below left: by contrast, the hedgehog, when threatened, curls into a tight pincushion, denying predators a toothhold.

mincemeat of any one of them individually.

Defensive and offensive formations of this kind often have as much to do with the survival of the group as of the individual animal. Indeed, among animals in which instinctive behavior dominates learned behavior—such as ants—individuals in the front line may be programmed to sacrifice themselves for the benefit of the group. The leading ants in a march, for instance, will unhesitatingly drown themselves to form a raft over which later ants can safely march. At the other end of the scale, among humans, it generally takes powerful indoctrination and desperately threatening circumstances before individuals can be manipulated into such suicidal behavior. Nevertheless this latent aggression is there when it is needed, part of the basic behavior program we carry in our inheritance.

When it comes to the survival of the super-group, the collection of all animals of the same kind—the species—the strategies are written into the program in even more basic ways. In fact, it could be said they *are* the program.

When we looked at the way life on this planet began, we saw that two kinds of acid (both of them compounds of carbon, hydrogen, oxygen, and nitrogen) played the crucial role. One kind, amino acids, link together to make proteins. The other kind, nucleic acids, have the power to organize the production of protein. They are in effect both the recipe and the mixing bowl. In a living cell the nucleic acids are not scattered haphazardly about but kept tightly organized in a sequence unique to the creature of which the cell is a part. If the nucleic acids were organized in a different sequence, they would dictate the structuring of different proteins, and therefore of a different cell, and therefore of a different individual. It is the sequences that are all-important; change one and you change all. *And some rate-change quenches all change: it is you that are one pint tall.* And if you find that italicized sentence a little odd, let me explain that it uses precisely the same letters and punctuations as the sentence that preceded it. It even keeps nine of the original 14 words intact. Here is a more radical re-ordering: *A cellular act is to strangle a queen in one hand: hey-get at the champions.*

An Arabian oryx sprinting over the Namib Desert, startled by the airplane from which this photograph was taken. Their impressive turn of speed enabled this species to survive until men with machine guns and Cadillacs came along. A determined campaign by the World Wildlife Fund and Phoenix Zoo has helped to save them. The task is made easier because they breed readily in captivity.

The two rearranged sentences read more like codes than plain English. You can't say they have *no* meaning but you can't imagine the circumstances in which you'd read them straight through without a moment's unease. To put it in a more general way, the 26 letters of our alphabet can be assembled to make an astronomical number of words and those words in turn can be combined, together with various punctuations and spaces, to make a near-infinite number of sentences. Most of them will be utterly meaningless in all conceivable circumstances, full of "words" such as *xamduff* and *gensputtle*. The rest—those that by stretching our imagination we can call vaguely "meaningful"—will mainly consist of sentences like the two rearranged ones above. By far the smallest set will consist of sentences whose meaning is clear—the sort of sentence we are most used to reading.

It may sound odd to say that the truly meaningful sentences are a tiny minority—especially when we realize that all the meaningful sentences written since the dawn of history and all those spoken since the birth of speech do not amount to more than a small part of the total of all possible meaningful sentences. Truly the mind shrinks

The bright markings on this stink bug warn other animals of its nauseous flavor.

When threatened, musk-oxen will form themselves into a tightly defensive ring in which the strong shield the weak.

from even contemplating the vast number of all possible sentencelike arrangements of the handful of symbols on a typewriter keyboard.

But—and here is the really mind-boggling part—suppose that the typical word had *tens of thousands* of letters. How many possible sentences do you think could be written then? There is no hope of assessing the numbers. Yet that is the scale of complexity which exists in the making of proteins. Proteins are like words with tens of thousands of letters each. And the strings of nucleic acids are like mammoth encyclopedias composed of millions . . . tens of millions . . .

Right: soldier ants crossing water, partly on a leaf but partly on the suicidally drowned bodies of the column's pioneers.

Above: like wartime shipping convoys schools of fish have a much better chance than individuals of surviving a difficult migratory journey through dangerous waters.

hundreds of millions . . . of such words—the precise number varies with the complexity of the organism. That is the encyclopedia into which evolution has written its billions of changes. And the tens of millions and perhaps hundreds of millions of species that have come and gone (for death is the natural fate of species as well as of individuals) have each arisen by random changes in the words in the encyclopedias.

Each such change means at the very least that the new protein is not like the old; it may mean a far more radical alteration, producing a new kind of organism (just as a light tap on a bottom can of

beans in a supermarket display pyramid can lead to what you might also call a "radical alteration"). A string of such changes can lead to organisms so different that they cannot breed with their siblings and cousins; they are the first of a new species.

Most of these random changes produce nonsense words, turning meaningful sentences into meaningless ones. The resulting organism is weak and incapacitated—in some way less viable than its forebears. But every now and then comes that rare change that improves the organism and fits it better for survival. To round this off in terms of our encyclopedia analogy: suppose all encyclopedias up to a certain moment in time specified "and all free men are equal." That's part of a recipe for what history tells us is a viable though unedifying society—one of free men and slaves. You've probably guessed the change—same words, different order: "all men are free and equal"—a recipe, few would doubt, for a much better society.

If all this seems a little remote from the real world of living things, let us turn back to that world and see how the process has worked in actual changes that naturalists have been able to record and study. This is how species evolve.

One of the most often-quoted pieces of research in this context is the classic work of H. B. D. Kettlewell of the University of Oxford; just recently it has developed a new twist to its tail. Kettlewell studied the history of the peppered moth, a light-colored moth that can stay well camouflaged when it settles among lichens on tree trunks. At least, *most* of them were light. A few—so few that collectors prized them as rarities—were dark. Their dark color made them conspicuous, an easy mark for marauding birds, and the black form survived at all only because it was hardier, which partly compensated for its color disadvantages. But that was before 1850. Came the Industrial Revolution, and a pall of soot settled down-wind from the factory areas, far out into the country. The lichens died, poisoned by soot. The tree bark turned black. Now it was the dark rarities that were inconspicuous; the

Dutch tulip fields are like an open-air diagram from a genetics textbook. Each plot here is the handiwork of the plant breeder, who chooses among thousands of genetic variations to preserve and multiply those that are most economic and marketable— particularly color, size, season, and disease resistance.

129

pale forms were suddenly the easier mark. By 1900 the once-rare black varieties made up over 90 per cent of the population. Only in the remotest rural areas were the original proportions preserved, and not just in Britain, but throughout Europe.

Things stayed that way until the 1950s, when the story took a new turn. European governments and local commissions began enforcing new clean-air legislation, and one of the first things to be forbidden was solid soot emission. The air in and around the cities is now cleaner than at any time since about 1600. The result, as you might expect, is a return to the status quo: the light form is staging a comeback as its advantages reassert themselves; the dark form, despite its greater hardiness, is once again an easy target for the birds. Altogether naturalists have dis-

covered about 50 other species of moths in which a rare dark form has enjoyed a brief one-century heyday, thanks to the Industrial Revolution and the tardy enforcement of clean-air ordinances.

This example reveals one of the secrets of survival at the species level: variety. If the tendency to dark coloring had been absent among these moths, many of them might now be extinct. The species that becomes so uniform that it is suited to just one very local set of conditions is sealing its own fate. This is especially prone to happen where it colonizes a remote island and becomes adapted perfectly to life there—so perfectly that it can soon survive nowhere else. It is no accident that among the world's rarest and most threatened bird species are half a dozen from the Seychelles, at least an equal number from the Fijian islands, and the Galápagos finches. All are

perfectly adapted to environments that man is changing. They have nowhere else to go.

We have seen other examples of survival by variety in earlier pages: the warfarin-resistant rats, and the bacteria that are nourished by antiseptics, for instance. Those were species in which there were, so to speak, changes present in the background ready for an environmental change to mobilize them. But in any widespread and successful species we can see that the process is continuously at work. One fascinating example is found among gulls. In eastern Siberia lives the Vega gull. It has a darkish mantle (back and wings) and dull flesh-colored legs. As we go eastward across the Bering Strait, then across North America and the Atlantic to Britain, we notice a continuous change toward a lighter mantle and more strongly flesh-colored legs. The ultimate

form is the British herring gull, with the lightest mantle and the strongest-colored legs. The American herring gull is an intermediate form. But travel westward from Siberia and we see quite a different pattern of change: the mantle gets darker and the legs get yellower. The extreme is again found in Britain—the lesser black-backed gull—with the Scandinavian black-backed gull as a halfway stage.

So here is a continual variation toward two extremes from the centrally placed Vega gull of Siberia. And where the two extremes overlap they are so different as to be different species. The lesser black-backed gull is a migratory inland scavenger, whereas the British herring gull is a year-round cliff-dwelling resident. So, genetic changes are not just dormant, waiting for a change in the environment to select them. They

The picture sequence on these two pages illustrates the story of the peppered moth, told at length in the text. The first picture represents the pre-industrial situation, where the lighter moths have the advantage among the light-colored trees; the black moth, being more visible to predators (like the black-cap on the far right), is a rarity. The next picture shows the advantages reversed when industrial grime covers the vegetation; here the white moth is the rarity. In the third picture, antipollution codes have restored the status quo and the black variant of the peppered moth is once more becoming rare.

131

are continuously being called forth (or suppressed) by a constant process of external change.

Clearly with this great reserve of variety to draw upon, only the most catastrophic environmental change poses any threat to the gull. It is on the ability to make that variety in the first place that the success of a species depends. This is one of the mysteries of modern biology: the genetic material—the stock of nucleic acid—in some species is much more *labile* (likely to change spontaneously) than in other species. This phenomenon occurs throughout the living world but it is perhaps most intelligible and easiest to grasp among that unique group of living things, the viruses. It is, in fact, arguable whether viruses are living creatures in the full sense of the word, because basically they are nucleic acid material perpetually on the scrounge for some other living cell to expropriate as a workshop.

Most viruses are constant in their character—fortunately so, for that allows us to produce vaccines against the few that threaten us. Those responsible for polio and measles, for instance, have not changed in the three or four decades we have studied them in detail and the vaccines pioneered in the 1950s are still effective today.

The gulls illustrated here are all members of a continuously varying group that spans the Northern Hemisphere from Britain around again to Britain. The Vega gull of Siberia is the intermediate type. Westward from Siberia the leg and wing colors change in a direction that culminates in the lesser black-backed gull of Britain. Eastward similar changes culminate in the British herring gull.

Vega gull

Scandinavian black-backed gull

132 Lesser black-backed gull

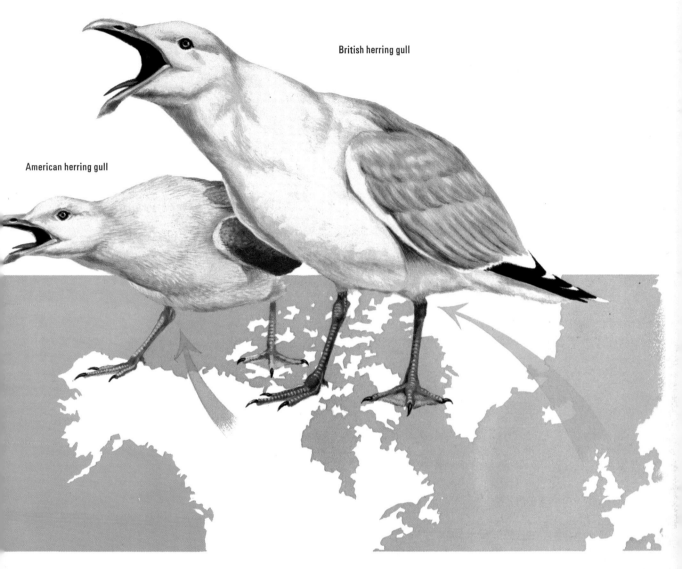

British herring gull

American herring gull

But the influenza virus is highly labile. As fast as we make vaccines and as fast as our bodies develop natural immunity, it changes its form slightly and slips under our defenses. Usually the changes are small, so that some of our immunity is preserved. But every so often (it used to be every 18 years until vaccines speeded up the whole process—now it is about every 12 years) the virus produces a major change, possibly by cross-breeding with closely related wild strains that infect animals other than man. Against this new form all our acquired immunity and all our vaccines are useless, so we get a worldwide 'flu epidemic, spread rapidly via the world's airways. Our only hope of meeting such changes is to do what workers have done at the Pasteur Institute in France—they have artificially speeded up the natural evolution of the virus in the laboratory so that we know what changes are likely in the wild and can prepare vaccines to meet them.

But none of this adequately explains why some viruses are so genetically labile and others so fixed. And, as we have seen, the phenomenon is found throughout life's kingdoms. Human genes are remarkably labile. The changes in human and near-human forms over the last 20 million years still baffle their most expert students. In contrast there are reptiles, fish, and lower creatures that have not changed substantially in tens or hundreds of millions of years because their environment has not changed sufficiently to force them to adapt accordingly.

This difference of lability is even found in different cells in the same body. In an unborn human baby, for instance, the white blood cells are so amazingly labile that each generation is different from its parent cells! And when you realize that generations of cells are only 8 to 10 hours apart, you can imagine the stock of variations that build up in a few months. The variations are minute—akin perhaps to several thousand copies of this book in each of which just one word had been changed. But they are the secret of the white-cell army's success in dealing with invaders. No matter what sort of invader comes in, somewhere among the white cells will be at least one that, by this chance variation, is tailor-made to battle with it. As on the large scale, so on the small—lability is one of the keys to success.

Curiously enough, it does not pay to be too successful too suddenly. To illustrate, let us take the example of an oil company who ran a gas sales promotion campaign one summer. It gained them an extra 5 per cent slice of the market. That may not sound much, yet it upset the entire petroleum-oil business, and the repercussions took years to smooth out. What a lesson in ecology they learned! There they had a delicate and complex system, developed over the years and kept going only because they had evolved a kind of balance between cutthroat competition and the commercially prudent granting of territories and licenses. The balance was much too fine to adjust to a sudden 5 per cent shift; the whole structure was threatened.

The living world is full of examples of a similar kind. In any given environment or location there are vast numbers and varieties of living things all ostensibly in keen competition for the same food and the same territory. But look a little closer and you will see that they all behave as though there were unwritten agreements and understandings limiting such competition, and the resulting balance is the basis of the whole system's stability.

To round off this first volume and draw its many threads together, let us study how such a system may arise. Let us start a mere twinkling of an eyelid back in geological time—10,000 years or so—when the last of the great ice ages was past and the ice sheets were receding from northern America and Europe.

It is still cold and there is a lot of bare rock, ground down and rubbed clean under the pressure of hundreds or thousands of feet of ice overburden. Soon the rock gets pitted and cracked by rain, frost, and sunshine. Water that falls in the little hollows dissolves some of the minerals and makes a weak, life-sustaining brew. Lichen spores blow in on the wind from slightly friendlier climates. They quicken in the water and take hold on the rock. Some of them produce enough acid to dissolve more rock releasing more nutrients. The lichens use solar energy to create new living material.

In the folds of lichen, and in the hollows and pools, fine sediments of dust and windborne soil collect. The pioneer lichens die, to be replaced by others. Dead lichens begin to form humus in the sparse soil, and in time there is enough to support more than simple bacteria and fungi. Springtails, mites, and other tiny creatures move in, then their predators—spiders and other arachnids. As they die they further enrich the soil.

Soon it is rich enough to support mosses, which help to bind the soil in a way impossible to lichens. Over the generations the weathering of rock, the drift of windborne particles, and the death of generations of plants and animals make the soil still thicker and richer. It holds water better during longer dry spells, so more sensitive plants—grasses, and herbs such as ragweed and horseweed—move in. Birds and winged insects are swift to follow, bringing with them, perhaps in the mud on their feet, the spores of other soil organisms and microorganisms. Soon the soil is alive with earthworms, threadworms, eelworms, and others. In time, shrews, moles, and other mammals will thrive on these soil organisms, just as mice, rabbits, deer, grouse, woodcock, prairie chicken, dotterel, and other ground birds will move in to feed on the grasses and other plants or to eat its lesser animal life. *Their* predators, too, will follow: coyotes, foxes, wolves, and falcons among them.

The grass becomes a tall, thickly matted natural windbreak. A keen wind may ruffle the fur of the large animals that stand above the grass, but down there in those few inches above ground level is an utterly different climate— warm and humid, ideal for the tender shoots of seedling shrubs such as heath and hawthorns.

The herbivores, or plant-eaters eat most of the seedlings but enough survive to change the character of the area yet again, from grassland to heath or grassland scrub. Perching birds,

The shrinking Matanuska glacier, Alaska, reveals in part some of the stages in the gradual colonization of bare rock as described in the text. The lowest ground, kept cool and damp even in summer by meltwater, has a tundra-type vegetation composed mainly of lichens and mosses. Higher up it gives way to coniferous forest. In the foreground, farthest from the influence of the retreating glacier, we see the pioneer saplings of a new deciduous forest. Each of these areas supports its own characteristic community of animals.

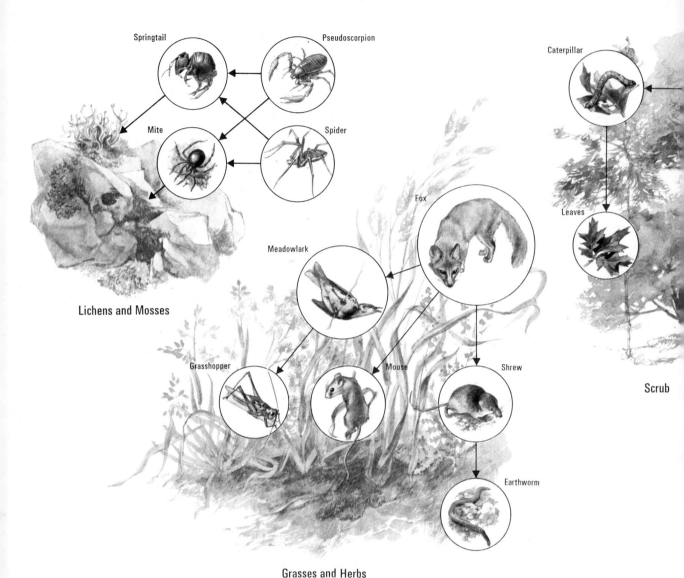

Springtail

Pseudoscorpion

Caterpillar

Mite

Spider

Lichens and Mosses

Fox

Leaves

Meadowlark

Scrub

Grasshopper

Mouse

Shrew

Earthworm

Grasses and Herbs

These paintings show four typical stages in the natural progression from bare rock to broadleaved forest. The species shown are typical of North America but a similar progression for, say, Europe would be roughly comparable and the kind of predator-prey relationships (shown by arrows) would be identical. The relationships actually shown here represent only a fraction of the tens of thousands of similar "chains" that could have been drawn. Yet, simple as they are, they demonstrate two basic facts: all food chains end in plant matter, and the relationships grow more complex as the sequence progresses. Such richness is the basis of ecological stability.

which nest in shrubs, move in, followed by *their* predators, which range from snakes to birds of prey such as hawks. Finally, trees grow, first in scattered stands, then in woods that ultimately merge to form a forest. The development of trees heralds the arrival of yet other species—woodpeckers, sowbugs, bark beetles, tree squirrels, and so on.

Each of the stages we have just looked at consists of a community of interdependent plants and animals. The early ones, by enriching and deep-

ening the soil, paved the way for their own ousting. The whole succession assumes that the general climate has changed to permit each of the stages to proceed through to its successor. But if that assumption is not true, if the land that started as bare rock uncovered by glacial retreat is too cold, too windy, too dry, too high, or has too great an extreme between high summer and midwinter, the sequence will remain stationary at one of its stages, or will be diverted along another pathway to a different climax—

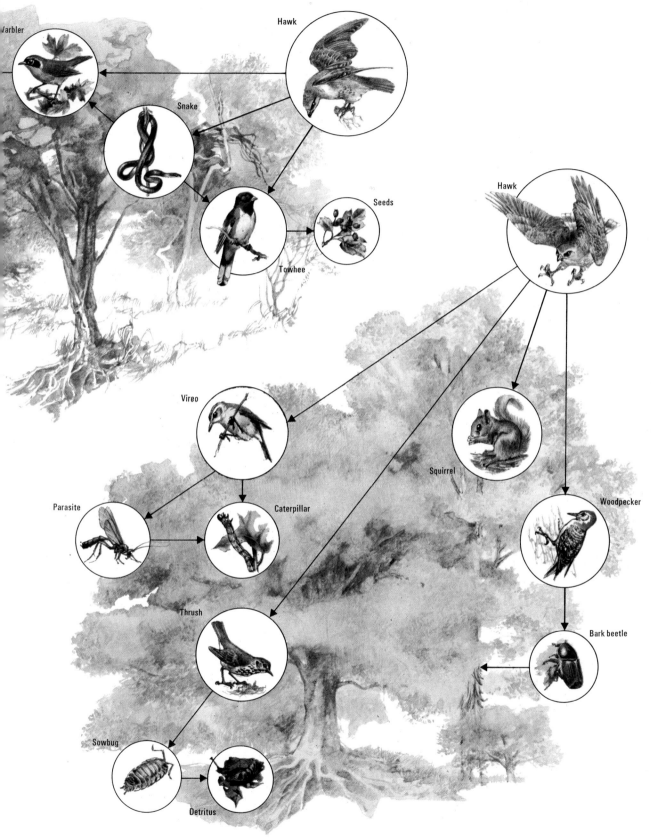

Warbler

Hawk

Snake

Seeds

Towhee

Hawk

Vireo

Squirrel

Woodpecker

Parasite

Caterpillar

Thrush

Bark beetle

Sowbug

Detritus

Hardwood Forest

bog, perhaps, or alpine meadow, or chalk hill, or prairie, or coniferous forest.

Generally speaking, each stage represents an increase in the number of types of plants and animals and the richness of their interrelations. The broadleaved forest with its plentiful clearings and open high ground offers an amazingly rich and varied community, exceeded only by tropical rain forest, which has the advantage of year-around warmth, rain, and light.

To put it another way: each part of the earth's surface offers different conditions of warmth, rainfall, light, wind, and altitude. Yet whatever extreme we may encounter, the communities we find there will all be tending toward some stable climax situation, which will require some external change before it is modified. The external change may be the arrival of a new species or a general drift in the climate. But it will, inevitably, tend toward another climax. And the thing that distinguishes all climaxes from all the other stages in a succession is this: the climax is the most interlocking, and above all most stable system, that the region is capable of supporting.

The study of such systems and the successions that lead to them is the basis of the science of ecology. Although the term (then spelled *oekologie*) was coined over 100 years ago, in 1869, by the German zoologist Ernst Haeckel, it is only in recent years that the science has claimed widespread public attention. This new-found interest stems from a widening realization that man is now the biggest single cause of changes in the world's many ecosystems. Earlier attitudes, right up until the 1960s, were colored by our short-term successes in the physical sciences and engineering. A troublesome river? Throw a dam across it. A hill or mountain in the way? Punch a tunnel through it. Need houses? Pave over the landscape—thousands of square miles, if need be. A surfeit of garbage? Dump it in the bottomless ocean. Muscles not enough? Supplement their energy, mine out the coal, tap oil and natural gas. Hungry? Take the most productive plants and animals and spread them over the face of the earth at the expense of less productive varieties.

"Solutions" of this kind have led to big short-term payoffs. But in the long term they nearly always lead to a simplification of the ecosystem, to a reduction in its richness, to an undermining of its stability. The hoped-for long-term advantages are vanishing before our eyes, leaving us to face a future that now indeed looks bleak. It is a future in which natural resources are depleted; in which the genetic variety of some wild populations has vanished, effaced by the uniformity of purpose-bred strains, in which soils thinned by ignorant misuse yield less and less each year; in which an ever-increasing, ever-hungrier human population cries ever more insistently for the millenium now—while urgently needed long-term action gets indefinitely postponed yet again in favor of quick short-term payoffs.

Our only hope of breaking this vicious circle is to *understand*: to understand what we are doing and why it can never work; to understand the world of which we are a small although dangerous component; to understand that life cannot be plundered for ever as we have plundered it these centuries past; to understand that, used with tenderness and care, it can be coaxed into yielding for as long as the sun continues to shine; to *understand*. That was our purpose in making this volume; we hope it is yours in reading it.

A skein of cormorants, etched in black against the dying day symbolizes the freedom and beauty of the natural order. That order is increasingly threatened by the spread of human civilization. Shall we learn too late that of all the Earth's resources this natural order is and always has been by far the most precious?

Index

References in *italics* are to illustrations or captions to illustrations.

Picture Credits

Cover: Magnum/Marilyn Silverstone
Title page: Animals Animals © 1973
Contents: © 1972 Time/Life Inc./ Rentmeester

9 R.I.M. Campbell/Bruce Coleman Ltd.
12 Peter W. Bading, Alaska
13 Adam Wolfitt/Griggs
16(T) Dr. Edward S. Ross
16(B) Photo Researchers Inc.
17(L) Cornell Capa/Magnum
17(R) Keystone
18 James Simon/Bruce Coleman Ltd.
19 Norman Myers/B. Coleman Inc.
20(L) Josef Muench, Santa Barbara
21 George Rodger/Magnum
22(L) H. Reinhard/ZEFA
22(R) J. L. Patel/Pitch
23(L) Dennis Brokaw
23(R) H. Reinhard/ZEFA
24 P. Lefebvre/Pitch
25(T) Eric Hosking
25(B) Paul Freytag/ZEFA
26(TL), Dr. Georg Gerster/The John
27(B) Hillelson Agency
27(TR) The Bettmann Archive
28(L) Norman Myers/B. Coleman Ltd.
28(TR,C) Norman Tomalin/B. Coleman Ltd.
28(BR) R.K. Murton/Bruce Coleman Ltd.
29 Jane Burton/Bruce Coleman Ltd.
30(B) Clem Haagner/B. Coleman Inc.
31 Mike Nathan
32 A. Ross/Bruce Coleman Inc.
33(T) Chandrakant K. Shah/Frank W. Lane
34(TL) Harald Schultz/B. Coleman Ltd.
34(TR) Jane Burton/Bruce Coleman Inc.
34(BL) J. Launois/Black Star, New York
35 Jen and Des Bartlett/Bruce Coleman Inc.
36 Peter Bading/ZEFA
37 Wangi/Jacana
38 Leonard Lee Rue/B. Coleman Ltd.
39(L) S.C. Bisserot/Bruce Coleman Inc.
39(R) Russ Kinne/Bruce Coleman Ltd.
41(B) G. Vienne/Pitch
42(L) Emil Schulthess/Black Star, N.Y.
43(T) F. Erize/Bruce Coleman Ltd.
43(B) P. A. Milwaukee/Jacana
44 Jan Lindblad/B. Coleman Ltd.
45 P. A. Milwaukee/Jacana
46-7(B) Jane Burton/Bruce Coleman Ltd.
47(T) F. Erize/Bruce Coleman Ltd.
48(T) G. Vienne, P. Bell/Pitch
48(B) Bruce Coleman Ltd.
49(T) Jane Burton/Bruce Coleman Ltd.
49(B) A. Aldebert/Jacana
50 Eugen Schuhmacher, München
52(T) Bruce Coleman Ltd.
52(B) John R. Brownlie/B. Coleman Inc.
53(T) Tom Myers/Photo Researchers Inc.
53(C) Tom McHugh/Photo Researchers Inc.

53(B) John R. Brownlie/B. Coleman Inc.
54 A. Rainon/Pitch
55(R) Marilyn Silverstone/Magnum
56(B) Phillippa Scott/Photo Researchers Inc.
57(T) Eric Hosking
57(BR) Hans Silvester/B. Coleman Ltd.
58 David Hughes/B. Coleman Ltd.
59(T) Bruce Coleman Ltd.
59(B) Ted Gruen/Bruce Coleman Inc.
60(L) Robert Schroeder/ Bruce Coleman Ltd.
60(R),61 David Hughes/B. Coleman Ltd.
62 A. Rainon/Pitch
63(T) David Hughes/B. Coleman Inc.
63(B) Emil Schulthess/Black Star, N.Y.
64(T) W. Schraml/Jacana
64(B) Jane Burton/Bruce Coleman Ltd.
65 Robert Dunne/Photo Researchers Inc.
66(T) S. C. Bisserot/Bruce Coleman Ltd.
66(B) Jane Burton/Bruce Coleman Ltd.
67(TL) Jane Burton/Bruce Coleman Ltd.
67(R) S. J. Krasemann/Photo Researchers Inc.
68(L) Sundance/Jacana
69 Peter Gimbel
70 Kojo Tanaka/Animals Animals © 1973
71 Jane Burton/Bruce Coleman Ltd.
72(BL) Jane Burton/Bruce Coleman Inc.
73(L) Peter David
73(R), Russ Kinne/Photo Researchers Inc.
74(B) Ministry of Agriculture, Fisheries and Food
75(T) Sergio Larrain/Magnum
75(B) John Markham/B. Coleman Ltd.
77(T, R) Jane Burton/Bruce Coleman Ltd.
77(BL) Simon Trevor/B. Coleman Ltd.
78(L) Ian Beames/Ardea
78(BR) F. Park/ZEFA
79 K. Ross/Jacana
80(B) Dr. Georg Gerster/The John Hillelson Agency
81(T) Roberto Bunge
81(BR) Dr. Edward S. Ross
83 Russ Kinne/Bruce Coleman Ltd.
84 Russ Kinne/Photo Researchers Inc.
85(T) Picturepoint, London
85(B) Al Giddings/Bruce Coleman Inc.
86(T) Eric Grave/Photo Researchers Inc.
86(B) Dr. G. T. Boalch
87(T, BR) Oxford Scientific Films/ Bruce Coleman Ltd.
88(TL) Janet Finch/Frank W. Lane
88(TC) Eric Hosking
88(BL) Jane Burton/Bruce Coleman Ltd.
88(BR) Camera Press
89 © 1972 Time/Life Inc./ Rentmeester
90 Ernst Haas/Magnum
92(C) Barry Paine

92(B) Charlie Ott/Bruce Coleman Ltd.
93 Robert Dunne/Photo Researchers Inc.
94(L) Norman Myers/B. Coleman Ltd.
94(BR) Neville Fox-Davies/Bruce Coleman Inc.
95 M. Sire
96 Josef Muench, Santa Barbara
98 Dr. John B. Free
99(TR) Jane Burton/Bruce Coleman Ltd.
99(B) W. Treat Davidson/Frank W. Lane
101 Dr. K. Biedermann/ZEFA
103 Jane Burton/Bruce Coleman Ltd.
106 A.A.A. Photo/Picou
107(R) Auerbach, F.R.P.S., London
109(T) Hayon/Pitch
110 Picturepoint, London
112-3(T) Oxford Scientific Films/Bruce Coleman Ltd.
112-3(B) Jane Burton/Bruce Coleman Ltd.
114 Derek Bayes/Aspect
115 Watson-Jones, *Fractures and Joint Injuries*, 4th ed., Livingstone, Edinburgh, 1962
116 Dr. James D. Hirsch, The Rockefeller University
118(L) W. Renaud/Jacana
118(TR) Jane Burton/Bruce Coleman Inc.
118(BR) Dr. F. Sauer/ZEFA
119(L) David Houston/B. Coleman Ltd.
119(R) Louis Quitt/Photo Researchers Inc.
120(L) Simon Trevor/B. Coleman Ltd.
121(TL) George Holton/Photo Researchers Inc.
121(TR) Jane Burton/Bruce Coleman Ltd.
121(BL) Mike Nathan
121(BR) Graham Pizzey/B. Coleman Ltd.
122(T) Ernest Wilkinson /Animals Animals © 1973
122(B) Jack Dermid/Bruce Coleman Ltd.
123 Professor Irven DeVore
124(T) Jane Burton/Bruce Coleman Ltd.
124(B) S. C. Bisserot/Bruce Coleman Ltd.
125 G. D. Plage/Bruce Coleman Ltd.
126(L) Keystone
126(R) Jerry Hout/Photo Researchers Inc
127(T) A. J. Deane/Bruce Coleman Ltd.
127(BR) Gerard Munschy/Jacana
128 George Rodger/Magnum
132(CB) after W. Höhne/ZEFA
133(TR) after Bruce Coleman Ltd.
135 Binois/Pitch
139 Kojo Tanaka/Animals Animals © 1973

Artist Credits

David Astin 109; David Nockels 15, 100, 130–1, 132–3; Roger Pring (design), 105, 108 (finished artwork by Studio Briggs Ltd, London); Peter Warner 40, 41, 111, 136–7; Brian Watson/Linden Artists 10–11.

MAN AND NATURE
Part 2
Natural Man

by Robert Allen

Series Coordinator Geoffrey Rogers
Series Art Director Frank Fry
Art Editor Roger Hyde
Design Consultant Guenther Radtke
Editorial Consultant Malcolm Ross-Macdonald
Assistant Editors Allyson Fawcett
Bridget Gibbs
Copy Editor Damian Grint
Research Enid Moore
Ann Fisher

Contents: Part 2

Editorial Advisers

MICHAEL BOORER, B.SC. Author, Lecturer, and Broadcaster.

MATTHEW BRENNAN, ED.D. Director, Brentree Environmental Center, Professor of Conservation Education, Pennsylvania State University.

PHYLLIS BUSCH, ED.D. Author, Science Teacher, and Consultant in Environmental Education.

KLAUS-FRIEDRICH KOCH. Assistant Professor of Social Anthropology, Harvard University.

VERNON REYNOLDS, B.A., M.A., PH.D. Lecturer in Physical Anthropology, Oxford University.

Introduction "It's not natural" is a common criticism of actions we dislike or do not understand. But how do we judge? In the sense that human beings are as much animals as are tigers or butterflies, all our actions are natural. At one time we regarded ourselves as morally superior to the other animals. But by studying animal behavior we have learned to marvel at the ability of other species to regulate their numbers, to ritualize and minimize violence, and so on, and now we consider man—potentially so violent, licentious, and greedy—as the most unnatural of animals.

Of course neither extreme is correct. Anthropologists have long recognized how misleading it is to use one cultural group—such as the people of the Western industrial countries—as the representatives of the whole of humanity. To look at natural man we must choose examples from those cultural types that have survived longest: the hunter-gatherers—peoples who live by hunting wild animals (including fish) and gathering wild plants. However, because societies that live substantially, though not completely, by food collecting often have similar characteristics to those that depend entirely on it, the term "natural man" refers not simply to pure hunter-gatherers but also to hunter-gardeners (people with a mixed food-collecting, food-cultivating economy).

From surviving and recently extinct hunting societies we can learn a great deal. They can help us answer some of the most vexing questions troubling us today. Are we innately violent and greedy? What do we mean by good health and a sound diet? What is the best way to bring up our children? Are we capable of living in harmony with our environment?

Unfortunately, fewer and fewer hunting societies remain. Their numbers have been rapidly reduced since the development of agriculture, by the more numerous and powerful farming peoples. But there is still a little time to help the remaining representatives of natural man choose a meaningful and dignified future for themselves. If we do, we will benefit from the great many things of lasting value they have to teach us. Perhaps in the process we may find a better future for ourselves.

From Apes to Man

Man has become man through the complex process of evolution. Given different environmental pressures at different points in his evolutionary development, he might have become a very different creature. Man belongs to a group of mammals called primates and his nearest relatives are the apes. He and the apes share the same ancestors, an idea some humans have found humiliating. One woman is said to have reacted to Darwin's theory of evolution with the exclamation: "Descended from the apes! My dear, we will hope that it is not true. But if it is, let us pray that it may not become generally known."

Man differs physically from his fellow primates in a number of important respects. He is unable to grasp with his feet. Formerly his big toes may have had the same capacity as his thumbs, as do those of the majority of the other primates. Most of the primates are tropical forest dwellers. They use their hands and feet for grasping branches rather than for walking on the ground. Man's ability to stand upright has enabled him to use his feet for walking and his hands for doing all kinds of intricate work involving great dexterity.

In some other respects, however, man is more or less the same as other primates, retaining features that reflect his forest background. His teeth, as with those of all primates, are multipurpose. They are not specialized as are those of cows for chewing grass, squirrels for gnawing nuts, and tigers for tearing meat. Rather, they are capable of dealing with a variety of foods, vegetable and animal. The position of our eyes is roughly the same as that of other primates. Most of the animals have eyes on either side of their heads, so possessing a wide range of vision. We have them in front, which reduces their horizontal range, but enables us to see an object with both eyes at once. This is a vital attribute for judging distances accurately, of the greatest importance to animals that live in trees.

Our closest relatives are the members of the two ape families—that containing the gibbons, and that containing the chimpanzee, the gorilla, and the orang-utan. We share with them the lack of a tail, the disposition of our internal organs, and much of the structure of the brain.

The oldest remains of an apelike creature dis-

Orangutans (left) share the same ancestors as man. They have become successfully adapted to their forest environment in Southeast Asia. Man, however, has become adapted to a great many environments besides the forests of the tropics. The Australian Aborigine above, for example, was able to survive successively in grassland, scrub, and desert.

Richard Leakey with the skull found by his colleagues near Lake Rudolf in northern Kenya. His preliminary datings suggest it is some 2.9 million years old. The skull is exciting evidence that the genus Homo may be much older than has been believed.

covered so far are those of *Parapithecus*, found in the lower Oligocene strata of Egypt and some 30 million years old. Part of it resembles the modern tarsier, a primate but not an ape or a monkey. This lends some support to a much disputed theory that men, apes, and monkeys are descended from tarsierlike ancestors. Many more apelike remains have been found in the Miocene strata (12–26 million years old) of Africa and Asia. Some resemble the modern gibbons, chimpanzees, gorillas, and orang-utans. One, *Proconsul*, looks as if it might have been an ancestor of the chimpanzee, although it has a number of manlike features. The fossil apes, *Dryopithecus*, also have manlike attributes, notably their arms and legs, which look as if they were less specialized for tree-dwelling than those of the modern apes.

The most controversial of the manlike apes is *Australopithecus*. A number of its remains have been found in Africa, but opinion is divided as to whether it is an ancestor of man. The recent discovery by Richard Leakey of a skull as old as *Australopithecus* is certainly an oddity. Some skulls have been found in caves with the remains of the crushed bones of other animals as well as cracked shells. This has led to *Australopithecus* being described as "an animal-hunting, flesh-eating, shell-cracking, and bone-breaking ape."

But no modern ape has a diet like this.

Part of our difficulty in tracing the evolutionary story of the apes and man is due to the environment in which they lived. We know that mankind was born in the forests of the tropics and developed in the grasslands. But tropical forests are probably the least favorable places for the preservation of fossil remains. Thus, it is extremely difficult to discover how man left the forests, in what form, and exactly how he has changed since then. Archaeologists and prehistorians are not yet in a position to answer precisely the question: "Where did modern man come from?"

One thing we can be sure of. Modern man did not come from one single spot in the world. This is not how evolution works. We are the result of a considerable intermingling of races of different evolutionary stages of man over a very wide area. For example, toward the end of the Pleistocene ice age, Europe, western Asia, and North Africa were inhabited by the Neanderthal race, *Homo sapiens neanderthalensis*. These people were no more than five feet tall, but were heavily built, with thick necks, large heads, and in some cases bigger brains than ours. Their bones were heavy, their jaws massive with big teeth, and they stooped. About 75,000 years ago, the Neander-

The diagram (right) shows the changes in proportion between the brain (colored area) and face as man evolved. Compared with chimpanzees, modern man has a much larger brain, about twice the size of that of the great apes. This increase in brain size is associated with the development of speech, improved memory and ability to store information, and especially, the ability to reason.

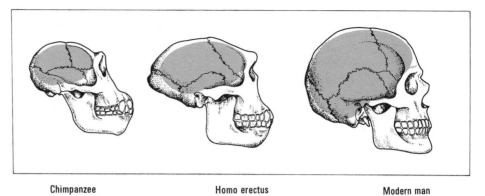

Chimpanzee   Homo erectus   Modern man

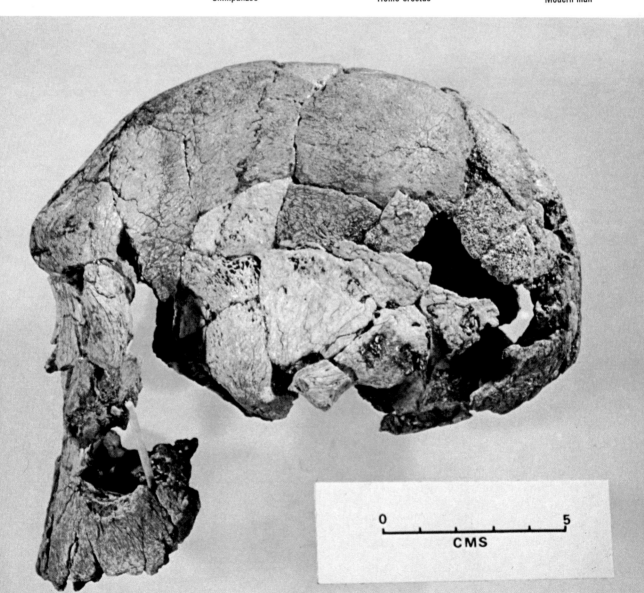

Above: the skull found by the Leakey team. In shape it is more like that of modern man than that of Australopithecus, *but the cranial capacity is rather small.*

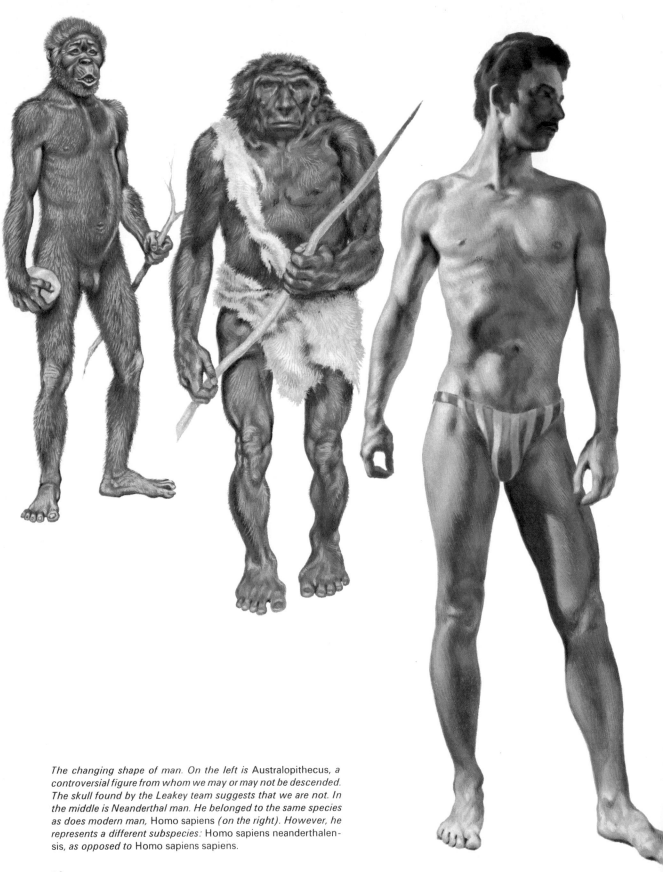

The changing shape of man. On the left is Australopithecus, *a controversial figure from whom we may or may not be descended. The skull found by the Leakey team suggests that we are not. In the middle is Neanderthal man. He belonged to the same species as does modern man,* Homo sapiens *(on the right). However, he represents a different subspecies:* Homo sapiens neanderthalensis, *as opposed to* Homo sapiens sapiens.

thals were replaced by a race that is very definitely modern man, representatives of *Homo sapiens sapiens*. These people also had large brains, were up to six feet tall, and are called Cro-Magnons.

It is not known precisely where the Cro-Magnons came from, although a clue has been found in the series of human bones found in the caves of Mount Carmel, Israel. These range from Neanderthal-type bones to Cro-Magnon-type ones. It is therefore possible that the ancestors of the Cro-Magnons moved north from Africa and that Israel was where the two races met. Probably the Cro-Magnons interbred with the Neanderthals, but the former eventually replaced the latter by virtue of their superior disease resistance and culture inventiveness. Some anthropologists have suggested that there are modern European populations which still carry a few Neanderthal genes.

Why did man leave the trees and lose his particularly apelike characteristics? We can only speculate. Possibly his ancestors lived at the margins of the forest. Maybe this was because, by an accident of genetics, they were not as skilled as the other primates at moving about the trees. More probably, they were simply better adapted to the forest edges. By modifying their diet and behavior they could utilize clearings and the productive forest edges. Individuals would obviously have encountered each other and bred together. Naturally, these individuals would have had more chance of survival and would have been genetically favored. Gradually, distinct populations would have emerged, able to utilize a greater variety of environments, such as grasslands, than conventional apes. These populations would have developed those characteristics likely to improve their utilization of such environments: the ability to walk, to handle a greater diversity of objects, to eat a greater range of foodstuffs. Above all, as apes evolved into men, they ceased to specialize.

Man is not the fastest running animal, nor the strongest swimmer. He is not the strongest animal, nor the most agile climber. He is not unique as a tool-user. He is not the only creature that can dwell in grasslands, forests, mountains, or even deserts. But no other animal is capable of doing all of these things, as man is.

Among those features unique to man are his ability to tolerate a greater range of environments than other species and also his ability to conceptualize, for which he had to develop his brain. Each enlargement of his brain improved his capacity to conceptualize and each improvement in his capacity to conceptualize improved his survival—which in turn favored those human beings with the more developed brains.

Thus by degrees there emerged a new species. Exactly when it did so is very difficult to say. It depends entirely on one's definition of man. Is the upright posture most significant? Or his tool-making abilities? Or his cranial capacity? At all events, the latest date is 600,000 years ago; while the earliest date may be pushed back by Leakey's skull discovery to roughly 3 million years ago.

Evolution ends only with extinction. We may take it that, like all species, we are still subject to the evolutionary process. But for some time now, the pace of man-induced change has been so fast—and is getting faster—that we have not responded with conventional biological adaptations. Rather, we are adjusting culturally, evolving new institutions and behavior patterns. We are not unique in this. There is the famous example of the English blue tits, which have learned to peck through the tops of bottles of milk, so that they can get at the cream. They did not have to develop new beak structures to do this. They simply developed a new behavior pattern, a new habit.

This cultural adaptation has one obvious advantage over physiological adaptation: it is much faster. However, it has one great disadvantage, too. It permits a species the illusion of full adaptation. For example, as a species we have evolved under sugar-scarce conditions. The sugar in our diet used to come only from what was naturally present in ordinary plants and from honey. It is to be expected, therefore, that as soon as we started eating sugar in large quantities, our bodies would show signs of maladaptation. So, of course, we have bad teeth. As a result, we have introduced the cultural adaptation of the dentist, who in effect enables us to go on having bad teeth.

A study of human evolution teaches us about the remarkable flexibility and adaptability of man. But it also teaches us that evolution proceeds fairly slowly, and that we might be wise not to attempt to impose too many sharp changes on ourselves too quickly. The nature of our more inflexible biological and psychological requirements can be appreciated best from a study of our past and in particular from that most fascinating part of it, the era of natural man.

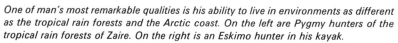

One of man's most remarkable qualities is his ability to live in environments as different as the tropical rain forests and the Arctic coast. On the left are Pygmy hunters of the tropical rain forests of Zaire. On the right is an Eskimo hunter in his kayak.

!Kung Bushmen of the Kalahari

The Bushmen of southern Africa are the most thoroughly studied surviving examples of natural man. Before they came under pressure from alien white and black peoples they inhabited the whole of the region, but now those that remain as hunter-gatherers are largely confined to the least hospitable areas of Botswana, with scattered outliers in Zambia, Rhodesia, Angola, the Namib Desert, and the Transvaal of South Africa. Most of the 55,000 Bushmen alive today have become laborers and stockmen on farms and ranches, or vagrants on the fringes of them; but there are still some 1600 Bushmen in Botswana, living by hunting game and gathering wild plants, more or less as their ancestors have done for many thousands of years.

The land is poor, with very little rain. There are no permanent rivers, although after exceptionally heavy rain low-lying areas become flooded. These flooded areas eventually shrink to pools that can hold water for up to six months after the end of the rainy season.

Although it is so poorly watered this part of the Kalahari Desert is not really desert at all. It is relatively thick thorn scrub, with many trees such as acacias, interspersed with other broad-leaved trees and shrubs. Nonetheless, the environment is harsh enough to make it extremely difficult, if not impossible, for the uninitiated to survive in it—and it is certainly less fertile than the country that supported the majority of Bushmen in their heyday.

Yet they live well. The Dobe !Kung (the exclamation mark denotes a click sound made by the tongue on the roof of the mouth), who are the best known of the Bushmen, eat more protein than the British. Indeed, each person's daily protein intake, 93.1 grams, is exceeded by only 10 countries today. A third of their protein comes from meat, principally warthog, kudu, duiker, and steenbok, followed by gemsbok, wildebeest, springhaas, and guinea fowl. The rest comes from a remarkable nut, the mongongo or mangetti nut, which also has a very high content of other important nutrients and calories. It gives a large crop, can withstand prolonged periods of drought, and can lie on the ground for as long as a year without rotting.

The lush environment of southern Cape Province, South Africa. Before the arrival from the north of Bantu tribes, the native Bushmen enjoyed these surroundings unchallenged.

A herd of wildebeest in the Kalahari Park. These animals are an important source of meat for the Bushmen. On the right a Bushman hunter displays his weapons and a typical array of plant foods. Both these pictures show how arid are the desert and scrubland in which the Bushmen live, in contrast to the richer areas formerly available to them, yet they still eat well.

A Bushman hut. It is made by the women from grass and sticks, and is easily assembled. It provides adequate shelter from sun, rain, or wind, although when the nights grow cold, as they often do, people sleep outside around the fire.

The food supply is varied and remarkably easy to obtain. A time-and-motion study has been made of the hours spent by adult Bushmen hunting and gathering. It was found that they never spent more than 32 hours a week searching for food, and that the average was half that—or just over two hours a day for a seven-day week!

Bushmen communities consist of camps, which vary in size throughout the year. Each camp is based on a waterhole, is largest during the rains, and breaks up into units as small as a single family during periods of drought. At such times, the only sources of moisture might be the fluids from a newly killed animal and melon juice.

Camps constantly fluctuate in size irrespective of the availability of water. This is because the communities have no rigid social structure, but are simply groupings of relations and friends, who get on well together, and find it convenient and pleasant to work and live with each other.

Right: each Bushman camp is based on a water hole. Here a woman on a foraging expedition drinks at a desert pool.

Men do the hunting. Women gather the plants. The men will hunt either alone or in pairs, and will normally cover between 8 and 15 miles in search of an animal. Sometimes a hunter is unlucky and finds nothing, in which case he will probably return with nuts, roots, and perhaps an animal such as the leopard tortoise, which is easily caught, so that he won't arrive in camp empty-handed. It is most unusual for a hunter to bother to stay out all night. He knows that some-

Above left: !Kung Bushman hunters returning to camp with a duiker, a small antelope. Above right: Bushman arrow poison is made from grubs (top) by crushing them in a bowl (lower) made from the kneecap of a giraffe.

thing is bound to turn up another day.

When the hunter comes across the track of an animal, he trails it until he is almost upon it. This requires stealth and a good knowledge of animal behavior. He must get close because his bow is small and weak, and will shoot accurately only over short distances, What kills the animal is the poison applied to the arrow-tips. The poison, taken from grubs, is potent but non-persistent. This means that the animal dies over-night, but by the time the meat is butchered it is perfectly safe to eat.

Once he has shot his prey, the !Kung hunter does not bother to follow it. He knows that if he does so, the animal will only run farther away. If he has shot it early in the morning, he will seek out some of the other men, and together they will butcher it into pieces small enough to carry back

to the camp. If the animal is killed in the after-noon, it will not be butchered until the following morning. There is then the possiblity that the body will be plundered by a lion or hyena, but this is a risk that the Bushmen accept.

In groups of three to five the women gather plants. Besides mongongo nuts, they collect baobab fruit, sour plums, marula nuts, melons, and various roots. These are carried home in the women's karosses, garments that serve as dress and carrying bag. The women are generally back by mid-afternoon and never stay out overnight.

A man hunts and a woman gathers whenever he or she want to. Nobody tells them to do any-thing. On any given day, no more than a half, and on average a third, of the able-bodied adults will be out getting food. The rest will be relaxing, making and repairing tools, fashioning ostrich

Three Bushmen catching a springhaas (or Cape jumping hare, a large rodent). Above, one of them has dug a hole, then another prods the animal out if its burrow with a long pole. Below, the digger grabs the animal as it rushes from the scooped-out hole.

Bushman women with the melons they have collected. These are a useful source of water as well as food.

A !Kung Bushman scraping a skin in front of his hut. Animal hides are never wasted. They are used to make karosses, combined cloaks and carrying bags for use by the women, and smaller skins are made into slings for carrying infants.

eggshell jewelry, gossiping, entertaining visitors, or themselves visiting relatives and friends. The men spend much of their time discussing hunting, the whereabouts of game, and so on. They work slightly longer hours than the women, but less regularly. The women will probably work all morning and for much of the afternoon for two to three days a week: plants are reliable and stay put, so their collection can be made a fairly routine activity. By contrast, because the movements of game are so irregular, a man might work intensively for three to four days and then do nothing for weeks. He may have bad luck, be off form, or feel it inappropriate for him to hunt.

With the !Kung people, this seemingly casual and unconcerned activity yields an abundance of vegetable foods, and for each man, woman, and child, on average a half pound of good meat every day. There are three reasons why this is so. First, although the Kalahari scrub might seem inhospitable to us, familiar as we are with lush meadows and well-stocked supermarkets, it is in fact quite rich in food resources. Secondly, the Bushmen have considerable expertise on the whereabouts and properties of plants and on the behavior of animals, which they utilize with

great skill. And thirdly, the Bushmen share whatever they have.

The Bushman ethic of sharing is most important. It means that nobody, young or old, goes in want. Plants are shared only among the women's immediate family, including aged dependants. All able-bodied women gather, and their two to three days' work is enough for a week's supply. If, however, a woman has been unable to collect anything, she will be supplied by her companions.

Meat, on the other hand, is shared throughout the camp. Strictly speaking it belongs to the owner of the first arrow to lodge in the animal, and this may not necessarily be the hunter, and could be a woman. The meat is first divided between the arrow-owner and the members of the party who helped to hunt and butcher it. Each then distributes his share, a man giving first to his wife's parents, then to his own, then to his wife and children, followed by his brothers and sisters and those of his wife, and finally to any of his other relations who are there, to his friends, and those from whom he has received meat in the past. Each of the people to whom he has given meat will in turn give some of his share to others, adopting a similar order of priorities.

23

This regular pattern of exchange ensures that everybody in camp is given meat and that over a period of time everybody's share is equal.

Because they are confident of their environment's constant ability to yield food, the !Kung make no attempt to create a surplus. They store nothing, and would consider anybody who did so an antisocial hoarder.

Sharing is not confined to meat. Nothing that is not essential for survival, such as a bow or a kaross, is regarded as a personal possession. Jewelry or any other nonessential item might be "owned" by an individual, but someone else need only ask to borrow it, and he will not be refused. Such "possessions" often go through a long process of borrowing and sharing, a practice that reinforces individual relationships. Indeed, the whole custom of sharing is very important for social cohesion.

The main practical reason why the Bushmen are not acquisitive is that they are nomadic. Nobody wants to be burdened with possessions when he or she moves around a lot and has to carry them. Since the Bushmen have no pack animals, the total weight of each individual's possessions never exceeds 25 pounds, a load that is easily borne. A family's belongings, for example bow and arrows, musical instruments, pipes, cooking pots, water pots, jewelry, and children's toys, will go into a pair of sacks no larger than overnight bags.

This lack of acquisitiveness, besides being sensible, has been elevated into a social value. Generosity, nonviolence, and a propensity for laughter, are considered admirable virtues.

The sharing ethic also means that old people are looked after, long after they have ceased to be "productive," even in the unusual event that the old person is without relatives. The proportion of men and women over 60 is 10 per cent—smaller than in the industrial countries of Europe and North America, but significantly greater than in the nonindustrial countries of the tropics. Similarly, the level of infant mortality lies between that of the rich third of the world and the higher rate of the poor two-thirds.

Generally speaking, the life of the !Kung Bushmen is not only easy, but also relatively free from disease. Their happy physical circumstances are matched by a harmonious social life, of which the sharing ethic is but one example. This is not to say that life is entirely free of tensions. But the !Kung fear violence and try to avoid conflict.

Above: !Kung Bushmen sharing meat. Meat from all but the smallest animals is always shared out according to a set pattern. These are Nyae Nyae !Kung, and they are not so well-off as the Dobe !Kung, described in the text.

Left: a group of Bushman children and old and middle-aged women talking. The anthropologist Richard Lee reports that 10 per cent of the population of the groups he studied were over 60 years old, and some were considerably older.

!Kung parents often try to arrange marriages, but their attempts are rarely more successful than any modern parent's attempts at matchmaking. Trial marriages are common, and between the ages of puberty and the age of 30 an individual may go through a number of experimental marriages. During this period, too, divorces are common; the person who wants the divorce simply leaves the other. Friendly relations are generally quickly restored, and sometimes an estranged couple will live with their new partners in the same camp.

Once they are past the age of 30, however,

25

An old Bushman in a medicine (trance) dance. The dance is an important way of maintaining harmony in the community, and occurs spontaneously about once a week in a large camp.

tive people in the world." It is very difficult for an outsider to distinguish between a dialogue of exaggerated abuse and a real dispute. Most arguments rage and then collapse in verbal battles of Shakespearean richness. In the middle of the uproar a bystander might crack a joke or one of the antagonists might make a particularly absurd play on words: the whole camp dissolves in laughter, and the dispute is over.

Occasionally, however, the grievance is more serious, in which case other members of the camp have to intervene to keep the peace. If this happens, a few days will elapse and then one or both of the disputants will leave with their immediate family. The dispute will not be given as the reason for their departure, but some pretext will be chosen such as the intention of going off to a different area where the food-plants are said to be better or the game more abundant.

Camp fission—the practice of leaving one camp for another, so that each camp is in a constant state of flux—is a most effective way of avoiding violence. Yet sometimes, as in all communities, tensions are more general and widespread, and something less ordinary, more dramatic, is required to resolve them. This is the trance dance.

The trance dance is also called the medicine dance, for its explicit function is not simply to release tensions, but to cure sick individuals. More accurately, the acknowledged motive for such dances will be either entertainment—the expression of sheer *joie de vivre* as when the hunting has gone particularly well or when there are a lot of welcome visitors in camp—or healing. In any case, some curing will be done by the men in trance; and whatever the stated motive, the dance's most valuable function remains the relief of tension.

Trance dances occur on average once a week in large camps, once a month in small ones, although being spontaneous their frequency varies greatly. The women sit in a circle, shoulder to shoulder, facing the fire. They provide the music by singing and clapping. The songs and rhythms are traditional, but the women enjoy inventing variations on them. The men dance around them, moving counter-clockwise and clockwise by turns. The old people and the children sit around separate fires outside the dance circle.

The dance does not begin until after dark. Some of the women light a fire and begin to sing. They are joined by others, and the men are stimulated to dance. Only their legs move, the

Bushmen stabilize their marital life and their marriages become permanent. The constancy and resilience of the relationship thereafter is possibly due to the great deal of liberty both parties enjoyed beforehand.

Often the man will have undergone some sort of probationary period with his wife's parents, who wanted to assure themselves of his qualities, particularly his ability to bring back meat. The length of this period varies, of course, and is subject to the inevitable fluctuations of camp life.

!Kung Bushmen enjoy a good argument. They have been described as "among the most talka-

This old man is in a trance and is laying his hands on another man, thus "curing" him.

rest of their bodies remaining quite stiff. Their feet stamp out a vigorous, highly syncopated beat. After about two hours, the men start to go into a trance. No drugs are used: the trance is due entirely to the high degree of concentration, to a decrease of carbon dioxide in the blood caused by the dancer's rapid and deep breathing, and to auto-suggestion. Those who first go into trance are supported by their companions who are still awake. Once they are fully in trance, the men move among the singers and spectators, especially those who are sick, "curing" them by laying their hands on them. This is the high point of the dance. Naturally the men do not go into trance simultaneously, but after each one has done so, and has performed the act of curing, he will go into a very deep sleep. The dance usually lasts all night—its most intense periods being just after midnight and at dawn—so it is very exhausting.

It is not easy to bear the intense experience of

Above: a Mbuti Pygmy camp in a clearing in the rain forests of Zaire, with its intimate association of human dwelling and natural habitat. In many places all over the world people have exchanged similar such environments for other, less congenial habitats such as this Hong Kong shanty town (right).

the trance dance, and young men often go charging into the bush or into the fire at the center of the circle of singing women. Since they might knock themselves out or seriously burn themselves or someone else, the more experienced men have to restrain them. When he is experienced, a man can channel his emotional energy and go into controlled trance, often twice a night.

Obviously a 12-hour trance of this nature has a purging effect on the community, involving as it does everybody in camp. In the course of this extremely intense experience any residual tensions still left, despite the various ways employed by the Bushmen to reduce them, are released.

According to Thomas Hobbes, the 17th-century political philosopher, life in the state of nature was "solitary, poor, nasty, brutish, and short." He had no evidence for this assertion—indeed there is a good deal of evidence to the contrary.

We have seen that, despite their comparatively unfavorable environment, the Bushmen of the Kalahari enjoy a life of reasonable abundance, longevity, good health, harmony, and entertainment. Although Europeans and Americans might find it uncomfortable, they should bear in mind that the Bushman standard of living is exceeded by only a minority of those people alive today.

We know that, before they were pushed out by more powerful farmers and herdsmen, most of the Bushmen lived in much more generous environments than that of the Kalahari, and we may safely assume that their standard of living was consequently even higher.

The best accounts of those other surviving hunter-gathers whose homes are in the most favorable parts of the tropics (between latitudes 30° North and South) show (although not so precisely) that their lives until recently were also good. In fact, it is probable that all hunter-gatherers living in environments to which they were adapted enjoyed high-quality lives.

This is especially significant when we consider that all but a minority of mankind have been hunter-gatherers living in just such environments. The skull found at East Rudolf in Kenya by Richard Leakey is evidence that men have been around for almost 3 million years. For 99 per cent of this time they lived by hunting and gathering, much as the Bushmen do today. Of the estimated 80,000 million men who have ever lived, only six per cent have done so by agriculture, less than four per cent by industry, and the rest by hunting and gathering.

It is therefore probable that abject poverty, squalor, epidemic diseases, and senseless violence are, in fact, recent aberrations. We have come to regard them as our natural lot, unless we can be protected from them by our technological ingenuity and the legislatures and bureaucracies of our industrial civilization. Mankind was spared them for the greater part of his experience. However, that is not to claim that conflict, illness, and hardship were absent, simply no more prevalent than among the other higher animals.

What went wrong? If it is true that for thous-

The Lewis Glacier, Mount Kenya. Extreme climatic and environmental changes caused at the end of the Pleistocene glaciation may well have disrupted man's stable relationship with the rest of nature, provoking his still continuing population explosion.

Map showing the extent of the ice cap toward the end of the Pleistocene glaciation, and illustrating the global distribution of natural man, past and present. Remote as these tribes are, none of them is completely untouched. The Eskimos are increasingly influenced by industrial society, and the Sioux lost their lands long ago—although some of them are pioneering a revival of the old values in a modern context. With the opening up and development of the interior of Brazil the Brazilian Indians have come under pressure, and for some time the Pygmies of Zaire have lived near the invading Bantu, with an unusual mixture of freedom and semi-dependence. Although many Bushmen have been educated into new cultures and are attached to ranches, a substantial proportion still live in their traditional style—unlike the Australian Aborigines, whose culture has been eroded.

Eskimos   ● Sioux Indians   Brazilian Indians *Beicos de Pan*

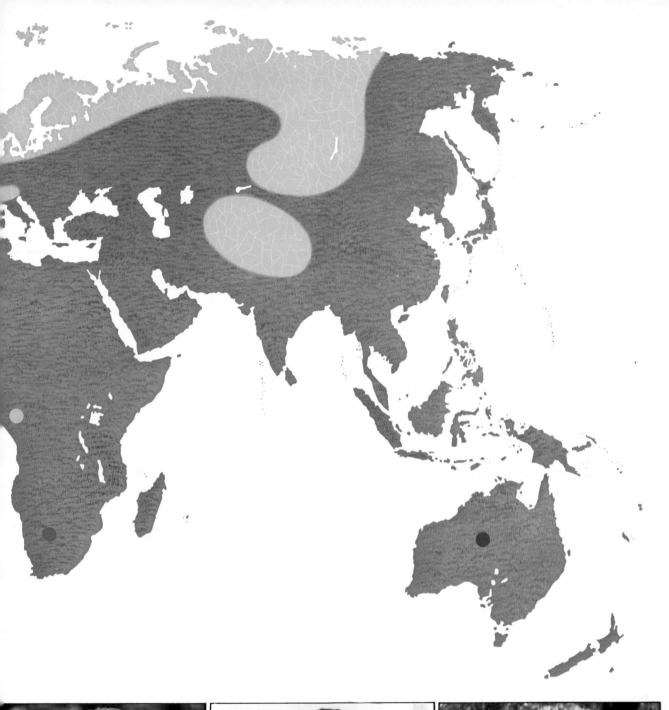

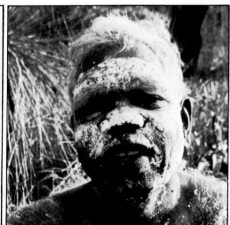

Pygmies

Bushmen

Aborigines

ands of years men enjoyed a high standard of living—so high that it was not bettered for a significant proportion of the Western population until after the Industrial Revolution—why did he throw it all away? Why didn't he know what was good for him?

We can only guess. We know that until about 11,000 years ago, the human population was small and stable. In the past people believed that this was due to a suppression by crude environmental factors such as disease and famine, much as it was in our more recent past before the development of public sanitation and so on. Now careful, less prejudiced studies of anthropologists over the last 30 years have revealed enough evidence to strongly suggest that the role of crude environmental factors was insignificant. Our ancestors' populations must have been regulated in part by infant mortality, but largely by infanticide, abortion, and contraception.

Obviously individual couples must have had strong pressures upon them to make them resort to these methods. That of hardship would be easy to understand, but, with conditions as favorable as they were, plainly hardship did not apply. It is most likely that there were certain cultural controls, impulses built into the culture, which stimulated communities into regulating their numbers before they exceeded the carrying capacity of the environment. We have very little idea what these cultural controls were, but we know they must have been related in some way to environmental conditions. Many other animals regulate their populations, and it has been found that the secret of their success is a subtle early warning from the habitat—such as an artificial, socially determined notion of density—which triggers off population control. This is plainly more adaptive (and more pleasant) that breeding right up to the point of collapse from starvation or epidemic, or both.

So it must have been with men. A part of the complex relationship between culture and environment was a feedback that triggered off the

As man's population grew too large to be sustained by the hunting way of life, he was forced to turn to agriculture and the domestication of animals. Relatively early on, he developed the remarkably efficient system of the rice paddy. This photograph shows rice terraces in the Philippines.

mechanisms of population regulation before the habitat was jeopardized.

These controls were of course unconscious. They had to be, otherwise anybody could modify or abandon them for, no doubt, excellent short term reasons, but with disastrous consequences in the long term. However, there is one inevitable disadvantage to internal controls of this nature; they are incapable of responding to conditions outside their evolutionary experience. All organisms are capable of adaptation, man no less than the others, but it is a basic law of all biological systems that there is an optimum level of adaptation. If an organism adapted to every conceivable change in the environment, it would be incapable of adapting to normal conditions of stability. Thus organisms such as man tend to be able to adapt only to a given range of change; if the change is too radical the species will be unable to adapt to it.

The last great advance and retreat of the Pleistocene ice cap between 12,000 and 9000 years ago, caused tremendous changes in climate. These, in turn, caused marked modifications of the environment, so marked that entire species of game were wiped out or were forced to move to other areas. They were followed by man, who now found himself in environments of which he had inadequate evolutionary experience. The controls that formerly regulated both his numbers and his relationships with other species could no longer operate. This enormously accelerated the dispersals and movements of mankind, which brought about the extinction of many Pleistocene animal species, the population by man of the Americas, and the domestication of plants and animals.

Some peoples remained in the environments they knew and maintained stability. A few others restabilized at a later date. They were quickly outnumbered, for the majority embarked on an expansionist course that has continued up to the present day: a sharp rise in population until it is suppressed by natural disaster; then comes some technological innovation that counteracts the disaster, and the population expands again. Thus it continued until the introduction of preventive medicine and public sanitation. These two factors released populations from the epidemic diseases brought about by overcrowding, which itself originated at about the same time as farming and stock raising, at the end of the era of natural man.

Left: in sharp contrast with the intensive use of the hillside in the picture opposite, is the ranching of sheep and cattle. Here sheep are being sold in New South Wales, Australia.
Below: a rock painting from the Tassili region of Algeria. It shows that cattle once grazed an area that is now the Sahara Desert.

Natural Man and his Environment

There are five different ways of getting food: hunting, fishing, gathering, agriculture, and the domestication of animals. As we have seen, the first three are natural, farming and stock-raising being recent innovations. It is also believed that man did not start fishing until some time after the beginnings of hunting.

Hunting is the subsistence activity associated most with natural man, although most hunter-gatherers depend on it for no more than 30 to 40 per cent of their total diet (by weight), the rest comes from the gathering of plants. Nevertheless hunting remains as important nutritionally as gathering, and more important psychologically.

This is not surprising. In the first place the eating of meat usually induces a feeling of great well-being. Most people still like nothing better than sitting down to a good steak; and it is really quite amazing how fish is scorned as a substitute for meat, even in those areas where fish are cheaper and easier to obtain. In the second place there is great drama in the hunt, in the idea of man pitting his strength and his wits against another animal—risking himself for a meal for the entire community.

This idea has survived among peoples who are no longer hunter-gatherers. The Majangir of southwest Ethiopia, for example, get most of their food from gardening and honey-collecting, and not more than 15 per cent from hunting. African buffaloes and elephants are the only animals considered to have power or life-force, and of the two the buffalo is preferred for its flesh and the courage and skill required to kill it. Songs and dances about the food quest are mostly concerned with the successful hunting of buffalo.

A number of people consider game the only proper food, whether or not vegetables and fruit make up a greater proportion of their diet. The Bushmen will describe themselves as "hungry" if they have not eaten meat, even though they may have gorged themselves on plant matter.

To this day, hunting plays a part, however minor, in the lives of Europeans and Americans, particularly in the country. Fox hunting, water-fowling, and potshots at pigeons and rabbits testify to the prevailing attachment to the hunt.

Above: a Pygmy hunting a buffalo. This is an unusual picture, as the Pygmies have a healthy respect for buffalo and usually regard hunting them as foolishly risky. Right: two Bushman hunters crouch low as they stalk an animal in open grassland.

There are many hunting techniques—some involving entire bands, others the individual alone. The one requiring most people is the drive, a method suited to open areas such as grassland and tundra, where there are large migratory herds, and where there is relatively little cover for the lone stalker. The Eskimos used to take advantage of the annual migration of the caribou (a kind of reindeer) to drive a herd into a lake. They then took to their boats and shot the animals at leisure. Their kill was never wasted, however, for the meat was stored in ice and the

Napore tribesmen gather at the start of a hunt in the Karamoja district of Uganda. These men do not live by hunting, as they are pastoralists (herdsmen), but wild meat is an important supplement to their diet.

remains that the men aboard are hunting. Fishing is also one of the world's most popular sports.

As with land hunting, there are a great many methods and tools for hunting. Some Amerindian peoples are adept at shooting fish with bow and arrow, others at spearing them. But perhaps trapping and poisoning are the most effective.

A remarkable variety of traps are made, ranging from a few bundles of reeds to complex structures made with great care and skill. People such as the Sanpoil, who lived in the plateau area of southwest Canada, took great care of their traps, because they depended upon them for their survival through the hard winters. A Salmon Chief was appointed for the entire period of the salmon runs (from May to October) and his job was to decide who should empty each trap and how the catch should be shared. He had total control over all activities associated with fishing, taking particular care that all the traps were in good order. This included making sure that no woman went too near them, or near any part of the salmon stream for that matter, lest she damage them by her presence alone. If a woman did get too close, the Salmon Chief had to beg the salmon to ignore the offense.

Many of the Indian peoples of South America have a considerable knowledge of fish poisons. The most common method is first to partially dam a stream with branches to minimize the risk of fish escaping. Then to cut down vines and beat them so that the sap runs into the water. The sap has the effect of stupefying the fish, which float to the surface where they can be caught with ease. The poison does not remain in the fish, or at least not in a form that is harmful to humans. There are many such fish poisons, and the Amerindians have an extensive knowledge of them. This knowledge has already helped in the advance of pesticide chemistry (for example, the insecticide Derris is derived from an Amerindian fish poison), and undoubtedly could be utilized much more—in the development of new drugs, for instance.

Once a fish has been caught, of course, it must be kept fresh. It would be extremely difficult in the tropics, for instance, but, since fish is just one of a number of foods eaten there, and its occurrence is regular it is not a problem. However, in areas like the Pacific Coast of Canada fish made

Turkana fishermen with hand nets on Lake Rudolf, Kenya. Netting fish is one more method of hunting invented by man.

A Kalapolo Indian fishing on the Xingu River, Brazil. Great accuracy is displayed in hitting the fish.

up at least half the total food supply and although astonishingly abundant at times they were also scarce at others. Peoples like the Tlingit, the Bella Coola, and the Nootka, had therefore to devise means of storing the fish for months on end, particularly during the snowbound winters.

In the summer, the Bella Coola took immense catches of humpback and sockeye salmon, halibut, and lingcod, and dried them on racks in the sun. In the autumn, other varieties of salmon were taken, such as cohoe and dog, and these were smoked indoors out of the rain. The sockeye and dog salmon kept best because they are fatter than the others.

The fat from the richer fish was often rendered into oil. When the dried fish were eventually eaten they were dipped into this oil, which provided the Indians with valuable fats and carbohydrates. Salmon eggs were allowed to get high and were then made into something resembling cheese. Clams were also preserved, first by steaming and then by drying them. Among some of the peoples of the Pacific coast, the dried fish were kept in pits, but generally they were stored in baskets and boxes that were then placed on racks inside each home. Apparently the smell was quite intense.

On the other side of the Pacific, the Ainu of Japan trained their dogs to catch fish for them. The men used to take 20 or 30 dogs along the shallow sandy bays. At an agreed point, half the men and dogs would stay where they were, while the other half moved on a farther 200 yards or so. At a signal, both groups of dogs would swim out to sea in a single file. Then the men gave a shout and the dogs wheeled around toward each other until the heads of the two files met. Then at another shout the dogs swam ashore in a crescent. Any fish between them and the shore were driven inexorably toward the beach. As soon as it felt the bottom each dog would grab a fish and take it to his master, no one else. His recognized reward was the fish's head. Each man kept the fish brought to him, together with his fair share of any of the fish that had fled onto dry land.

The Ainu were one of a number of food-collecting peoples for whom fish was the most important element in their diet. This is not surprising in view of their geographical position. Most food-collectors living in the far North (North of 60°) depended largely on meat; most of those, like the Ainu and the Bella Coola, who lived in the intermediate latitudes (from 40°–50°) depended largely

A Waura Indian of Brazil, killing a fish by biting it.

43

on fish; while most of those living in the tropics and subtropics (0°–39°) depended largely on the gathering of plants.

Gathering, like hunting, is still practiced today, more for fun than anything else. People walk the fields and hedgerows in search of nuts, blackberries, and mushrooms, not because it is an essential part of life but because it is a pleasant change from the office, or fun for the kids. Plants that were once exclusively gathered are either no longer eaten or are deliberately cultivated. The exceptions are seaweed, still gathered in vast quantities by the Japanese and to a lesser extent by the Welsh; truffles, gathered by the French and the Italians simply because they cannot be grown; and, until 1968, wild rice.

Wild rice is, strictly speaking, not a rice at all, but a separate type of grain in its own right. This delicious food, besides being the staple diet of the Chippewa Indians of Minnesota, is highly valued as a luxury by many Americans. Wild rice is still gathered by the Chippewa, even though in most

Ojibwa (Chippewa) Indians still harvest wild rice in the traditional way. Here they assemble on Rice Lake, Minnesota.

other respects they follow an industrial way of life, however impoverished. This is basically because the hand-gathering of the rice is a vital link with the past, but also because it grows in such a way as to make manual harvesting much better for the rice beds than mechanical harvesting. Unfortunately, wild rice is now being grown by white Americans in paddy fields, and thus a valuable and traditional living is progressively being wrested from the Indians.

For most peoples, however, the gathering of wild plants was once of the greatest possible importance. This being the case, it is interesting that it was left almost entirely to the women of each group, while the men were charged with hunting and fishing. Thus, even now, among the Western Desert Aborigines of Australia, women are the chief providers and spend one-third more time than the men on food collection and preparation. Occasionally the men deceive their womenfolk by telling them they are going hunting, and then, once they are well away from the camp, spend the rest of the day on sacred carving or

Ojibwa Indians bagging up the hand-gathered harvest. Strictly speaking the grain is not rice at all, but it is very nutritious.

An Eripagtsa woman from Brazil is watched by her child as she gathers wild honey—a much-sought-after delicacy.

some other activity less strenuous than the hunt. When they return empty-handed, their excuse is one to which the women are fairly well accustomed. They saw little game and the hunting was very difficult, they say.

The Tiwi of northern Australia are well aware of the economic importance of women. In this respect they are considered as more important than men, although this insight is used to justify not women's liberation but polygamy, the marriage of many women to one man. When a missionary once tried to persuade a Tiwi elder with a particularly impressive retinue of wives

that this accumulation was impious, the aborigine answered: "If I had only one or two wives I would starve, but with my present 10 or 12 wives I can send them in all directions in the morning and at least two or three of them are likely to bring something back with them at the end of the day, and then we can all eat."

Many sorts of leaves, seeds, roots, fruits, berries, nuts, and mushrooms are gathered, and different groups of food-collectors have differing preferences, from the Mongongo nuts of the Bushmen to the fruit called mundjutj collected by the Aborigines of Arnhem Land. They leave the fruit until it is wrinkled like a prune, then they rub it with a red ocher and allow it to go dry until it is hard and brittle. Wrapped in bark it will keep for months, until it is pounded into a

Some aquatic animals are gathered, not hunted. Here, a group of Australian Aborigines gather shellfish on the shore.

paste, mixed with kangaroo meat, and eaten.

Common to all peoples living in regions warm enough for bees, however, is a passionate fondness for honey. Honey is a food esteemed universally, and especially by natural man. The Majangir method of obtaining it is typical: a few men go off with gourds, an axe or large knife, and fire-sticks. They keep a sharp eye on the trees, and when they see a few bees obviously going in and out of a hole in one of them, they set to work. One man uses the fire-sticks to light a fire, while another takes the axe to the hole to enlarge it. A bundle of twigs chosen for their tendency to smoke is placed on the fire, and when they are smoking they are put by the hole, as it is widened still more. The smoke stupifies the bees, and they allow the men to raid the nest almost unstung.

The combs, dripping with the delicious fluid, are withdrawn and put into the gourds—apart from those that are consumed on the spot. Sometimes a part of the comb is left and the hole repaired, to encourage the bees to return.

During certain months of the year, the Majangir and a number of other peoples are seized with an irresistible craving for honey. The Mbuti Pygmies become obsessed with it, and dance and sing and talk about nothing else. The Majangir take their honey in three ways; straight from the comb, by chewing on the wax until all sweetness is gone, when the wax is spat out; diluted in

The first stage in slash-and-burn gardening. With only a hand-ax, an Amerindian man fells one of the larger trees.

48

water to make a nonalcoholic and surprisingly refreshing sweet drink; and mixed with water and a special bark that they gather and powder. This mixture is slowly heated overnight, and the fermentation properties of the bark act so fast that by morning a drink has been produced as dry as red wine, with the alcoholic strength of beer, and tasting of honey.

Farming cannot really be said to be a "natural" activity, and different farming methods grade subtly from one to the other. Probably the oldest method is slash-and-burn, or swidden, which consists of first felling the larger trees, then burning off the fallen wood and the scrub, and finally clearing the area ready for sowing.

This method sounds much more destructive than it is: in fact, provided it is practiced by a people whose numbers are stable, it is one of the safest and most productive methods known to man. The closer a group is to the social conditions of the food-collecting way of life, the more stable and natural is their method of cultivation.

Under such conditions, swidden imitates as much as possible the pattern of the surrounding vegetation so that the swidden garden tends to be almost as stable as the environment it has replaced. In the forest regions of the tropics, where slash-and-burn has been most successful, the pattern of vegetation is one of high diversity —a mass of different species. This diversity is duplicated by the swidden cultivators, such as the Tsembaga of New Guinea and the Hanunoo of the Philippines. The latter grow dry rice (that is rice in ordinary gardens, not in paddies), but their rice gardens contain a great many other plants besides. At the sides and against the fences there are often five different kinds of climbing beans. Next to them, toward the center of the garden, there is a mixture of grain crops, root crops, shrubs, and small food-bearing trees. These plants will all be ready for harvesting at the same time of year, when among them the vines of yams and sweet potatoes, and the leaves of the taro betray the presence of a growing store of rootcrops that will be ready some time later. Once the rice toward the center has ripened, it is replaced by the slower growing shrubs and trees.

The combination of so many species of food plants ensures that no time is lost between the ripening of one type of plant and that of another. It also means that the fragile layer of decaying plant and animal matter on the surface is not

The felled trunks and branches are then burned.

A man carrying away timber useful for poles.

49

destroyed by the direct rays of the sun or washed away by the rain. Instead the nutrients within it are taken up immediately by plants valuable to man. At the same time, of course, the beneficial effects of the sun are utilized to the fullest extent by converting the energy into a productive protective canopy of vegetation. Generally, some of the original trees are retained for the protection they give.

Swidden has been described as a natural forest transformed into a harvestable forest, and it is easy to see why. There is good evidence that slash-and-burn is more productive over the long term than more extensive methods. The Tepoztlan swiddens of Mexico yield double the harvest of continuously cropped fields, and the farmers of the West African hill districts abandoned their swiddens in the valleys for manured terraces only when raiders forced them into the hills.

Slash-and-burn is almost as easy a way of life as hunting and gathering. With only two hours' work a day, the South American Kuikuru can grow an acre of manioc. This provides some four million calories a year—so much that they can allow up to half the crop to be robbed by peccaries and ants.

As with hunting and gathering, so with farming there is division of labor between the sexes. The men do the heavy work of felling the trees, burning the debris, and clearing the ground; the women do the planting and harvesting. A swidden patch will last from three to seven years depend-

ing on its location, and yielding less and less each year as the nutrients are consumed. It must then lie fallow for 5 to 15 years. The forest is allowed to return, which it does in the form of secondary growth—the unkempt mass of vines, shrubs, and trees that people associate with the jungle of adventure stories. If the secondary growth were left alone it would gradually be replaced by true forest, but normally after 15 years at most the nutrient cycle is sufficiently re-established for the growth to be cleared for yet another garden.

Although this means that each man would not have to clear a new garden very often, if he worked by himself he would have infrequent bouts of intensely back-breaking work. But in fact the men co-operate with one another, thus providing longer periods of more continuous—and less strenuous—work.

Different peoples have different staples—the crop on which they depend most. In Southeast Asia it is rice, in the forests of Africa it is yams, and in the African grasslands it is millet and sorghum. At the time Europeans first came to the Americas, the Indians were growing about 120 different plant species, of which maize was the staple in North America and the Central American highlands, potatoes in the Andes, and manioc (cassava) in the forests of Central and South America. It is somewhat startling that modern man has not domesticated any new staples—that all of our major food plants were domesticated

Clearing the garden (left) and harvesting (above). The men do the heavy work of clearing and preparing the gardens; but the women do the planting and sowing, look after the plants, and then finally harvest the produce.

51

shortly after man ceased to be truly natural. All we have done is improve on the work of farmers very much like the people still practicing slash-and-burn today.

Herdsmen are the true nomads of the world, roaming over much greater distances than hunter-gatherers who, although they move around much more than we do, tend to do so in a relatively confined area. Most herdsmen, on the other hand, will stay put only until their animals have grazed out the area and they are forced to move on, covering great distances in this way.

Generally, the animals domesticated by herds-men, or pastoralists as they are known, were once native to the area—for example, the reindeer of the Lapps in Europe's Arctic north. There is one great exception to this rule, however. The cattle of the African pastoralists—the Fulani of West Africa, the Masai astride the borders of Kenya and Tanzania, and the Karamojong in the wildest part of Uganda—were introduced into Africa from Asia about 4000 years ago, but since then

they have become a dominant part of the African scene. To people like the Masai and the Karamo-jong they are a source not simply of food, but also of riches and prestige. The main food of these herdsmen is cow's milk and the blood obtained by cutting the jugular vein in the cow's neck. Only a small incision is made, so that the cow can continue giving blood with as little ill effect as we suffer when we donate blood to the hospital blood bank. Cattle are a measure of a man's wealth and a constant source of pride to the Masai. He will part with a cow only with the greatest reluctance, as for example, when he has to pay the bride price.

Domestic animals are important, not merely to pure pastoralists, but to less specialized farmers as well. Among the Melanesian peoples of New Guinea and the smaller islands of the western Pacific, pigs are valued socially as much as they are nutritionally. For example, the Bomagai-Angoiang of New Guinea give every one of their pigs personal names and practically make them part of the family. Pigs are always part of

Above: reindeer are the only species of deer to have been domesticated. Few kinds of animals have been domesticated by man.

the bride price, and are killed whenever someone is ill or dies. They play an important part in the ceremonial life of New Guinean peoples — ceremonies, and occasionally even wars, occurring only when pigs are in good supply, so that a fine feast is assured.

Although generally the pigs are owned by the men, they are looked after by the women, who can cope easily with one or two, but begin to grumble if they have to care for more. The attitude of the men, however, is that the only good pig is a cooked pig and in the tedious period between birth and the pot, pigs must stay with the women. As one anthropologist, writing of a people called the Karam, puts it: they feel that "women are always potentially dangerous because of their child-bearing capacities and menstrual activities, but you have to live with them. Pigs are also filthy creatures, but you have to live with them too."

Masai herdsmen of Kenya and Tanzania with their cattle.

Young Turkana boys tending a herd of camels. Among pastoral peoples children start work early in life.

54

Now that Eskimos have high-powered rifles, their one-time respect for animals has changed to relative indifference.

From the very moment of birth, hunter-gatherers and hunter-gardeners are made aware of their intimate relationship with the rest of Nature. The Hupa of northern California used to take the remains of the infant's umbilical cord and place it in a young spruce. They believed that the child would be identified with the tree and grow as strongly. The Polynesian Tokelau follow a similar custom, placing the afterbirth and umbilical cord in the ground, and planting over it a coconut tree, thereafter regarded as the child's.

Many North American Indian tribes sent their adolescent boys on spirit quests. They would go alone into the forests and mountains, fending entirely for themselves, until they were visited by the spirit of a plant or animal. This would then be their guardian for the rest of their lives, and would aid them in the hunt.

Natural man does not distinguish quite as sharply as we do between man and the other animals or between man and the rest of Nature. He has a much more realistic appreciation of the interdependency of man and the living world about him. This awareness is expressed in ways that we might find sentimental or mystical or just odd, although an increasing number of people today are coming to realize that natural man's religious attitude to his fellow species is probably more scientific than our mixture of indifference and hostility. Certainly it is more conducive to survival in the long term.

The Eskimos had every reason to feel hostility

Above right: an Eskimo hunter alone in the harsh environment he has learned to come to terms with. Below: an Eskimo woman cooking seal meat. None of the animal is wasted.

toward their incredibly harsh environment, yet they did not. In the business of kill or starve, which so many people, ignorant of the abattoir and the factory farm, now find so cruelly un-civilized, the Eskimo was well aware that he had no more right to live and eat than did his prey. Consequently, he developed a strictly moral code of behavior toward the animals he hunted. Whenever a polar bear, or a seal, or a whale (any mammal in fact that came from the sea) was killed, the wife of the hunter would welcome the spirit of the dead creature, offer it a cup of fresh water, and ask it to return to its fellows to tell them that it had been treated properly.

The Nemadi of Mauretania hunt the addax, an antelope of the Sahara Desert. Whenever a Nemadi hunter is about to kill one he asks its forgiveness. Sometimes the respect given to

57

animals by hunting peoples is extended even to highly dangerous ones. For example, the G/wi (the stroke denotes a click sound made by the teeth) Bushmen of Botswana have been seen to remove scorpions carefully from the camp to prevent them straying into the fire. And the Dorobo of Kenya will not kill any snake that enters a hut at night, but will see that it is sent politely on its way. This, they say, is because their ancestral spirits live underground with the snakes, and emerge at night for a stroll, so no one can be sure that a snake is not some relation. The prohibition against killing snakes does not apply in daytime.

The Dorobo also have a tremendous love of the forest in which they live. They feel respect and friendliness toward the animals that share it with them. As one Dorobo has said: "The Dorobo know the tracks of all the animals, and they like also to see the animals. The animals are not bad, for we all dwell in the forest together. The intelligence of the animals is not like that of people, but it is not very different, for they also are intelligent. Every animal of the forest is alike; we eat some, others we do not; but we like them all. We, and they also, are of the forest."

The Mbuti Pygmies express the most vigorous affection for their forest home. The men refer to it as "mother" and the women call it "father." They are fully aware that the forest provides all their requirements—shelter, food, drink, and security—and that without it they would die. Their entire morality is bound up in the forest, quarrels and other offensive behavior being broken up with the admonition that the forest must not be offended. So closely do the Mbuti identify with their environment that young men have been known to dance alone apparently but actually, they say, with the moon and the forest.

Many other hunter-gatherers have a reverential attitude to plants. The Omaha Indians, for example, always left a pinch of tobacco whenever they picked a plant for its medicinal properties, for they believed that its healing powers were theirs only by the generosity of the plant.

Such attitudes are not confined to hunter-gathers. The Barama River Caribs of Guyana always take care to sprinkle beer on the trees they have to fell when they clear a new garden. They wish to placate the spirits of the trees so

Panare Indians of the Venezuelan forests resting in camp. Familiarity with the forest breeds confidence, not fear.

that they will not skulk malevolently in the surrounding bush but, when the new growth is big enough, will return to guard the swidden.

Perhaps the most complete of any people's identification with its environment is that of the Australian Aborigines. Until destroyed by miners and missionaries, the Aborigines were as much a part of the landscape as the rocks and cliff faces on which they painted their totemic designs.

Among the Wikmunkan Aborigines, for example, every clan had a totem: an animal, plant, or geographical feature with which it was closely associated. Every totem had a sacred spot from which it first originated. These would be bushes, trees, holes, or rocks, generally with water nearby. The killing of an animal or the injuring of a plant near its sacred spot was absolutely prohibited and bound to be followed by misfortune.

The sacred spot was called *auwa*, and ceremonies of increase were held there, when the clan appealed to the spirit of its totem to ensure a plentiful supply of the plant or animal concerned. The clan's senior men painted themselves with designs in white clay representing the totem. The ritual that followed varied according to the totem, but it could include stamping, hitting trees, sweeping the bushes, and making strange noises. In effect, each clan was making itself responsible for the abundance of those objects of economic and social value to the community.

The *auwa* of the bream totem is a small creek running into a major river. It is probably one of the bream's main breeding places. Beside it, ant hills have been arranged in a circle and in lines going east and west from it as if from the *auwa*. Whenever a man from the clan was speared in a fight, it was thought that his spirit went under

Above: an Aborigine rock painting of a fish totem. Below: Aborigines dancing a totemic dance. The Aborigines had a striking awareness of the unity of man and land, which was expressed in their culture until it was destroyed by Europeans.

Above: Australian Aborigines feel a powerful bond with the rocks and cliffs and other natural features that surround them.

water at the bream *auwa*. Another *auwa* was that of the plains turkey. This is a lagoon, and no one was allowed to swim there. Once, a man did so, and as soon as he emerged from the water he died.

It is hard for us to comprehend the deep love and respect the Australian Aborigines had for their totemic sites. All hunter-gatherers have a very close bond with the landscape that is their home and with the animals and plants that share it with them. But only the Australian Aborigines seem to have expressed this bond quite so strikingly—even obsessively—in their rituals and daily life.

Food-collecting survived as a successful way of life for so long because hunter-gatherers have a

highly detailed and comprehensive knowledge of their environment. Many observers, having heard their opinions with scepticism, have been surprised to find how accurate they were.

The explorer Humboldt, for example, when traveling in the Americas was struck by the crocodiles' strange habit of swallowing stones. It is a habit that has often been observed, but until recently was thought quite inexplicable. The Amerindians told Humboldt that the crocodiles retained the stones in their bellies, and this improved their stability and maneuverability under water. Humboldt thought the idea was simply a rather amusing native superstition and did not believe it. But recent research has shown that the Amerindians were right.

One anthropologist, Richard Nelson, was commissioned by the United States Air Force to study Eskimo knowledge of sea ice, the general term for the different types of ice that cover the Arctic sea. If an aircraft is forced to come down in the Arctic, it is essential that its crew know as much as possible about Polar survival techniques. Quite apart from the need to hunt, fish, and keep warm, it is virtually impossible to stay alive without an understanding of how ice behaves. Some ice is as safe as dry land, other ice may crumble or fracture into small floes. One large mass of ice may suddenly break away from another, or equally suddenly they may pack together with crushing force.

Richard Nelson found that the Eskimos could predict, with great accuracy, the likely behavior of the ice on which they were traveling, and that the rules they went by and their descriptions of the physical properties of the ice were of a high scientific standard. They were also expert at remembering their way in what to us is essentially a featureless landscape, and past masters at crossing ice so thin that, were it not for the Eskimos' technique, it would break under the weight of a man. Richard Nelson had some difficulty in believing the Eskimos at first, but in the end he wrote: "Those who live with Eskimos over a long enough period find themselves questioning less, and follow whatever they are told to do by their experienced native companions. It is my opinion that the information given by Eskimos relating to successful hunting or sur-

Eskimos, like all hunting peoples, have a formidable knowledge of animals. Here a group of them are preparing to use the properties of frozen fish for an unusual purpose.

The fish are laid end to end and wrapped in skins previously soaked in water. Before the skins freeze they are trampled into the correct shape. Thus sledge runners are made from frozen fish! The crosspieces are made from caribou bone or antlers. This extreme example of skillful improvization shows how the Eskimos use their knowledge of animals to the full.

Successful hunting demands silence. The otherwise highly voluble Bushmen keep absolutely quiet as soon as they see an animal. They have developed this sign language to tell each other what they have seen. The two-handed gesture above means buffalo. Below are some single-handed signs.

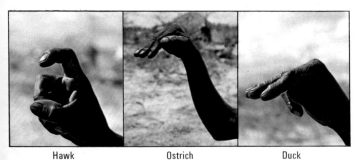

Hawk   Ostrich   Duck

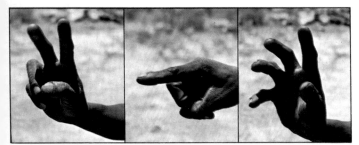

Scrub-hare   Springhaas   Porcupine

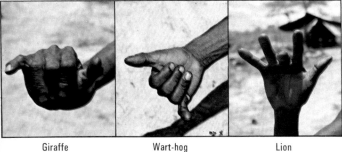

Giraffe   Wart-hog   Lion

vival techniques is nearly always correct and well-founded, regardless of how difficult it may be to accept initially."

Obviously, simply to have survived in such an environment is proof enough of the Eskimos' great knowledge, and this proof applies equally to their knowledge of animals. How else could they have hunted them? Yet many of the peoples who hunt with bow and arrow—for example, the Andamanese, Bushmen, Pygmies, and various Amerindian tribes—are singularly poor shots. At ranges greater than 60 feet or so they are most unlikely to hit their target, and their normal range is about 30 feet. However, their lack of technological competence is amply compensated for by their knowledge of animal behavior. So well do they understand the habits of their prey that they are able to stalk it and get close enough to it to make sure of killing it. By examining tracks, animal droppings, and vegetation that has been bruised or broken when animals have passed by or fed on it, hunting peoples can tell what their prospects are of getting meat that day. In this way, too, they know what species of animal is around, its age, sex, size, and condition, and where it is likely to be. They know the sleeping habits of animals, an obviously advantageous piece of information as there is no easier catch than an animal asleep. At the other end of the scale, some American Indians were able to run down deer by keeping them moving and by taking advantage of their tendency to run in an arc: the hunters simply traversed the shorter distance between the two ends of the arc. By contrast, the modern "sportsman," with his high-powered rifle and telescopic sight, or even with the latest archery equipment, can hunt successfully without even the knowledge to identify his prey by more than a distinction between game and stock.

Knowledge of animals was not confined to their behavior. The Aleuts had an impressive anatomical knowledge, and the multiplicity of uses found by the Eskimos for different parts of an animal is astounding. The blubber, heart, kidney, liver, spleen, and flesh of the northern sea lion, for instance, were eaten as food; the bones were made into clubs, root diggers, and

Above, right: Bushmen pretending to hunt ostriches. Right: Aborigines perform a ritual emu-mimicking dance. Natural man's knowledge of animal behavior often emerges in play and dance.

other tools, depending on their size; the flippers into soles for shoes; the intestines, stomach, and the tube connecting the mouth and stomach (the esophagus) were used for making jackets (the parka), trousers, and pouches; the sinews were used for binding and sewing; the skin as a kayak cover; the teeth as jewelry; the whiskers as decoration for hats; and the pericardium, (the sac enclosing the heart) as a container. The Majangir put the hide alone of an antelope to many uses: carpet, hat, a sling for carrying

infants, and sheaths for knives and fire-sticks.

In the past, naturalists and explorers have benefited greatly from hunting peoples' knowledge of animal life, and there is no doubt that serious students of animal behavior still do so. Quite as extensive as his knowledge of animals is natural man's knowledge of plants. We have already gained a great deal from this knowledge, as is shown by a list of plants we eat today which almost certainly we would not have known about if we had not seen them eaten by American

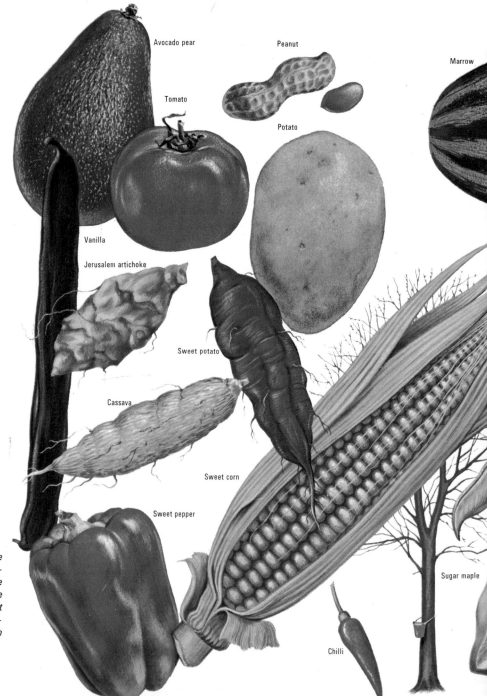

The Amerindians' gift to the world. There are 24 important food-plants that the hungry world would have been without had they not been discovered by the various Indian tribes of South and Central America.

Indians: maize (or sweet-corn), sugar maple, peanuts, sunflower seeds, Brazil nuts, cashew nuts, runner beans, french (or kidney) beans, butter beans pineapples, passion fruit, guavas, cocoa, papaya, avocados, marrows, tomatoes, sweet peppers, chilis, vanilla, potatoes, Jerusalem artichokes, manioc (cassava), and sweet potatoes. It can be seen that they include three vitally important staples—maize, manioc (a major food in Africa as well), and potatoes.

It is unlikely that those representatives of natural man still surviving will be able to introduce us to any more major food plants. However, there are probably many of rather more modest importance still awaiting either discovery or wider application. In this latter category are the mongongo nuts of the !Kung Bushmen. This highly nutritious food-plant would be of great value if it could be cultivated in arid lands such as those of Saharan Africa and the Near East. It is also probable that some tropical-forest dwelling tribes know of plants that could be used in

Brazil nuts

Kidney bean

Cashew nuts

Guava

Sunflower seeds

Butter beans

Pineapple

Scarlet runner bean

Cocoa

Papaya

Passion fruit

A Tukano from Peru collects the leaves of the coca plant. Many Amerindian tribes use cocaine and other plant drugs.

beverages. There are plenty of stimulating drinks on the market, but remarkably few genuinely soothing (non-addictive) ones. We are far more likely to discover such a plant by finding it in use among a forest people than by selecting plants at random or by experimenting in laboratories.

From the Amerindians we have also learned about important drug plants such as quinine, cocaine, and curare. Quinine is a well-known antimalarial agent; drugs derived from cocaine are used in dentists' anesthetics; and curare is a drug vital to safe and painless surgery. Cocaine comes from the coca leaf, chewed by the Indians of the Andes, while the many types of curare are various combinations of complex chemical compounds, used by the forest Indians as arrow poisons. It is from their formidable knowledge of such poisons that we are likely to derive most future benefit. A great many fish poisons, for example, remain to be investigated for properties other than their ability to stun fish. Some have already proved useful in bettering our understanding of nerve action. Another is the well-known insecticide Derris. The Barama River Caribs have long known about the insecticidal properties of *haiari*, the plant they use as a fish poison. They treat their tobacco plants with it.

On the other side of the world, the Andaman Islanders use a plant they call *jojonghe* to protect them on their frequent raids of bees' nests. Like many hunting peoples they are extremely fond of honey, and whenever they are about to collect some they smear themselves with *jojonghe* and put some in their mouths. This they chew, breathing the fumes on the bees. The effect is to repel the bees completely, and the honey robbers win their prize absolutely unstung. Only one anthropologist visiting the Andaman Islanders seems to have grasped the usefulness of such a plant. He took some samples of it and planted them in the governor's garden on the main island, so that as soon as they had flowered they could be taken to the mainland of India for identification. Unfortunately, the governor's gardener thought they were weeds and threw them away.

Another branch of natural man's learning of which there is a good deal of evidence but which is almost entirely unexplored, is his knowledge of oral contraceptives and abortifacients. The first are taken before sexual intercourse, the second after. The women of Efate, Gau, and Pentecost, islands in the New Hebrides group, know of a great many plants that they combine to

Some of the uses to which Amerindians put their knowledge of plants. Above left: Tukano Indians cure an after-the-party hangover with green pepper juice. Right: Colorado Indians from Ecuador use a red paste on their hair to repel insects. Below: a Tukano Indian prepares coca leaves. It was from the Amerindians that we learned about cocaine, now used in medicine.

make contraceptives or abortifacients, and that they claim are effective. Their use is a source of friction between the men and the women, for the women want small families while their husbands want large ones. None of the plants used have been tested. Nor have the plants used by the Lesu of New Ireland, which are known only to a few old men who sell the leaves whenever they are required. The situation is further complicated by the refusal of most Lesu women to admit they resort to the plants at all.

Again, it is in South America that research into abortifacient plants is likely to be most successful. The forests of the Amazon-Orinoco basin are rich in a great variety of species, and the Amerindians have a long-standing and intimate acquaintance with them. As we shall see in the next chapter, many of their populations are kept stable through the use of contraceptive and abortifacient plants, the safety of which have been tested by the living laboratories of the tribes themselves.

A fourth group of plants, of which South and Central American peoples in particular have a comprehensive experience, are the hallucinogens, the drugs used to induce trances and visions. As these are normally used in religion and medicine, they will be discussed when we deal with shamanism, in the next chapter.

Finally, natural man employs a wide variety of plants for their different mechanical properties. Besides making common use of gourds of all shapes and sizes for pots, cups, ladles, and dishes, the Majangir also use the bark of a number of vines that they turn into serviceable ropes, and of course they know what wood makes the best fire-sticks. Their houses are made from sticks, grass, and leaves, and are perfectly waterproof. But perhaps they are most skillful in their working of string, carrying bags, and baskets. Their string is made from various plant fibers, by hand of course, but the fibers are bound so well together that they appear manufactured. The carrying bags are made from beaten bark, are very strong, and are most attractive to look at— as indeed are the Majangir baskets, made from different types of cane to which a plant resin is applied to make them waterproof.

Some idea of the food-collectors' general knowledge of plants can be gathered from the fact that their classifications are often more complex than those of Western science. While our classification is based on structure, theirs is based on shape,

Above: Kamayura Indians in the Xingu National Park, Brazil, with bark canoes. Left: a heavily ornamented Eripagtsa mother and daughter. The woman is making a basket of plaited leaves.

taste, smell, and texture. If a botanist wishes to identify a plant he must wait until he sees its flower or fruit, but a hunter-gatherer uses a number of criteria for identification. Nor is his knowledge frozen in time and incapable of modification. The Pinatubo Negritos of the Philippines are—or were until the practice was missionized out of them—constantly improving their knowledge. If they found a plant they did not know, they would taken it home and discuss it with their colleagues.

Farming peoples as different as the Cubeo of Colombia and the Tsembaga of New Guinea have tremendous experimental curiosity and take great delight in trying out new crop varieties.

However, this willingness to experiment is allied with conservatism, and the experimenter will not commit himself to his new variety for many years, until it has been proved better or as satisfactory as the one it might replace. Again it is worth reminding ourselves that very few indeed of our food crops, and none of our major ones, are modern domestications, and it is those areas where the remaining representatives of natural man still live that are most likely to be the centers of the genetic diversity of plant species on which our food supply depends.

So far we have seen that natural man has developed a striking diversity of ways of gaining a living, an intimate and detailed understanding of his environment, and a harmonious relationship with it. All of these things, though essential, would be useless without any capacity to stabilize his population. We know that, in fact, hunter-

!Kung Bushman mother nursing a five-year-old child. Long lactation periods are an important contribution to hunter-gatherer population control. On average lactation periods last for three years, during which time fertility is suppressed.

gatherer populations remained virtually stable for a very long time, but until recently it was generally considered that this was because they were subject to starvation and disease of an intensity and frequency only rarely encountered today. Now, however, we know better. Not only do most hunting peoples feed well and easily; they are generally in relatively good health.

Very few full-scale studies of the medical status of pure hunter-gatherers have been carried out. But partial studies, such as that of parasites among Bushmen, reveal that they are much healthier than other, either rural or urban, peoples in the same area. Of the 12 species of parasitic worm found most frequently in rural African populations, only one (the hookworm) was found in Bushmen, and its incidence was not high. The general picture of hunter-gatherer health, life-expectancy, and longevity is that although they are not quite so good as are enjoyed by the average person in the industrialized countries of North America, Europe, Australasia, and Japan, they are much better than can at present be hoped for in the populous non-industrial countries.

It is more than probable that hunting man's health is at least marginally better than that of mixed gardeners and food-collectors—and it is among this latter category that the only full-scale studies have been made. Outstanding among them are those of J. V. Neel and his colleagues on the Xavante of Brazil and the Yanomamo of Venezuela, and Dr. Albert Damon's team from Harvard on the Nasioi and Kwaio peoples of the Solomon Islands.

Dr. Neel described the people he studied as "in general in excellent physical condition," a finding that has been amply borne out by Dr. Damon among the Solomon Islanders. Dr. Damon found that there was a sufficiently large proportion of them old enough for him to do a study on degenerative ailments such as cancer and heart disease so common in the industrial world. Yet such diseases were almost totally absent. In general both studies demonstrate that hunter-gardeners (mixed gardeners and food-collectors) suffer more from infectious and less from degenerative diseases than we do, and that on average they are probably fitter than we are.

Thus it is now accepted by a number of authorities that many hunter-gatherer and hunter-gardener societies stabilize their populations

House on stilts for single men and boys on the Solomon Islands. Separate accommodation for bachelors is a form of population control practiced by some peoples, the efficiency of which is related to the persistence and ingenuity of the young men.

Above: Tasaday men in the Philippines making stone tools. Right: a Tasaday mother with her children. The ability of the tribe to maintain a stable population, as well as the remoteness of their home, must have contributed to their isolation, until discovered in 1971. Now the delicate relationship between themselves and their environment is likely to be destroyed.

deliberately rather than involuntarily through starvation and disease. The means they have adopted are restraint, infanticide, abortion, and contraception. Restraint is practiced in the form of the post-partum taboo, a prohibition on sexual intercourse for up to three years after the birth of a child. This provides at least a minimum of spacing. Infanticide is obvious: the deliberate killing of the child as soon as it is born. It sounds horrible and barbaric to us, but the people who practice it have a good reason for doing so: to them, it is more important that the opportunity of all members of the community to live complete lives is not jeopardized by their having to cope with an excess of numbers. Among the Eskimos, female infanticides were more common than male ones. This is because the men, being hunters, live much more dangerous lives than do the women, and so get killed more easily. If there were as many girls as boys, when they grew up the women would eventually far outnumber the men. Abortion, both direct and by means of abortifacients, and contraception are as common as infanticide, and natural man has a profound knowledge of plants for these purposes, as we saw from the last section.

The mechanics of population regulation among hunter-gatherers and hunter-gardeners are of absorbing interest, but it is still more fascinating to speculate about the controls that stimulate people to resort to these mechanisms. That these controls are powerful is demonstrated by comparing the respective fates of two Amerindian tribes of Brazil, the Tenetehara and the Tapirape. Both tribes lived in virtually identical environments, but the Tenetehara were expansionist and the Tapirape were stable. Tenetehara women left their men if they felt they were insufficiently fertile. By contrast, the Tapirape took care to limit their families to two at most three children, and certainly no more than two children of the same sex. When the white man came to Brazil, both tribes suffered terribly from introduced diseases such as measles and smallpox and from raids by colonists and bandits. Both tribes were decimated, but only one recovered. The Tenetehara continued to be expansionist, their numbers began to increase, until today their population is greater than ever before. The Tapirape, however, continued to regulate their numbers as if nothing untoward had happened. Unfortunately, such control although advantageous for a vigorous

population is disastrous for one that has been reduced to almost nothing—and today the Tapirape tribe is extinct.

This tragic example can be repeated from other tribes. What is the nature of such powerful controls? Nobody knows, and regrettably virtually no research is being conducted on the subject. What is still more confusing is that while the controls appear suicidally powerful among some people, they are highly fragile among others.

The Havasupai, for example, are a small tribe of North American Indians, who live in an enchantingly beautiful canyon in Arizona. During the 200 years for which there are written records, their population has remained stable—except on two occasions. The first was in 1906 after a two-year measles epidemic that halved the population. Interestingly, the population recovered and appeared to stabilize itself. The second occasion occurred with the arrival of a hospital service leading to an expansion of population.

The cause of this rise in population is not that people who formerly would have died from illness are now being saved. It is something quite different. As far as we know, Havasupai numbers were kept down in the past in four ways. The first was a post-partum taboo of two years, and the second was the use of contraceptives, whose effectiveness has not yet been tested. The third was the reduced fertility of the men, as a result of their practice of taking frequent steam baths. It has been suggested that the exposure of the adult men to very hot temperatures, followed by very cold ones when they plunge into the icy stream, lowers fertility by reducing the production of spermatozoa.

The fourth way, and probably the most significant, was abortion. This was a generally accepted way of removing unwanted children, particularly those conceived out of wedlock, until the hospital was built in the locality. Then the Havasupai started having their children in hospital, and abortions virtually ceased. For the first time in their history they had illegitimate children—and a growing population.

By carrying out multigeneration studies of peoples such as the Havasupai, the Tapirape, the Bushmen, and the Andaman Islanders, it may be possible to discover not just new contraceptive drugs, but more significantly what makes a people unconsciously desire to limit its population. For it is only among such people that the answer to this important question can be found.

Havasu Canyon, Arizona, the home of the Havasupai Indians. Until recently, they were able to regulate their numbers so that they remained at peace and could be contained within their cliff-bound home without spreading into the surrounding desert.

Natural Man and his Fellows

Violence is commonly associated with natural man. There are probably two reasons for this. The first is that hunting animals is considered a violent act. We have seen, however, that although finding and killing prey stretch the intelligence and physical prowess of hunters, they hunt with no more aggression than the minimum required to key them up. They certainly feel no aggression toward the animal, and are generally at most reverential, at least neutral.

The second reason is that a society such as ours is fascinated by violence. The anthropological accounts that have greatest impact are the highly colored ones in which the people have strange practices and are particularly violent. Cannibalism, for example, holds a peculiar interest, and is often attributed to a tribe as a regular dietary practice when it is only an occasional ritual one—or not even practiced at all. Thus much more publicity is given to the rather warlike peoples of New Guinea than to the relatively peaceful Semang of Malaya.

Most hunter-gatherers are not at all violent. The !Kung Bushmen have a horror of fighting because, as they say, "someone might get killed," while the Australian Aborigines are exceptionally skilled at ritualizing their aggression. This is not really as surprising as it may sound. Hunter-gatherer bands are small, rarely being larger than 25 people, adults and children. As we shall see, they have little sense of property, and in any case they have nothing worth stealing. Nobody owns land, they simply have the right to hunt animals and gather plants on it. No work is so onerous that anybody would want another person to do it for him. Yet all, both male and female, are needed to do their bit. For these reasons, there is absolutely nothing to gain, either from warfare or from individual acts of violence. Yet of course there is a great deal to lose: life itself, a reduction in the work force, or simply an unpleasant disruption of the community.

A lot of subtle effort is put into preventing such disruption, or smoothing things over when it occurs. There are tensions, in hunter-gatherer communities as there are in ours: one person might feel his share of meat has been inadequate or unfair recently; another might be considered

Many Australian Aborigines ritualized violence, turning potentially dangerous situations into outbursts of fiery rhetoric. Whenever quarrels looked as though they were going to become violent, onlookers would intervene to calm the participants.

by a member of the community not to be pulling his weight; a third might just be going through a patch of surliness and bad temper.

The community will first try to bring the offender into line in such a way as not to make him more aggrieved and aggressive. If he will not be gentled into line, and his behavior seems to be more disruptive than the effects of an open rebuke, then increasingly he will be ostracized by his fellows. Nobody will laugh at his jokes, his questions will go unanswered or be met with irrelevant and totally unsatisfactory replies. All his attempts to make conversation will fail, being met less with silence than with vagueness and indifference. This is not quite the same as putting a person "in Coventry." It is much less obvious and not so overtly hostile. The general idea is to make it clear to the offender that he has done wrong and is publicly disapproved of, but at the

Above: Jalé warriors, New Guinea; the main party watch as their vanguard set fire to a neighboring village. Below: the body of one of the Jalé warriors, killed in ambush.

Jalé warriors, ornamented with shells and bird-of-paradise feathers, celebrating their success with a victory dance.

same time to leave him room for maneuver, an opportunity to pretend that nobody has really noticed, while he turns over a new leaf and makes amends. In other words, there is a general, if subconscious, recognition that if somebody causing disruption is corrected carelessly or heavy-handedly then the disruption will spread and grow; that the wisest course is to make sure that remedial measures are subtle, and reduce the likelihood of further disruption.

If things go wrong and the dispute spreads so that the band is, for example, divided into two opposing factions, then the most likely course is not war but fission. Hunter-gatherer bands are constantly splitting and then coming together again in different combinations of families. Clearly, if one family finds itself temporarily incompatible with another, it is preferable that they go their different ways for a time rather than foment a full-scale battle between their men. Such fission is the tendency not only among most hunter-gatherers who find no difficulty in moving, but also among hunter-gardeners. For example, the Cubeo of Colombia, like many southern Amerindian peoples, live in communal long-houses, occupied by a number of families. Inevitably, however, for a time one family might not get along with the others. Rather than remaining in the long-house, causing increasing friction until perhaps everybody leaves or somebody resorts to violence, the family will simply abandon the long-house and build a separate hut nearby. Here they will live until the tension subsides.

Aggression is a useful behavior pattern for all species. The problem is to prevent it deteriorating into violence. Most species have developed ways of solving this problem, and natural man is no exception. Here, Chimbu warriors and their women of the New Guinea Highlands are indulging in a harmless war game, which ritualizes, and thus absorbs, excess aggression.

This is not to claim that there are no fights between individuals or battles between groups. If such normally effective controls fail for some reason, armed conflict does break out, sometimes disastrously. The Majangir of Ethiopia are, for the most part, peaceable and friendly. They avoid disputes preferring to laugh off difficulties and differences of opinion. Resentments can smolder beneath the surface, however, only to explode under the influence of too much alcohol. Normally, whenever beer or honey wine is to be consumed, a sufficiently large number of people hear about it for there to be enough to make people merry but not enough to make them uncontrollably drunk. Unfortunately, the system is not entirely foolproof and occasionally the drinking is confined to too few people. Men whose drinking is controlled by scarcity cannot develop self-control, and they then drink far too much. When that happens, and if there is indeed an undercurrent of resentment, then a violent quarrel may break out, all too often ending in the death of one or more of the participants.

Yet on the whole, the violence in hunter-gatherer disputes is effectively ritualized. The Tiwi of northern Australia, for instance, were superficially a violent people. They were given to frequent duels between individuals and battles between groups. The commonest cause of duels was jealousy. The Tiwi marriage system was such that nobody younger than 40 had a wife. This meant that their society consisted of old men with lots of wives, middle-aged men with one or two wives, and young men with no wives at all. The old men were very important, but not much fun for the young women, who also had to bear with the bossiness of the older wives. Thus when all the women went off to gather plants, the temptation for a young man and woman to pass the time in clandestine friendliness was irresistible. The old men knew this, and were therefore constantly accusing their juniors of seduction. This inevitably led to a duel—which consisted of the old man haranging the young man and then loosing off his spear at him. Because he was not just old but also furious the senior was more than likely to miss his target, so the youth was in little danger. In fact, if he was wise he deliberately allowed himself to receive a small wound so that honor could be satisfied all around.

Group disputes were almost as innocuous. Each individual in the war party spent most of the time haranging his opposite number, after which everybody threw their spears. The battle ended as soon as somebody was wounded. Sometimes this was fatal, and as often as not the injured party was a spectator; but never was there the kind of slaughter we associate with medieval warfare, modern terrorism, or gang violence.

Wrestling is another way of absorbing excess aggression among the Amerindians. The picture below shows an attack posture, below right, a clinch, and the one on the right, a throw.

Most people's image of leadership among natural man is the splendidly war-bonneted Red Indian chief. But the situation is, of course, much more complicated than that. To begin with a number of societies had no leadership of any kind, and while most hunting peoples did in fact have a head man, his powers were greatly restricted. Furthermore, many American Indian "chiefs" attained their positions simply because their bands were under attack by the white man. The institution of chief was a response to a highly unusual and stressful situation, when it was essential that the mildly anarchic state of affairs that normally pertained among Amerindian communities be transformed into an organization capable of resistance. Indeed, the failure of the Indians to defeat the invaders can be attributed partly to their absurd trustfulness of the white man's good intentions, but largely to their failure to centralize authority under one man. People described as chiefs often had complete control over only a few families, the rest obeying them only in extremely favorable and unusual circumstances. Europeans had the greatest difficulty in understanding this, and rarely did so, which explains their frequent accusations that the chiefs were fickle and treacherous. Even when relations were peaceful, the white men insisted on dealing only with one man, whom they described as chief, because this simplified matters, and was after all the way Europeans conducted their affairs.

Few hunter-gatherer leaders had any great authority, for their societies were truly democratic. It was very rare for a headman not to do his own hunting and fishing, and his wife not to do her own gathering. He had no servants and no special privileges. In fact he was often materially *less* well off than his fellows. He derived his authority from his prestige, and prestige was won in a number of different ways, a particularly important one being generosity. The ethic of not hoarding, together with that of sharing, are very important among hunter-gatherers. It follows that to gain prestige a man had to be even more generous than the norm. One anthropologist leaving the tribe he was living with was grateful enough to the chief to present him with an antelope he had shot. Somewhat embarrassed, the

A typical image of tribal leadership: the Northern American Indian chief. Often, however, the chief emerged only in response to the new, threatening situation caused by the arrival of the white man.

The African chief is another popular image of tribal authority. The chief shown here is Winyi IV, Omukama of Bunyoro, in Uganda.

chief refused the gift, asking the anthropologist to give it to somebody else, lest the jealousy of the band be aroused against him.

Prestige is also won by skills such as hunting, by a sense of humor, and by an ability to smooth over disputes. If there is a quarrel and the headman does not settle it, he is likely to be roundly abused by some of his people. If he intervenes too obtrusively he will be attacked by the disputants for being overweening and authoritarian! It would be surprising, therefore, if headmen really enjoyed their position, and, indeed they have few rivals for the job. It is perhaps because of this that succession to leadership is usually by birth.

This does not mean that there are "royal families" among hunter-gatherers. If the head-

man dies his son or brother may replace him; but only if his fellows regard him as suitable. The authority of a headman is limited to advice, which is usually followed because of his prestige. But if his people think little of him, he will be utterly ignored, and will soon relinquish his position to someone else. Among the Cubeo, for example, it is the responsibility of the chief to see that the communal house is built. The Cubeo are not hunter-gatherers, relying to a large extent on gardening as well as hunting and fishing, but they illustrate a principle common among truly food-collecting peoples, The *maloca,* which is what the communal long-house is called, normally lasts for about five years. When a new one must be built, the headman will set up the main beams with his brothers and sons. At that point, if they still approve of him, the rest of the men in the community will join in and help. However, if for

Above: Winyi IV receives his tribal elders in the royal compound, and below, the Bunyoro royal trumpeters blowing their sacred horns covered with cowrie shells. Such authority and its trappings within a tribe are absent among hunting peoples.

some reason he no longer commands respect, none of the other men will bother. This will be a clear sign to him that he should give way to somebody else, which he will do.

His replacement will probably be one of his sons or brothers, though it could also be somebody from outside his family. The reason why the new leader is more likely to be from the old leader's family, is that a son or close male relation will tend to model his behavior on that expected of a chief. Thus he will already have acquired prestige by showing what a generous and moderate man he is. Whoever he is, he will be the community's choice, because the people can clearly demonstrate to any prospective leader whether or not he can expect their co-operation.

This system, in a way rather like the four-yearly presidential elections in the U.S.A., is plainly an effective way for the community to keep its leader up to the mark. In the case of a man becoming chief on the old leader's death, a new house must be built, however new the existing one is; and this, too, is obviously an excellent way of demonstrating whether or not he is acceptable.

Apart from the single, rather restricted, position of the leader, communities of natural man have no hierarchy or class system. This is possible firstly because wealth does not flow in the direction of authority, as it does in our society—and in fact the wealth, such as it is, flows away from authority. Secondly, the communities are very small, which means they can be truly democratic. When everybody knows everybody else, when expertise is shared, and when there is plenty of time to discuss things fully, then it can be guaranteed that decision-making will be democratic. This means that it is extremely difficult for a hierarchy or class to be established. As soon as any individual or group tries to dominate, the rest of the community resorts to the usual sanctions to prevent it.

This is not to say that communities were completely unstructured. Apart from kinship alliances, which will be described in a later section, a number of peoples had special groupings—such as the dyadic partnerships of the Netsilik Eskimos. These consisted of two men getting together and agreeing to be trading partners, or to share names, or to exchange wives. The function of these partnerships was probably to reinforce loyalty in an environment hostile enough to make community cohesion of the utmost importance.

But on the whole, natural man has little need of institutionalized community cohesion. There is little difficulty in getting food and everybody knows how to, so that only the old, the infirm, and the very young have a genuine physical need for others. Hence the tendency to fission and the marginal authority of the headman. Thus, what the headman can give his people is limited to his experience and his capacity to resolve conflicts, which is not to say that these qualities are not highly important. This extreme flexibility and reduced central power is valuable in that it

Men building a longhouse. Among southern Amerindians it is the job of the headman to organize house-building, and it is a sign of his unacceptability if he receives no cooperation.

minimizes the possibility of inter-band battles, although of course this makes the community correspondingly vulnerable when faced with a strongly centralized enemy.

Religion is probably the area of natural man's life about which it is most difficult to generalize. It is also the least easy to understand. Religion is not a separate compartment of natural man's experience as it often is of ours. It is the expression of all his values, of his total world-view. Few hunting peoples have any conception of a single God, one creator of the universe, or if they have they are not much concerned about him. They are animists, populating the world about them with spirits, some good, others bad. The Majangir of Ethiopia, for example, believe in a rainbow spirit, which is both good and bad. Good because it stops excessive rain, but bad simply by virtue of its tremendous power. All creatures have power, the Majangir believe, but something with very great power, such as a strong spirit, is dangerous to something that is relatively weak such as an ordinary man. Power is comparable to heat. Human beings have an average blood temperature of about 98°F, and if they were exposed to a heat source of say 298°F they would be completely consumed. This in effect is what is said to happen when a Majangir is exposed to the rainbow spirit: he falls ill with a fever, and will probably die. Fortunately, the tribal chief and his male relatives, because of *their* power, are able to force the rainbow spirit away whenever it is encountered, thus protecting their people.

Men (and women) with unusual knowledge of the spirit world are known as shamans or medicine men. They are the exceptions to the generalization that there are no specialists among hunter-gatherers and hunter-gardeners. Everybody knows something of ritual and the medicine with which it is associated, but the shaman knows a great deal more than anybody else. Again there are exceptions even to this rule; for the Bushmen have no shaman, most of the men being capable of joining in the medicine dance and other religio-medical activities.

Perhaps the most interesting shamans are those of the Indians in Central and South America, for they have a most impressive knowledge of hallucinogenic drugs. These they will use by smoking or chewing them, or having them blown with painful force as a snuff up their nostrils. The best known example of such a shaman

Top: a Navaho (northern Amerindian) shaman at work. First, a ritualized design is "painted" with colored powders in the sand. Next, above, the shaman scatters corn (maize) as an offering to the spirits, so that they will help him cure the patient.

is Don Juan. This "man of knowledge" of the Yaqui tribe of northern Mexico is still alive. He is highly skilled in the use of three hallucinogenic plants—peyote, jimson weed, and the psilocybe mushroom. Because he knows them so well, he can use them to experience a completely different reality to the natural one known by us. It is a world of dreams and hallucinations, a world that we would find highly unreal. Once

Above: the completed painting in the sand. Round it are baskets of colored powders, and prayer sticks, and rattles. Below: the shaman sings his invocations, while his patient sits inside the sacred picture area so that the spirits can cure her.

inside it, however, its reality and its great beauty and power are overwhelming. It is also extremely dangerous. Only an expert like Don Juan knows how to control the effects of the drugs he takes, or to cope with the events of this other reality, which to the novice are quite terrifying. Unless the drugs are taken under supervision of a shaman as part of the long and difficult task of being a shaman apprentice, they are more often than not killers.

The use of trance by shamans is the commonest way in which they communicate their power and special knowledge. Outside the Americas hallucinogenic plants are not widely used to induce trance. More general are the self-induced trances, such as those of the Bushmen in their medicine dances. The shamans are skilled at hypnotizing themselves into trance, or they may be peculiarly sensitive to certain stimuli that help them go into a trancelike state. Some shamans have neurotic tendencies, which the community has sensibly socialized by giving them the opportunity to become shamans.

Many shamans resort to tricks and dramatic devices to help their patients to be fully responsive to their treatment. The intention of such tricks is not to deceive, they are not "mumbo-jumbo," but more the equivalent of the Western doctor's bedside manner or the placebo pills given to people just to satisfy them that they are being properly looked after. The Comanche shamans

Above: a Karaja man who has scarified his body cleans the blood off his skin. Scarification is often done ritually, but also frequently out of vanity. Right: Kamayura flute players in Brazil praying for an end to the rainy season, so that they can start fishing again. The women are not allowed to hear the flutes being played, for they are regarded as very sacred.

Above: a Kraho shaman of Brazil curing a child. He sucks out evil and blows in good, a practice that survives among us when we "kiss things better." Left: a southern Amerindian inhaling a hallucinogenic snuff. Such drugs are used with great expertise by shamans to assist communication with spirits.

Amerindian totem poles such as these near Ketchikan, Alaska, were common among the peoples of the northern Pacific coast.

used to work in pitch darkness. With the aid of drums and the curious noises they could make from different parts of the tent (they were highly effective ventriloquists), they induced the patient and his relations to believe that the sickness was caused by a monstrous demon, and that the shaman was grappling with it. As the fight proceeded both patient and audience were driven to a climax of terror, followed by exquisite relief as the shaman vanquished his opponent. This invariably had a remarkable psychological effect on the patient, whose belief that he was now past the crisis point significantly aided his recovery.

Among the Australian Aborigines, religion and the activities of the medicine man were largely expressed through totemism. In order for the medicine man's power to be effective he had to develop a particularly close relationship with an animal. It was generally believed that he worked with the help of or through the totemic animal, in other words that the animal actually acted for him. Because the relationship was so intimate, the medicine man would not eat his totemic animals, and they in turn protected him.

The possession of totems was not confined to medicine men. Everybody had one; and in southeast Australia there were special sex-totems, representing the sex division in each tribe and emphasizing solidarity within the sexes. Among the Worimi tribe the men's totem was the bat, and the women's the woodpecker. If the men hurt or insulted the women's totem, or vice versa, there would be a violent quarrel or even a fight. This sexual totemism was allied to the belief that men and women had different ancestral origins.

There were also special totems for clans and other divisions within tribes. Members of a clan regarded themselves as related to their totemic animal as much as they were to the other human members of their clan. Such totemism has two important functions. The first is a social one, whereby the bond with people believed to have descended from the same ancestor is reinforced. The second is a natural one, whereby the individual is strongly and persistently reminded of his dependence on the rest of the natural world.

The totem was not necessarily an animal. It could just as well be a plant, a rock, a spring, a cliff, or any other natural feature. Reverence would be expressed toward the totem in a number of different ways: either by refraining to eat or injure the animal or plant; or by a dance associated with it; or by painting designs descriptive

An Australian Aborigine painted with totemic animals.

of it or actually on it if it was a physical feature such as a cliff. These designs were, and sometimes still are, major art forms in their own right, and the Aborigines are justly famed for them.

Clan totemism was, broadly speaking, of three types: matrilineal, patrilineal, and "geographical." A matrilineal clan was one whose members were related to the mother's line. A patrilineal clan was one whose members were related by the father's line. And a geographical clan one whose members depended not on relationship but on the totemic site nearest to which they were born or conceived. The function of matrilineal totems was social reinforcement. The function of patrilineal and "geographical" totems was the promotion of spiritual beliefs and of the cult-life. It was around such totems that the activity known as dreaming was centered.

The dreamtime is eternal, both past and present at once. In the dreamtime, the great heroes of the past are still alive, and their totems are alive

and part of them too. Dreaming is, therefore, an action that is not controlled by restrictive notions of time and space. A man who is a member of such a totem is strictly enjoined to preserve and keep secret the myths, rites, and sacred totem sites, and to hand them on to his son. Membership of a patrilineal or a "geographical" clan is thus equivalent to membership of a secret society.

The lack of preoccupation with personal property is one of the main distinguishing features between natural man and ourselves. Land, the means of production, is never owned by hunter-gatherers. Anybody can hunt, fish, and gather wherever he or she likes. There are restrictions, but these are not imposed because anyone owns anything, but out of a general recognition of what is best for the community. For example, under the guidance of their headman a Bushman band will probably discuss where the women should gather plants in order to get the highest return without straining the long-term capacity of a particular area to supply them. And the Sanpoil of Canada appointed a Salmon Chief to ensure the fish were harvested in the best way.

Instead of land ownership people have usufructory rights, the rights to the fruits of the land. Once a root has been dug up, a fish caught, or an animal shot, then it is owned by somebody. However, the owner cannot do what he wishes with it. Generally, plants and very small animals, such as rabbits or birds, are shared only among the family, although if anyone else is hungry he will not be refused. However, large animals—anything bigger than a small antelope—are shared throughout the entire band.

There is an elaborate system for the division of meat, which varies from people to people, but a typical one is that of the !Kung Bushman. Although the meat "belongs" to one person he does not really own it but is responsible for initially sharing it out among the men who were on the hunt. These men will then further divide their share among relations and people from whom the family has received meat in the past. Often the "owner" of the meat will have the privilege of having a choice cut—for instance the liver or the rump—but whenever a large animal is killed everybody will get some meat. The only thing that really varies each time an animal is caught is the distribution route on which each joint actually travels.

One obvious reason why only the larger animals are shared is that it is impossible for a single family to consume them unassisted. They could of course attempt to do so over a few days, but the meat might go bad before they have

Left: Dobe !Kung Bushmen hang strips of meat and (center) a Dyak of Borneo lays out venison to dry. Right: Nyae Nyae !Kung Bushmen share out a meal. Meat preserving and meat sharing are common practices among most hunting peoples.

All the items on this page are considered by the Bushmen to be personal possessions, but they are still readily shared. Above: a Bushman playing the Bushman "violin." Right: a man applies poison to his arrows. Below: simple storage utensils, such as these pots, bowls, and ladles, are made from gourds.

finished it. In any case, any attempt to keep so much would be disastrous: it would provoke a great deal of ill-feeling and be an open invitation to theft. This of course is the main reason why meat is so scrupulously shared. For, although meat is more perishable than plant foods it can be kept for a while, even in the tropics: the Ethiopian Majangir char and lightly smoke their meat so that it is still perfectly edible after a week. But without meat-sharing there would be little material incentive for people to form communities (although there would still be psychological ones), nor any point in a code of morality which regarded stealing as so reprehensible that only a social outcast would practice it.

In most communities of natural man, in fact, theft is virtually unknown. No doubt this is in large part due to the size of these communities. They are so small that everybody knows what everybody else is doing, and they can even identify footprints. There is thus a practical disincentive to stealing: it is impossible to avoid

An Amerindian woman making a hammock. Hammocks are not considered common property. This does not cause any problems because all women are able to make them.

being detected. Because theft is so improbable, it is considered as serious a crime as murder.

Apart from food, there is not much that natural man can own. There are clothes, which are generally never more than a leather cloak, and often as little as a belt for holding leaves or grass; and there are weapons and cooking pots, all easily replaceable items. Finally, there are ornaments and other objects of aesthetic value, including musical instruments. Often a true sense of ownership can be attributed only for those objects absolutely essential to survival. Generally, however, the property values relating to food apply to the other items as well. It is wrong to hoard, it is good to share. If someone asks for something, he must be given it. Possessions such as these move from one person to a great many others because it is considered antisocial to refuse a request for any of them.

Some agricultural peoples have similar attitudes to property as have hunter-gatherers. For example, among the Lesu of New Ireland, land is not owned by anybody until it is first cleared. A man has the right to clear a garden at any place where none has existed. As soon as it is cleared it is owned, and no one may take any of the produce without the owner's permission. The principle of reciprocity—exchanging goods and services over a period of time—is also well established. Among the Bomagai-Angoiang of New Guinea this extends to the giving of gardens or parts of gardens to other women besides the wife. The idea is that the man clears a plot and then gives it to his wife in exchange for the produce grown in it. But he also gives plots to his sisters and to widows. The advantage of this system is obvious: food production is more assured because it is less likely to be subject to poor planning, or

Sweet-potato cultivation in New Guinea. Gardens such as this are private property when they are cleared.

to a single woman's wrath during a marital dispute; and because different gardens will be planted by different women at different times, so that as one is exhausted another is ready for harvest. The same principle applies when one man gives a pig to another. He knows that sooner or later he will be given a pig in return, probably when he is more in need of one. And in the meantime he does not have the bother of looking after a troublesomely large herd, or preventing the pig breaking up his or his neighbor's garden.

Reciprocity means that nobody goes uncared for. Old people who have looked after their children will be cared for by them in return. It also ensures social cohesion. In theory it would be possible for a single family to be totally self-supporting, but people need company as well as food, and they also need long-term insurance against disaster. By exchanging goods and services between them, families build up a series of obligations and rights that cement them into a community. Because they can support themselves, families can temporarily leave the community when tensions become unbearable. On the other hand, because they are obliged to return any gifts made to them by others, and are also owed gifts in return for the ones they themselves have given, they are bound to come back. Thus, the combination of fission and reciprocity provides the community with optimum flexibility and cohesion.

Among some peoples the principle of reciprocity has built up into an elaborate exchange cycle that extends over thousands of miles. For example, the best stone axes came from a certain part of Australia while other parts boasted particularly fine ochers and dyes for painting. Consequently these localized valuables often traveled great distances between tribes and bands of one region and another. No economic class of tradesman was established, however, since reciprocal arrangements assured that each trading partner was obliged not to hang onto his property: there was always somebody he owed something to.

Status is knowing where you stand in relation to your fellows. Status, and the striving for prestige in order to improve status, are very old. All societies of natural man, and probably all societies, share this concept. Natural man values status rather more than possessions. There is no indication of status among his possessions, as

A Corroboree, or Aborigine trade and exchange ceremony, in Arnhem Land, Australia. Trade in items such as stone axes and paints and dyes once extended from tribe to tribe right across the continent.

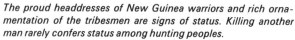

The proud headdresses of New Guinea warriors and rich orna-
mentation of the tribesmen are signs of status. Killing another
man rarely confers status among hunting peoples.

there is in our society. On the contrary, as we
have already seen, the reverse is the case, a man's
status depends in large measure on his generosity
in giving away his possessions.

This is not true of all hunting peoples. For
example, the Indians of the Northwest coast of
America amassed prestige through wealth and
even kept slaves. However, they are exceptional:
in general, hunter-gatherers find other ways of
gaining prestige, and the system rarely becomes
hierarchical. There is no ranking order from
people with high status to people with low status.
People remain equal, whatever their status, so

that a man will enjoy great esteem without gaining any privileges or even any obvious sign of respect from his fellows. The main differences in social relations between a man with little prestige and a man with a lot is that the latter's advice on matters about which he is esteemed will be listened to carefully and probably followed; and his fellows will be more favorably disposed toward him.

Prestige can be won by a person performing the role expected of him, to the best of his ability. The man who takes care over his hunting, fishing, weapons-making, garden-clearing, or house-building will be respected. So will the woman who diligently gathers or grows plants, makes a good home, and so on. The person who plays music, or carves ornaments, or in any other way harmoniously fulfills his role in the community will be in good standing with it. Whoever works hard and is generous, whoever is good-humored and friendly, in other words whoever boosts community morale whenever he or she can, will enjoy high status. On the other hand, anyone who is lazy, mean, grumpy, and ill-disposed toward his fellows will be shunned.

A skilled hunter, who brings large supplies of meat into the community, will be very much respected, although again, he will not be considered superior to one less lucky or adept. Indeed, his success will be attributed less to his skill than to his obviously harmonious relationship with the animals. Since it is believed that you must respect animals or they will simply not be there to be killed, it follows that a successful hunter must have a good relationship with his prey. Thus he will be in harmony with his en-

Prestige is won by fulfilling one's role as well as possible. Among the Makuna people of Colombia, one male role is that of boat-maker. The boats are made from tree trunks. First the bark is removed, then the tree is hollowed out and this process is accelerated by burning. The craft is then shaped with fire and chisel and finally launched.

vironment, and he will be of high moral stature. Accordingly, he will be valued as a "good" man rather than as a "clever" one.

This does not mean that there are no powerful men within these small communities. Some will have stronger personalities than others. They may have greater oratorical skill, or be better hunters, or harder workers. Particularly among hunter-gatherers it will be possible to accumulate more and thus be more generous and consequently still more influential. Among the Majangir, for example, the size of your garden depends on the number of men you can attract to help you clear it. This depends on the amount of obligation you have built up in your favor—by providing meat and especially by providing honey wine. The provision of honey wine in turn depends on the number of hives you have. The hives are made from hollowed-out logs and are placed high up in trees. Making and placing them is extremely hard work and it is best to get help. But help will only come from those obliged by your generosity to give it to you!

If a man wishes to enjoy great prestige he must have more than his fellows to be generous with, He must therefore work very much harder. An exceptionally hard worker will have a larger garden and theoretically it should be possible for him to pass this on to his children, thus creating something like a system of large landowners among relatively impoverished peasants. This does not happen because of the key role of generosity in the winning of prestige. The "richer" and more influential a Bomagai-Angoiang "big man" is, the more he must give away. He will support widows and orphans without expecting them to pay him back. He will even give away parcels of his land without expecting any of the fruits of that land. The more he gives without strings, the greater his prestige. Because Bomagai-Angoiang "big men" give so much away they have, if anything, a keener sense of property than most, because unless you own you cannot give. But at the same time there is the clear recognition that if a few people own too much, the differential will destroy the whole system. Consequently, if a man has an unusually large number of pigs, his clansmen will resort to sorcery to make them sicken and die. Thus, there is no distinction between rich and poor, and status is a means of distributing wealth as well as conferring dignity.

The family is at the heart of community life and natural man is no exception in this respect. But the family means different things to different people. Among one people, for example, an uncle on your mother's side might be referred to as "father," or cousins be considered as brothers and sisters. This just means that kin terms such as mother or son reflect social rather than biological reality.

Human beings differ from other animals in that their offspring are weak and helpless for very much longer. The family is necessary to support and train children, and to equip them for adult life in their society. Social relations are more important than biological ones, and many kinship structures implicitly recognize this: as long as there are enough people responsible for looking after some aspect of the child's life, it does not much matter whether they are actually related. We have something similar to this in our society in the institution of the godparent. The godparents are responsible for the spiritual welfare of their godchild. In another society, they might be called simply father and mother, so that the child has two of each, and be responsible for other aspects of the child's well-being.

Tasaday families. This newly discovered people will have much of interest to add to our knowledge of family life.

Kin terms like father and mother formalize and strengthen the relationship. In many societies this principle is extended throughout the community, so that whenever one person has anything to do with another they both know exactly how they *relate* to each other, which is all that "relationship" means. This has the advantage of defining precisely what kind of behavior is expected: whether extreme formality, or casual joking; affection, or reserve.

Kin terms also define the obligations of those people to each other. Everybody is then clear who is expected to support whom in times of crisis, and who is obliged to give priority to whom before sharing with anybody else, and so on. This arrangement serves as an intimate version of the welfare state. Old people and orphans will not go without while they have at least some form of kin relationship with someone in the community. Indeed, among most hunter-gatherer peoples there are no orphans—except in the strict biological sense—as they quickly become part of other families. Old people are well cared for, too.

Because the function of the family is to provide support, a prospective husband's ability to look after his wife and provide meat for her family is the most important quality they will look for. Of course, as their communities are small they will know quite a lot about his character already. It is unusual for a marriage to be considered unsuitable by the parents of either party, since they would have had ample time to make it clear beforehand that the liaison was looked on with disfavor. Nonetheless, it is normal for a young Bushman, for example, to live with his wife's parents and to hunt for them. If during this period he proves himself a poor hunter he might be thrown out.

There is plenty of leeway in the matter, because, as among many hunting peoples, a couple is not considered married until the girl is pregnant. The logic of this is that marriage and the family exist in order to provide security for children, and if no baby is expected there is no point in them. This gives considerable scope for premarital experimentation.

The Mbuti Pygmies of Zaire have an interesting betrothal festival called the *elima*. The *elima* is partly a puberty rite for girls. As soon as a girl has menstruated for the first time, she is eligible for this rite. The young girls spend some time confined together in a hut where they are instructed

in contraception, abortion, sexual intercourse, childbirth, and so on, by the older women. The *elima* lasts from one to two months, and during this time each girl is entitled to leave the hut regularly to whip the boy of her choice—if she can catch him. If she does, he must enter the hut with her, and if she gives him permission, make love with her. After a while the lovemaking ceases to be by invitation only, and the boy may enter the hut whenever he likes—as long as he can successfully get past the older women, all armed with sticks and stones with which they bombard him. Although all boys suffer this treatment, the women aim more particularly at those they regard with least favor. This effectively stops anybody the women regard as unsuitable. During the last two weeks, if the boy is still with the same girl, he is considered betrothed to her and must stay with her. Once the *elima* is over, the young man must prove himself a good hunter, and as soon as he has done so, the couple may live together. Again, however, they are not regarded as married, until she becomes pregnant.

Divorce is generally simple among hunting peoples. If a couple ceases to get on, they part. If a woman feels she is not being adequately looked after by her husband, she will return to her father; and if a man feels his wife is not fulfilling her duties, he returns her to her father. But after an initial period of instability in the early years, most marriages become stable.

Child-rearing among natural man is characterized by considerable physical contact initially, a minimum of corporal punishment, and the use of example as the only educational strategy.

The most obvious physical contact that the infant has from birth is with his mother's breast. Hunter-gatherer and hunter-gardener children are fed at the breast for an average of two and a half to three years. The minimum period recorded being one year and the maximum six years. This does not meant that they are fed exclusively from the breast. Quite early on they are introduced to supplementary foods, usually exactly the same food as that eaten by the adults. The only difference is that the child's food is chewed up for him by his mother before she gives it to him. This practice might be regarded as grossly un-

Pygmy children spend most of their time with their elders and are, therefore, involved in all the various camp activities.

hygenic, but in fact it is just the opposite. The small number of germs transmitted to the child in this way give it immunity against disease. Studies among the Yanomamo of Venezuela have demonstrated that because of their contact with low-level populations of germs from food and from the dirt of hut floors and so on, children have as high a level of antibodies in their blood as United States children do after vaccination.

Normally, the child is given the breast on demand; and the readiness to feed infants in this way not only increases resistance against disease, but also gives them a tremendous sense of security. The most casual observation of very young mammals shows how much they need to be close to their mother, or some similar body—to be enveloped in physical warmth. Humans are no exception, and the highly physical response of hunter-gatherer women to their small children is a major contribution to the sense of security with which they grow up. Whenever a child cries it is given the breast, and until it has learned to toddle

it is always in someone's arms—if not its mother's, then those of its father, another adult, or an older child.

Among the Lesu of New Ireland in the Pacific, as soon as the child can toddle, the care of it is divided between various members of the family. The father will sit for hours on end playing with his children at home or on the beach. Small children are fondled a great deal by other adults besides the parents, yet they do not appear at all spoiled. Generally they are models of cheerfulness, crying only when hungry. After about the age of three they are not fondled nearly so much, however. They are treated with great affection but nobody coos over them any more. Their time is divided between their parents and children of their own age.

Bushmen parents are very indulgent, spending a great deal of time with their small children. The young ones remain with the woman, but as they grow older the children spend increasing amounts of time with adults of their own sex, learning by example their future role in life. The Bushmen resort to corporal punishment very rarely indeed. If they have a difficult child, they just make sure he is constantly in the company

A Waura Indian mother and child in Brazil. Amerindians, like most tropical hunting peoples, are indulgent toward children.

of an adult who will break him in, though not beat him.

The Siriono of Bolivia also enjoy passing the time playing with their children, and like the Bushmen, they rarely resort to physical punishment, preferring instead to shout at offenders. Among hunting peoples—particularly in tropical and subtropical environments—nonviolence is in fact the rule for the upbringing of children as much as it is for adult relationships. Hunter-gatherer parents tend to be harsher in colder lands, where possibly discipline needs to be enforced to a greater extent if people are to survive. This generalization applies only to hunter-gatherers and it is not claimed that latitude is by any means the only regulating factor or even the most significant one.

Education, also, is very similar among all hunting peoples. It is by involvement. Just as small infants have a lot of physical contact with adults, so children as they grow out of infancy continue to have a great deal of social contact

!Kung Bushmen mothers relax with their children. Bushmen adults spend much time playing with and cuddling infants.

with adults. Most of their time is spent with their elders, not because they are being looked after by them, but because it is considered normal and proper for children to be a part of all experience. They are not excluded from anything in which the adults normally take part.

Thus by the time they are about 10 years old, and often long before that, hunter-gatherer children will have done all the things their parents do—hunting, fishing, gathering, gossiping, and so on. Consequently they will already have a good idea of what plants and animals are good to eat or are useful for various other reasons. They will also know those that are poisonous, or dangerous in other ways. They may have known hunger, and they will certainly have eaten their fill after watching animals killed, butchered, and shared out. They will probably have seen their parents get drunk, and may well have seen them or some other couple make love. They may also have watched the birth and perhaps death of babies. It must be borne in mind,

Above: children watch a Solomon Islander carve a model canoe, and below, an Aborigine shapes a club. Left: an Aborigine mother and her children gather mussels. As they grow older, children spend an increasing amount of time with an adult of their own sex, thus learning their future role in the community.

however, that many hunting peoples do not have alcohol and a number are secretive about love-making and birth. Nevertheless very early on, the hunter-gatherer child will have seen more of life than a good many Europeans and Americans will ever see in their lifetimes. And at the same time, they will be learning their roles in life, how to play their parts in supporting themselves and the community. A small boy will be given a small bow, and with it he will shoot grasshoppers, graduating to rabbits and birds, until he is

Right: Aborigine children of the Pitjantjatjara people at play. Such play groups help a child to learn to live with others. Below: an old New Guinea warrior teaches a boy to shoot, and below right, Jalé boys practice arrow shooting in New Guinea. There are no formal lessons in the life-style of their people

capable of taking small antelope. He will learn how to butcher an animal, so that the skin is not ruined and no part of the animal is wasted.

A small girl will learn how to find and prepare plants, how to cook, possibly how to weave, and certainly how to sew. Besides basic skills such as these, both boys and girls will learn the customs, the traditions, the entire way of life of their people. They will not be instructed in them, but will simply pick them up through being totally steeped in them. Not all of them will be with adults for much of their time, however. Among some peoples, the boys go around in play packs; they fish and hunt together, and otherwise act as a junior version of the group formed by their fathers and the other men. In such cases, they are imitating the adults as a body rather than as individuals.

The period in a Western child's development that parents dread most is adolescence "the difficult stage." The children of hunting peoples do not appear to experience adolescence in quite so severe a form. They grow from boys and girls to men and women much more smoothly and rather more quickly. This is not because they mature physically much more quickly—normally the reverse is true. It is because by the time they reach puberty, they already know a good deal about how their environment and their community work. And although they still have a lot to learn they are allowed to do so as adults and not as part children, part grown ups.

The changeover from childhood to adulthood is usually marked by a puberty rite, although no one is regarded as truly adult until he or she is married. One such puberty rite—for girls—was described in the last section. An example of one for boys is the *aka-op* ceremony of the Andaman Islanders. The boy must dance all night until daybreak, when he goes into the sea for a couple of hours or so. Afterwards, he kneels on the ground in the open to have his back scarified. An older man takes an arrow and cuts three vertical rows of incisions in the boy's back. Each row consists of 20 to 30 cuts. When that is over, the boy sits with his back to the fire until the blood

clots. Throughout the entire operation and for some hours afterwards the boy must remain completely silent.

As soon as the wounds on his back are healed, a similar operation is performed on his chest. During the entire period, certain foods are forbidden him. These foods are normally staples so they are not all prohibited at once. To begin with, if he is a member of one of the coastal tribes, he is forbidden turtle, dugong, porpoise, various grubs, fish, shellfish, birds and a great many plant foods. When the men decide he can resume eating turtle and the other foods, they hold a turtle-eating ceremony. They kill a large number of turtles, and when they are ready they seat the boy on special leaves, facing the sea. The master of ceremonies then picks up some meat and fat of cooked turtle, takes them to the boy, and rubs his entire body with the fat. He then covers the boy's body in iron oxide, and feeds him with some of the turtle. The boy is then vigorously massaged, after which he is sprinkled with water and clay.

At this point, the boy is allowed to eat unassisted. But he may eat only turtle, and then only with a wooden skewer, because he must not touch the meat with his hands, and drink only water. And for two days and two nights he is not allowed to lie down, speak, or sleep. Some of the men and women talk and sing to him to keep him awake. On the third day, a belt and necklace made from a vine are put on him, and he is allowed to sleep. Later he can wash in the sea, after which various designs in red paint and white clay are painted on him. On the fourth day, the boy and the men helping to initiate him dance until the boy is exhausted. This dancing is repeated for the two following days, at which point the turtle ceremony ends.

The boy can now eat turtle, but is forbidden pork. Eventually he is allowed to eat pork and resume a normal life, but only after a pig ceremony as intricate and prolonged as the turtle ceremony. It is clear from this that the importance of the transition from boyhood to manhood is indelibly impressed on the boy. The rite is probably alarming and certainly fatiguing. It is almost inevitable that he will emerge much changed: no longer a child, but well on the road to experienced adulthood.

Above: a boy emerges after his initiation into the men's house. Below: Jalé dancers outside a men's house.

A young Kamayura girl emerges after months of enforced puberty seclusion, one of the ways of preparing for adulthood.

Natural Man
meets Urban Man

As soon as a significant proportion of the human species ceased to live in a stable relationship with their environment, it was probably inevitable that the existence of natural man would be gravely imperiled. However few in numbers the expansionists were at first, they were bound in the end to outnumber those that remained stable. No doubt it was also inevitable that the expansionists should not only take over natural man's land but also *feel* a bitter hostility toward him.

The treatment of natural man by urban man is probably the most despicable aspect of our civilization. Hunter-gatherer and hunter-gardener peoples have been raped, murdered, and exterminated; they have been tortured, humiliated, and enslaved. Whether for trade, conquest, greed, colonial aggrandisement, or the good of heathen souls, natural man has been either utterly demoralized or else driven to extinction.

The relationship between urban man and natural man is most fully illustrated in the plight of the Amerindians, especially those of the United States and Brazil. Today, peoples who once roamed free over a continent are now confined

The primitive log cabin of a modern northern Amerindian.

The interior of such a hut. These structures express the cultural limbo in which the Indians now live.

The wretchedness of dwellings such as this Eskimo hut reflects both the poverty and the loss of a way of life.

to about 200 reservations in 26 States of the U.S.A. These reservations vary in size, from the graveyard of the Mohawks—a few acres, large enough for the Mohawks to occupy only when they are dead—to the nine million acres of the Navahos in Arizona. They vary in quality, too, from lakeside woodland, as in Minnesota, to Arizona's desert.

Some 450,000 Indians live on these reservations, and about another 150,000 outside them. Although the size and quality of their reservations vary, they all have one thing in common—abject poverty. They suffer from housing so bad that one estimate has suggested that 90 per cent of all Indians live in nothing better than tin-roofed shacks, poor quality mud huts, rough shelters, and old cars. About 60 per cent of them have no water supply nearby, many people having to walk over a mile to fetch it. Although the Indians lived with these hardships before the enforcement of

the reservations they were a part of their culture. Now, with their culture changing under the influence of urban man, they still have to suffer these hardships, but enjoy neither the benefits of modern civilization nor the freedom of their original way of life.

Unemployment among Indians is at least 10 times higher than among other Americans, while their average wage is less than a quarter of the national average. Similarly, the average age of death for Indians is 43, compared with 68 for white Americans. A great many diseases are suffered much more by the Indians than by the rest of the population. For example, dysentery is 40 times more frequent, influenza twice as frequent. An Indian baby is less likely to reach the age of one than are other Americans to reach the age of 40.

Perhaps, however, the most humiliating aspect of the plight of the Amerindians in the United States is the educational system that has been imposed upon them. Most children are removed from their homes and sent to barracklike board-

ing schools. Not only do these schools alienate the children and partially isolate them from their culture, they also produce a suicide rate twice the national average for that age group. It is not uncommon for children as young as eight years to commit suicide.

Given their appalling conditions it is surprising that the Indians remain on their reservations. But they do, and what is more they have vigorously resisted any attempt to remove them or to reduce the reservations still further. For although the reservations are on the whole grossly inadequate—in terms of size and quality of land—they are all that the Indians have, the symbol of their culture, the home of their memories.

These reservations are the results of treaties between the U.S. Government and the Amerindian tribes. About a third were peace treaties, and the remainder were land cessions. In other words, the U.S. Government permanently guaranteed the Indians their reservation land in return for generally much larger areas of land ceded by the Indians. In all but a very few cases,

With little or no thought for their community requirements, the Eskimos are presented with dull lines of concrete huts.

the guarantees were for ever—for "as long as the rivers run and the grass grows"—and were promises that the Indians could occupy their reservations absolutely free of all interference by anybody. If the reservations were so small that the Indians could not hunt in them, then they were given goods and often a small annual grant in compensation. But much the most important aspect of these treaties was that they confirmed the principle of Indian sovereignty: in each case the U.S. Government dealt with an independent nation. Unfortunately, while it could not avoid confirming this principle, the U.S.A. in all other respects treated the Indians as racial and cultural inferiors. So great has been the white Americans contempt for their hosts, that they have consistently violated their treaties. Treaty land has been compulsorily purchased and annexed, even though under international law the treaties are valid. The Indians have never been accorded their rights as citizens of sovereign nations, nor have they been offered full compensatory rights as citizens of the U.S.A. Worse still, the land treaties were interpreted very differently by the Indians and by the Whites. As with many of the other representatives of natural man, only a few of the Indian tribes had any concept of the ownership of land. Most knew only of the right to use the land and enjoy the fruits of it. As a result, they ceded treaty rights very willingly, assuming that the Europeans wanted to use the land for no longer than a few seasons, and quite unaware that they intended to settle permanently.

By the 1880s, the United States had completed their conquest of the Indians, all of whom were by then confined to their reservations. But the shock of defeat and of the loss of so much land was followed by the still greater humiliation of a campaign to "civilize" them. Proud and independent hunters were forced to turn to farming, which in any case they were obliged to do since they no longer had enough land to support the food-collecting way of life. But the white Americans went further: they made it clear that they regarded hunting as a slothful and degrading activity, no substitute for the true and dignified labor of agriculture. Missionaries were given the run of the reservations and allowed to do what they liked in their task of converting the Indians. They appeared to accept it as their function to convert the Indians as much to the white American way of life as to Christianity. They outlawed Indian religions, rituals, and gatherings, not so much because they were pagan but merely because they were Indian. Despite overwhelming odds, however, many tribes managed to retain their councils and their basic social structure.

The Indians had also managed to retain a total of 139 million acres of land west of the Mississippi River, and were gradually becoming reconciled to a farming way of life. Then in 1887 the General Allotment Act was passed, which allowed the President to give tribal land to individual Indians. The theory was that the Indians should learn to farm like white men, individually and not communally, and that the communal land ownership of the Indians was hindering their progress toward civilization. In practice, how-

Navaho Indians sell beads on their reservation in the Little Colorado River Gorge, near the Grand Canyon.

In Canada, the arrival of the European gave the Indian the opportunity to sell furs at the cost of reducing game.

An Indian resets his snare after retrieving a hare. Hares provide an important and regular source of food for trappers.

Conflict still mars relationships between Indian and white American. The plaque above commemorates the tragedy of Wounded Knee in 1890, where 146 Minneconjou Indians, including unarmed women and children, were killed by U.S. cavalry and the shellfire from a Hotchkiss cannon.

In 1971 members of the sun dance cult, an Indian revival religion, came into conflict with tribal authorities who objected to their allegedly disruptive effect. Below, an Indian member of the cult in ritual dress taking part in a sun dance.

The conflict known as the Second Battle of Wounded Knee in 1973 deteriorated into an armed confrontation between Indians and white authority. Above: dancers gather around the sacred sun dance pole. In the background is the occupied church.

ever, it was a means of eroding the reservations. Once individual Indians owned the land one of the most important ways of holding the tribe together disappeared. But most of the Indians did not take up the offer, and in many cases it was assumed that they therefore did not want the land, and white Americans were allowed to settle on it. In this way over 100 reservations, largely in the Great Lakes, Pacific Coast, and Plains regions, disappeared. The loss of land did not end there. The plots the Indians were allowed to buy were too small to support a family, and were often re-sold to Whites. Between 1887 and 1933, 90,000 Indians were made homeless, and 91 million acres of their land were lost, two-thirds of the little they were allowed after conquest. This is

the prime cause of much Indian poverty today.

In 1934, the situation was partially alleviated by the Indian Reorganization Act, which recognized the Indians' acute economic and cultural need for land. An annual grant of $2 million was allocated for the purchase of land, and during the next 10 years 50 million acres were bought for the tribes, and much land was improved by intelligent conservation measures. The architect of the Act was John Collier, the only Commissioner of Indian Affairs with a true appreciation of Indian needs. He alone realized the absolute necessity for maintaining the tribal community if the Indians were not to collapse into a demoralized third-class citizenry.

Unfortunately, his successors have not been so enlightened, and since the Second World War the preoccupation of the U.S. Government has been to detribalize the Indians as quickly as possible, whether they like it or not. This was the aim of the 1953 termination bill, which, under the guise of terminating what was described as a humiliat-

A teepee was set up at Wounded Knee as a neutral negotiating place between the Indians and Federal officials.

ingly paternalistic relationship between the Government and the tribes, in fact allowed the Government to arbitrarily end Indian title to land without reference to the people affected. Fortunately, the Indians and their friends have managed in most cases to resist the bill, but not before a number of tribes have been effectively eliminated by it. The Klamath tribe of Oregon, for example, suddenly found itself being told that unless it gave up its land without fuss it would not be entitled to compensation. The result was that in one stroke it lost its treaty rights, which although more honored in the breach, are still a vital legal weapon. In addition, the tribes simply ceased to exist as a distinct entity. Then, as the land was no longer owned by the tribe but by individuals, it ceased to be tax exempt. The timber stands were sold and the proceeds distributed among the members of the tribe, each one receiving about

$43,000. None of them were used to a cash economy, let alone to handling so much money, and of course they spent it as fast as they could. Finally, the Klamath people were easy prey to white people who wanted their land and persuaded them to sell it cheaply.

The termination bill is barbaric for two main reasons. First, it strikes at the root of Indian dignity, removing their security without making any real attempt to help them adjust to a workable alternative. And secondly, it violates not just the Indians' treaty rights and the Federal guarantees that such rights would always be protected, but also the promises by treaty that the

Below: Indians occupied the Bureau of Indian Affairs in November 1972. The building was to them a symbol of 100 years of bureaucratic oppression. They even prepared Molotov cocktails in case police stormed the building (above).

Above: Dennis Banks, director of the American Indian Movement, a militant and activist organization that campaigns for Indian rights, speaking outside the Bureau of Indian Affairs.

Indians would have permanent and inalienable title to their lands.

The Indians of North America have rarely been treated honorably by their European conquerors. They have been often deceived, slaughtered, and humiliated. It might be assumed that the Americans of today would be anxious to make amends for the inhuman behavior of some of their forefathers. Sadly, this seems far from the case.

The Indians of the United States, however,

126

have a distinct advantage over the Indians of Brazil and the other countries of tropical South America. For while those of the North are now experienced in the ways of the white man and are learning to fight with him on his own terms, their brothers in the South have no meeting points with the dominant culture save those of disease and the gun.

Out of the estimated 1 to 5 million Amerindians who lived in Brazil, only about 75,000 are left. Some of them have been reduced to the squalor of the shanty towns, while others belong to virtually isolated tribes. These latter still hunt, fish, and garden as they have done for thousands of years. They are still truly natural men, but they are highly vulnerable to the depredations of the city men.

Brazil's Indians have been decimated by disease and by violence. They have no resistance to diseases such as measles, smallpox, tuberculosis, and the common cold, which have spread like wildfire with devastating effect. Those who have managed to survive such diseases have often fallen prey to the greed of the white man. The rest have been utterly demoralized, either directly by missionaries who have censured their customs, or indirectly by the invading culture. The technological gimmickry of our way of life, while it

does not offer an appealing substitute for their own culture, quite often undermines the Indians' faith in it. To be deprived of faith in all that you value can be as devastating as being deprived of the means of subsistence.

There have been attempts to try and do something about the Amerindians' plight. In 1910, the great Candido Rondon inspired and helped to found Brazil's Indian Protection Service (SPI). Under him the Service helped to alleviate much of the suffering and to prevent further hardship. It helped secure tribal lands and it provided some sort of medical and educational assistance. It was deliberately neutral about religion, and stood for the honoring and respect of the tribal way of life. Thanks to the early work of the SPI, many tribes survived that would otherwise have disintegrated.

Unfortunately, the SPI soon became subject to political pressure. In the 1930s, Rondon quarreled with President Vargas, and the SPI was almost disbanded and lost its financial support. A country whose Constitution guarantees the Indians' possession of their lands thereafter found itself unable to uphold that guarantee for want of a strong enough protection service. With its ludicrously slender budget, the SPI found itself forced to employ men unfitted to the task. Often it lacked enough money for elementary medical assistance, let alone for legal aid in land disputes.

Such legal aid became decreasingly available as it grew increasingly necessary. Ambiguous phrasing in the Brazilian Constitution made it possible for states to take control of Indian lands from the Federal Government, thereby making the constitutional protection of those lands worthless. Many Indians were forced to flee their homes and local politicians curried votes by persuading their electorate that Indian land was theirs for the taking. Occasionally such people were taken to court, but usually such actions came to nothing.

The years following World War II witnessed a succession of scandals. In the 1940s and 1950s, the great Xavante tribe was reduced to a handful of despised groups, squatting at mission stations or on the edges of the cattle ranches that took over their territory. The Cayapo were destroyed by disease—transmitted by expeditions sent out to save them from rubber tappers who would otherwise have massacred them. The remnants of a number of other tribes decimated by disease were either slaughtered or driven off their land. In 1967, the Brazilian Government ordered an enquiry into the plight of the Amerindians. The result was the Figueiredo Report, which demonstrated that many of the SPI's 800 employees were corrupt, and exposed a history of cruelty. The SPI was subsequently abolished and replaced by a new organization called the National Indian Foundation, or FUNAI. Unfortunately, up to now FUNAI seems to have been unable to protect the Indians from alien diseases and from land-

Below: the new Amerindians of the tropics. Integration and assimilation generally means a collapse into poverty.

Right: the trans-Amazonian highway slices through the forests of Brazil, endangering the habitat of the Indians.

grabbers, still their two greatest scourges.

This is not to say that the Amerindians lack helpers. Their two greatest ones came from the SPI itself. They are the Villas-Boas brothers, Orlando and Claudio. In the late 1940s, they joined an expedition to the upper Xingu River. They stayed behind to form the Xingu National Park. In this area, the indigenous people have been able to live as they wish, free from outside interference. And into it, the Villas-Boas brothers have brought other tribes—the ones threatened by development or colonization. These peoples are not kept as museum pieces, but are free to live as they wish, being provided with technical and other education as they require it. Most, however, have chosen to continue their traditional way of life—living proof that there are other ways of helping the Indians besides stealing their lands and forcibly assimilating them. The Xingu National Park has been under more or less constant pressure, and the Villas-Boas brothers have had to fight many battles to stop encroachments on the Park and even prevent its total abolition. They were remarkably successful, until in 1971 a presidential decree removed a third of the Park containing the beautiful forest and river lands to which the Indians are adapted, giving them in exchange open bushland—land which is quite unsuitable.

Discouraged by this inexplicable blow, the Villas-Boas Brothers have announced their intention of giving up. They and the handful of dedicated men and women like them who battle on within FUNAI and similar organizations need as much help as they can get, from whatever quarter. So do the Amerindians and the other tribal minorities like them scattered across the tropical regions of the world. One of the few organizations formed specifically to meet this need is the London-based Survival International.

Left: the two men who founded the Xingu National Park in Brazil, Claudio (left) and Orlando Villas-Boas. Below: the Villas-Boas brothers, pioneers of the struggle to save the Amerindians, pictured with some of the Indians they have befriended.

An airstrip in the forest, hacked out by the Villas-Boas team so that a tribe could be persuaded into the Xingu National Park before its lands were destroyed by industrialization.

A young Amerindian using an outboard motor. The Indians in the Xingu Park are free to live their traditional way of life, adopt a modern one, or choose a compromise, as they wish.

In 1967, a handful of concerned individuals got together to form an Amerindian Protection Trust. When news of the Figueiredo Report was published, they joined with others to form the Primitive Peoples Fund, a charity dedicated to helping tribal minorities not just in South America but all over the world. Later still, the trust changed its name to Survival International, though its objects remain unchanged: to secure the traditional land rights of tribal minorities, to provide them with legal and medical assistance where necessary, and to help them either to preserve their way of life or to adapt to modern ways according to their choice. Survival International has sent out survey expeditions to Brazil and Indonesia to assess the position and needs of tribal minorities in both countries. It compiles an up-to-date dossier on tribal minorities through-

The Villas-Boas' plane brings the brothers and their team to all the tribes in the Xingu Park, who warmly welcome them.

out the world. And it provides as much aid as funds allow.

Bodies such as Survival International play a vital role in helping peoples so unused to the ways of the industrial world that they are unable to help themselves. But peoples such as the Eskimos, the Australian Aborigines, and the North American Indians, have begun to help themselves. Former generations of these peoples remained bewildered by their fate and by the technological ingenuity and sophisticated double-talk of the white man. But their children have learned the ways of the dominant culture, evaluated them, and elected to lead their own way of life. They have chosen the weapons of white society to fight for a synthesis of what they judge to be the best of traditional customs and the best of modern ones.

As might be expected, this development is most marked in the United States. There are a number of political and cultural groups among the Indians of the U.S.A., whose main object is the continued survival of their people as living tribes. One of the most interesting and encourag-ing developments is the adaptation of industrial techniques to the traditional way of life by some of the tribes.

The most famous example is that of the Yankton Sioux in South Dakota. The Yankton are descendants of proud hunters, and they wanted to benefit from modern technology without suffering the kinds of social and emo-tional destruction that is associated with full

Mining is often presented as an opportunity for wealth, but for the North American Indians, who lack both the skills and the inclination to mine, it means only the ruin of land.

industrialization. They began by converting their community hall into an electronic components factory. Soon they were providing jobs for 40 of their men and were much respected by the companies they supplied for their strict adherence to delivery dates.

In time they decided they would like to expand, not because they had fallen in love with profits or wanted to consolidate their position, nor for any other business motive. It was simply that they were anxious to help their brothers, the Santee Sioux, who lived on the other side of the Missouri River. With a larger plant, they could provide jobs for 50 of the Santee men during the lean winter months.

They needed $8000 for new tools, so they sent a spokesman to the Bureau of Indian Affairs in Washington to ask for the money. The Commissioner was impressed and sent one of his specialists to find out if the factory was as efficient as it sounded. The specialist returned saying it did

indeed have promise and recommending a grant of $115,000 in order that the existing makeshift factory could be replaced. His plans included landscaping, a multilane highway, all the trappings of a modern industrial estate.

This was exactly the sort of situation that the Indians most disliked. All they wanted, their spokesman said, was $8000 so that they could carry on with their own version of progress and not somebody else's. He had to go back to his people empty-handed. The Bureau of Indian Affairs had its own ideas about development and thought the Yanktons' rather absurd.

Fortunately, the Yanktons got their money from the Episcopal Church of Boston. Today, their factory is a model of its kind. There are no labor disputes and there is no time clock. Each man can come and go as he pleases. He can work conventional hours and take conventional holidays, or he can work nonstop for a week and take a whole month off. He gets paid a basic minimum, and then anything above that depends on how much work he says he has done. Because the Sioux are still capable of living a true community life, they trust each other and behave responsibly toward each other. Accordingly, they enjoy more freedom than we do, and a more rewarding working life.

Natural man's relationships with urban man have entered a new era. Those peoples who are still leading relatively traditional lives are close to being entirely eliminated. They require vigorous protection by all nations if they are to survive at all, and slowly, groups are being formed all over the world to press for such protection and to help provide the means for it. Those other peoples who suffered the traumas of contact with urban man some years ago have begun to learn not to rely on the parsimonious charity of the white man. They are learning, too, not to look up to the dominant culture, but to appreciate its many defects as well as its virtues. They have begun the arduous struggle for the right and the opportunity to lead their own lives as they wish, to fashion anew a culture that is not buried in the past—a modern one that is peculiarly their own.

Apart from humanitarian reasons and from the fact that we can discover many curious items of behavior from him, is there any point in trying to save natural man? Is there anything of real value that we can learn from him? The answer is yes. We can classify the sorts of information we can

Some attempt is being made to train Aborigines for life among the alien people and the alien culture that surround them. Many Aborigines, however, would simply prefer to return to their traditional land and way of life.

135

A lumberjack fells a tree in the heart of equatorial Africa. Habitats such as this forest should be maintained in their entirety for the benefit of the peoples that inhabit them, to conserve the plant gene pools, and for undiscovered data they may contain.

discover from natural man into two categories: direct and indirect. In the direct category comes his considerable knowledge of the natural world—his knowledge of plants and animals. In the indirect one, come the basic principles we can derive from a study of his social behavior and institutions.

All of today's surviving hunter-gatherer and hunter-gardener groups live in relatively undisturbed environments. These are also the world's most important sources of genetic diversity, of the plants and animals that form the gene pools of many of the foodstuffs and drugs on which we depend. The conservation of such genetic diversity is essential if the world is to continue feeding itself. This is because pests and diseases evolve new varieties faster than domestic plants evolve resistance to them. Accordingly, we have to hybridize new plant varieties in order to maintain and improve yields. We might take one variety of wheat noted for its high protein content and hybridize it with one noted for its resistance to fungal disease, for example. This work depends on the conservation of all the original varieties.

In addition, there are probably a great many plants with still undiscovered nutritional, medicinal, and mechanical properties. If the areas in which they live are destroyed, we shall never be able to use them and a priceless asset will have been lost. For these reasons, the United Nations Conference on the Human Environment, held at Stockholm in June 1972, strongly recommended that large tracts of forest, bushland, and grassland, be conserved as evolving plant gene pools. These habitats can only be conserved if they are maintained in their entirety, that is, complete with the peoples that inhabit them.

But having conserved these areas, what then? There is, of course, nothing wrong with leaving well enough alone; but it is of the utmost importance that we learn as quickly as possible what they contain. The tribes of hunter-gatherers and hunter-gardeners who live in them, have done so for thousands of generations. They have learned a great deal about the properties of plants there, and much about the animals. It is only sensible to find out what they know, before we do anything else. Unfortunately, this is not as simple as it sounds. It is not a question of going into the jungle with mobile laboratories, batteries of cameras and tape recorders, and squads of scientists skilled in interviewing techniques.

This is a recipe for getting false information very fast or no information at all. What are needed are ethnobotanists and ethnozoologists—men and women who know something of plants and animals, but more importantly are prepared to live with a tribe, without interrogating its members. Instead they should observe them closely, note exactly every use to which plants and animals are put, and simply seek the people's help in identifying them.

The study of natural man's social behavior and institutions is no less important and requires even more specialized techniques. First of all a thorough anthropological understanding of the tribe is necessary. In addition, experts are needed in whatever aspect is considered to be of prime importance, health, nutrition, and so on. The modern industrial world is troubled by many ills that may not necessarily be inevitable. They are probably products of our particular culture, rather than innately human. We can only find out whether or not we are naturally violent, greedy, or power-mad through a study of natural man. Similarly, we can learn from him a variety of ways of ensuring social harmony, of curing psychological disorders, and so on. This does not mean that we should adopt the Bushmen's trance dance or the institution of the shaman, or in any other way attempt to duplicate hunter-gatherer social organization. All it means is that by studying basic principles of such social organization, we can find out whether or not ours is constructed along the right lines, and if not, what reforms might be possible.

By the same token we can answer many difficult questions about health and what is the best type of diet through a study of hunter-gatherer health and nutrition. Again this does not mean to say that we should adopt identical menus to those of the Eskimos, or of the Andaman Islanders. It does mean that we might discover a vital nutritional principle that has so far evaded us or confirm others that at the moment are in dispute.

Both the industrial and the nonindustrial countries of the world face an increasing number of seemingly insoluble social and economic problems. Their solution requires courage and imagination, but imagination must not be entirely unfettered. It has to be restricted to what is humanly possible. The study of natural man, besides demonstrating the wonderful diversity of mankind, is exactly that—the study of the humanly possible.

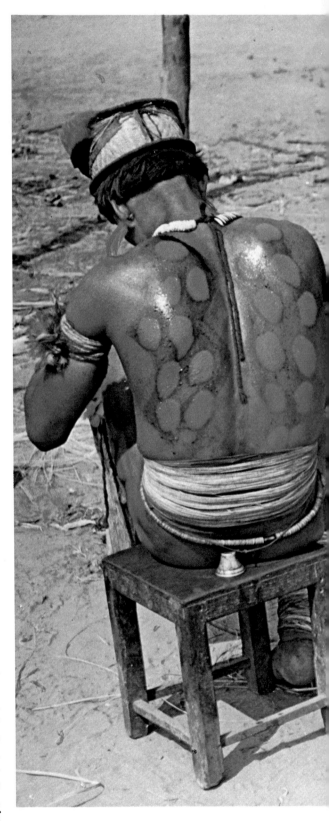

Kamayura Indians with their pets in the Xingu National Park. This is the only place in Brazil where the Indians can live as they wish. In spite of all their efforts the park is being dismembered, and the Villas-Boas brothers have resigned in despair.

Index

Page numbers in *italics* refer to captions to illustrations.

facient and contraceptive plants known by, 68, 70; children among, 110; ownership of cleared land among, 99

long-houses, of Cubeo people, 86–7, *88–9*

Maize (Indian corn), staple crop in North and Central America, 50–1, 67

Majangir people (Ethiopia): crafts of, 70; drinking parties of, 82; honey-gathering by, 47–8; hunting by, 38; prestige among, 104; smoking of meat by, 98; use of hides by, 66

Makuna people (Colombia), boat-makers of, *104–5*

manioc: cultivation of, 50; staple crop in Africa and South America, 51, 67

marriage, 25–6, 108

Masai people (East Africa), herds-men, 52, *53*

Mbuti Pygmies (Zaire), *28*; betrothal festival of, 108; and the forest, 58; hunting by, 38

meat: areas depending on, 43; in diet, 23, 36; drying of, *25*, *96*, *97*; sharing of, 23, *24–5*, *97*; smoking of, 97; stored in ice, 36

medicinal plants, 58, 68, 70

medicine, preventive, 35

Melanesia, pigs, in, 52

melons, gathered by Bushmen women, 20, *22*

milk, as food, 52

millet, staple crop in African grasslands, 51

missionaries, among Amerindians: in Brazil, 127; in U.S.A., 122

Mohawks, graveyard of, 120

Mongongo (mangetti) nut, 16, 67

Mundjutj fruit, Arnhem Land, 46

Napore tribe (Uganda), hunting by, *39*

Nasioi people (Solomon Islands), health of, 73

National Indian Foundation, Brazil (FUNAI), 128, 131

nature: natural man's knowledge of, 60–70; natural man's relation with, 53, 56–60; relation

with, emphasized by totemism, 95

Navaho people (North America): reservation of, 120, *122*; shamans of, *90–1*

Neanderthal man, 10, 13

Neel, J. V., on health of Xavante and Yanomamo peoples, 73

Nelson, Richard, anthropologist, 62

Nemadi people (Mauritania), and addax, 57

Netsilik Eskimo, dyadic partner-ships among, 89

neurotic characters, of some shamans, 92

New Guinea: bows and arrows in, *114–15*; headdress of warriors in, *102–3*; pigs in, 52; *see also individual peoples*

New Hebrides, abortifacient and contraceptive plants known in, 68

nomads, possessions of, 24

nonviolence, as Bushman virtue, 24

Nootka people (Northwest America), 43

Nyae Nyae !Kung Bushmen, sharing of meat by, *24–5*, *97*

Oil, from fish, 43

Ojibwa people (Minnesota), harvesting of wild rice by, 44, *44*, 45

old people: care of, 108; proportion of, in Bushman population, 24

Omaha people (North America), and medicinal plants, 58

orangutans, *8–9*

ostriches, Bushmen pretend to hunt, *65*

overcrowding, diseases of, 35

Paints and dyes, exchanges in-volving (Australia), 100

Panare people (Venezuela), in forest camp, *58–9*

Parapithecus, fossil ape, 10

parasitic worms, in Bushmen compared with other rural African populations, 73

peyote, hallucinogenic, 90

pigs in New Guinea, 52, 99–100

Pinatubo Negritos (Philippines), plant knowledge of, 71

Pitjantjatjara people (Australia), children of, *114–15*

plants: domestication of, 35, 51, 71; gathering of, *see* food gather-ing; gene pools of, 70, 137; hallucinogenic, 70, 90, 92, *92*; medicinal, 58, 66, 68; natural man's knowledge of, 23, 64, 68, 70, 137; *see also* food plants

poisons: on arrows, *20*, 68, *98*; on darts, *38*; for fish, 40, 68

polygamy, among Tiwi (Australia), 46–7

population, cultural control of growth of, 34–6, 71, 73–4, 76

potatoes, staple crop in Andes, 51, 67

poverty, recent aberration? 30

preservation of food: of fish by drying and smoking, 43; of meat by drying, *96*, *97*, freezing, 36, and smoking, 98

primates, 8

Primitive People's Fund, 132

Proconsul, fossil chimpanzee, 10

property, attitudes toward, 24, 97–100

protein, intake of, by Bushmen, 16

psilocybe mushrooms, hallucino-genic, 90

puberty rites, 108, 114, 117

Pygmies (Zaire forest), *14*, *28*, *32*, *33*, *109*; hunting by, *36–7*, 38; *see also* Mbuti Pygmies

Quinine, 66

Reciprocity, principle of, 99, 100

reindeer, of Lapps, 52, *52–3*

religion of natural man, 90–5

reservations, for Indians in U.S.A., 120–6

rice: in Philippines, (grown dry), 49, (grown in paddies), *34*; staple crop in Southeast Asia, 51; wild, 44, *44*, *45*, 45

rifles, of Eskimos, *56*

rock paintings: of fish totem, *61*; of Saharan game, 35

role, prestige from harmonious fulfillment of, 102–3

Rondon, Candido, founder of SPI,

Picture Credits

Key to position of picture on page: (B) bottom, (C) center, (L) left, (R) right, (T) top; hence (BR) bottom right, (CL) center left, etc.

Artist Credits